CHANGING LENSES

"Howard Zehr is insightful as he guides readers through the power of restorative justice and shows us why we need a new way forward."
—*Leymah Gbowee, winner of 2011 Nobel Peace Prize*

"Twenty-five years ago, Howard Zehr's *Changing Lenses* started changing the world. This new edition demonstrates the timelessness of its original insights. New material brings it up to date. Especially valuable are Howard's reflections in the final chapter on the movement he helped launch."
—*Daniel Van Ness, executive director, Centre for Justice and Reconciliation at Prison Fellowship International*

"This is such a needed book in a time when 'justice' is under so much review. This books points to not only a better system but a better self. It is perceptive, healing, and instructive. It gets at the spirit of improving our systems and the soul of justice."
—*Joel C. Hunter, senior pastor, Northland, A Church Distributed*

CHANGING LENSES

Restorative
Justice
for Our Times

Howard Zehr

TWENTY-FIFTH ANNIVERSARY EDITION

Herald Press
Harrisonburg, Virginia
Kitchener, Ontario

Library of Congress Cataloging-in-Publication Data
Zehr, Howard, author.
  Changing lenses : restorative justice for our times / Howard Zehr. --
Twenty-fifth anniversary edition.
    pages cm
  Includes bibliographical references.
  ISBN 978-0-8361-9947-5 (pbk. : alk. paper) 1. Restorative justice.
2. Restorative justice--Religious aspects. 3. Victims of crimes. 4.
Punishment. 5. Reconciliation. I. Title.
  HV8688.Z437 2015
  364.6'8--dc23
                                        2015005821

CHANGING LENSES:
TWENTY-FIFTH ANNIVERSARY EDITION
© 1990, 1995, 2005, 2015 by Herald Press, Harrisonburg, Virginia 22802
    Released simultaneously in Canada by Herald Press,
    Kitchener, Ontario N2G 3R1. All rights reserved.
First published 1990. Second edition 1995. Third edition 2005.
Library of Congress Control Number: 2015005821
International Standard Book Number: 978-0-8361-9947-5
Printed in United States of America
Cover and interior design by Merrill Miller

To order or request information, please call 1-800-245-7894
or visit www.heraldpress.com.

19 18 17 16 15   10 9 8 7 6 5 4 3 2 1

God is merciful and gracious,

slow to anger and abounding in steadfast love.

God will not always accuse,

and will not be angry forever.

God does not deal with us according to our sins,

nor repay us according to our iniquities.

—*Psalm 103:8-10, The New Testament and Psalms,*
    An Inclusive Version

CONTENTS

Foreword

I MET HOWARD ZEHR in 2007, when I invited him to speak at a conference on crime victims at Stanford Law School's Criminal Justice Center. As Howard finished his talk, Robert Weisburg, the center's long-time faculty director, excitedly whispered, "I've discovered what I want to be when I grow up! Howard Zehr!"

I was in complete agreement with Professor Weisburg that day. In the years that followed, I've taken every opportunity to learn from Howard, in the hopes that his prodigious heart and intellect would somehow be contagious.

It's no exaggeration to say that by asking us to change lenses, Howard Zehr has changed countless lives. Mine is among them. As a former victim advocate turned public defender, my heart was painfully pulled in different directions by our legal system. Reforms for one "side" always came at the expense of the other, and none addressed the inefficacy of punishment as a strategy for reducing crime. *Changing Lenses* offered the sole, true paradigm shift I had encountered in the realm of criminal justice reform. By centralizing crime victims' self-identified needs, Howard reframed accountability as an empowering reprise of the golden rule: *do unto others as they would have you do unto them.*

Here was a view of justice that could better meet crime victims' needs, while simultaneously ending our addiction to punitive confinement by believing in the power of communities to support their members when things go wrong. Howard's vision was so compelling that shortly after meeting him, I left the practice of law to see how his ideas could be operationalized in Oakland, California. Howard has been a friend and mentor to my work at every step of the way.

In the pages that follow, Howard writes, "Our understandings of what is possible and impossible are based on our constructions of reality. These constructs can and do change." Changing these constructs requires fearlessly replacing entrenched views that no longer serve us with new ones that do. Howard Zehr is such a thinker. It speaks volumes that Howard transferred to Morehouse College in the early 1960s and became the first white man to graduate from the historically black college. This act was an early expression of Howard's deep commitment to changing lenses, to walking with people who have been historically marginalized, and to placing himself in uncomfortable situations that would force him to learn, grow, and ultimately be of benefit to those whose lived experiences differ from his own. As you will see in the pages that follow, these personal commitments are reflected in his theory of justice.

It is these experiences that likely drove Howard to engage in the direct practice in the field he helped create. Howard is a rare academic with significant hands-on experience. In the years since the original publication of this book, he has personally facilitated dialogues between crime victims and those who harmed them, and has sat in countless restorative justice circles with communities across this country. Howard's commitment to continued learning—particularly about the racialized nature of punishment in the United States—is reflected in this twenty-fifth anniversary edition.

Yet this edition retains the timeless messages Howard offered twenty-five years ago. Most importantly, *Changing Lenses* continues to lay the deep, theological basis for Howard's more concrete offerings that guide today's restorative justice practitioners found in later publications. And while the text is Christian in its framing, as a Buddhist and atheist, I find *Changing Lenses* to be a universal call for equal compassion for those who have experienced harm and those who caused it.

Howard's capacity to see things from different angles is no doubt born of his eclectic personal and professional interests. First and foremost is his photography, followed closely by his love of pickup trucks, restoring vintage AM radios, a foray into beekeeping, and many other curious things. He brings what he learns from myriad sources to his justice work, and this is reflected in his writing. Equally present in Howard's work are his wry, understated sense of humor, his open heart, and his consummate storytelling skills. But above all, Howard's humility makes his work accessible—his writing feels like a dialogue with the reader. He remains open to new ways of seeing things every day. So when I find myself too wedded to Howard's framing of restorative justice, he gently reminds me that "restorative justice is a compass, not a map."

I offer a deep bow of love and gratitude to Howard for the compass he began to construct with this timeless text, and for delivering on his aspiration to a paradigm shift away from the binary view of justice, away from the notion of us / them, victor / vanquished, winner / loser. Away from a justice of sides toward a justice that heals.

—*sujatha baliga*
Restorative Justice Project
Oakland, California

Preface to the Twenty-Fifth Anniversary Edition

SOON AFTER MY fortieth birthday, I remember walking along the beach, looking over Lake Michigan at the distant horizon, contemplating this book. Like the indistinct shapes on the lake's horizon, the book seemed a kind of mirage, an idea shimmering in the distance, not actually real.

A friend and I were spending a few days at a nearby cabin to get away from work and ponder the writing projects each of us was anticipating. I was trying to envision the kind of book I wanted to write. Who was I writing for, what I was I trying to accomplish, what might it look like physically? One dimension was clear: I wanted to produce a book that did what Nils Christie's little book *Limits to Pain* had done for me on the issue of punishment. I thought of his book as a provocative essay, and that's what I wanted to write: a book that would encourage us to identify and rethink some of the assumptions we rarely examine and that would help us begin to dream of other possibilities. When I try to understand a new field, I look first for a good journalist who is interpreting the field. I wanted to approach this emerging book with a journalistic sensibility and to write accessibly, from an insider/outsider perspective, about the big-picture issues of crime and justice today.

By the early 1980s, the small victim-offender reconciliation programs in Kitchener, Ontario, and Elkhart, Indiana, had some years of experience, and the idea had spread to many other communities even beyond North America. The concerns for victims, offenders, and communities that had led to the approach in the first place remained central, but we had no real integrating conceptual framework for what we were doing. During this time, I began to put together the components of a framework, presenting this first to a national group of Catholic priests and nuns who were engaged in prison ministry. I began to use the term *restorative justice*, and with an inclination to alliteration, contrasted it with *retributive justice*. The first full publication of this framework was in a small book entitled *Retributive Justice, Restorative Justice*, published by Mennonite Central Committee in 1985.

Later, although I knew I hadn't invented it, I could not recall where the term *restorative justice* originated. Then some years ago attorney Ann Skelton from South Africa was working on the history of restorative justice for her doctoral dissertation and came to visit. I turned her loose in my office, and she found a book that included an essay by Albert Eglash.[1] Several times in that essay he mentioned the term *restorative justice*. The phrase is underlined in my book, and I remembered then that I had first encountered the term there. Anne later traced the term to the work of a German theologian in the 1950s.

I had found Eglash's essay somewhat helpful, but his vision certainly wasn't for restorative justice as I came to understand it. Eglash called for "guided" or "creative" restitution as a focus for justice. However, he put little emphasis upon victims'

---

1 Albert Eglash, "Beyond Restitution—Creative Restitution," in *Restitution in Criminal Justice*, ed. Burt Galaway and Joe Hudson (Lexington, MA: Lexington Books, 1977), 91–99.

needs or roles. In fact, he concluded the essay like this: "Any benefit to victims is a bonus, gravy, but not the meat and potatoes of the process."

As this suggests, *Changing Lenses*, and the concept of restorative justice as I have articulated it, owes much to many sources and discussions. The preface from the earlier editions said it well: It is a work of synthesis more than invention. This is especially true of this twenty-fifth anniversary edition, as the acknowledgements and citations make clear.

If I were writing *Changing Lenses* today, I would say some things differently. Nevertheless, rereading the book for this edition, I am struck by how current most remains. For this reason, and because the book has come to be viewed as a kind of classic, I have made only minor changes to the primary text except for chapter 9, which has been updated to include more recent developments. Also, I have added some notes and moved some material from appendixes into chapters, in the process adding a chapter 12. Finally, the resources section has been updated and expanded to include a variety of new teaching and study material.

I wrote *Changing Lenses* from a Christian perspective, but I had hoped to write it in such a way that it would resonate and be used much more widely. That has, in fact, been the case. I am honored that my friend sujatha baliga (she prefers her name uncapitalized), a practicing Buddhist whose creativity, experience, and wisdom I deeply value, has contributed the foreword.

A note about terminology: In recent years, many of us in the restorative justice field have become uncomfortable with labels such as *victim* and *offender*. Although they provide handy terms for criminal justice applications and cannot be avoided there, they are often not appropriate when applied in school settings. More importantly, as noted above, they are labels that oversimplify and categorize people. In fact, they can become self-fulfilling. As labeling theory in criminology points out, people tend to become what they are labeled. Alternatives such as *the person harmed* or *the person causing harm* are more awkward, but were I writing this book today, I would use such terms more often. Later in this edition I also raise some cautions about the term *retributive* and the retributive/restorative dichotomy around which my argument is structured.

Earlier versions of this book began with a case story. I introduced the central metaphor of the book—changing our lenses—much later. Now that this metaphor is so established in the restorative justice field, I introduce this metaphor first, before the story. So let's begin there: with the lenses we use to view crime and justice.

—*Howard Zehr*

Part I

The Experience of Crime

1

A Vignette

I **HAVE BEEN INVOLVED** in photography for many years. One of the lessons I have learned is how profoundly the lens I look through affects the outcome. My choice of lens determines in what circumstances I can work and how I see. If I choose a slow lens with a small maximum aperture, the image will be dim, and good-quality photographs may be hard to obtain under low light levels.

The focal length of the lens also makes a difference. A wide-angle lens is highly inclusive. It incorporates within the frame a multitude of subjects, but it does so at the cost of a certain distortion. Objects that are nearer become large, leaving objects in the background small. Also, the shapes of objects at the corners of the frame are altered. Circles become ellipses.

A telephoto lens is more selective. The scope of its vision is narrower, incorporating fewer objects within the frame. It too "distorts," but in a different way than a wide-angle lens. With a telephoto lens, objects are larger but distances are compressed. Objects appear closer to the camera—and closer to one another—than they are to the naked eye.

The choice of lens, then, affects what is in the picture. It also determines the relationships and proportions of the elements included. Similarly, the lens we use to examine crime and justice affects what we include as relevant variables, what we consider their relative importance to be, and what we consider proper outcomes.

We in the West view crime through a particular lens. The "criminal justice" process that uses that lens fails to meet many of the needs of either victim or offender. The process neglects victims while failing to meet its expressed goals of holding offenders accountable and deterring crime.

Such failures have led to the widespread sense of crisis today. An array of reforms to the criminal justice system has been attempted. The fads of today, such as electronic monitoring and intensive supervision, are simply the most recent of a long line of "solutions." Yet this system has shown itself remarkably resistant to significant improvement, absorbing and subverting efforts at reform. A French proverb seems true: "The more things change, the more they remain the same."

The reason for such failure, I will argue in this book, lies in our choice of lens—that is, in the assumptions we make about crime and justice. These assumptions, which govern our responses to wrongdoing, are in fact out of step with the experience of crime. Furthermore, they are out of step with Christian roots and even with much of our own history in the West. To find our way out of this maze, we will have to look beyond alternative punishments and even beyond alternatives to punishment. We will have to look to alternative ways of viewing both problem and solution. Indeed, the lens we look through determines how we frame both the problem and the "solution." This book is about changing the lenses through which we view criminal justice.

This book is about principles and ideals. It seeks—perhaps presumptuously—to identify and evaluate some of the basic assumptions we make about crime, about justice, about how we live together. It attempts to outline briefly how we came to have these assumptions and to suggest some alternatives.

Such an effort involves abstractions, but it cannot be limited to them. We must begin by entering into the actual experience of crime and of justice as deeply as we can. Only with a firm footing in such reality can we begin to understand what we do, why we do it, and, hopefully, what we might do differently.

But an understanding of the experience of crime is not an easy undertaking, and it is not one that most of us approach willingly. To confront what it means to victimize or to be victimized by another person sparks intense emotions that are often frightening and that we would rather ignore. Unless we have experienced crime directly, we may find it difficult to empathize fully. Nevertheless, we must try, realizing that the attempt will be incomplete and perhaps painful.

This book, then, begins at that point.

THE STORY

Many years ago, I sat with a seventeen-year-old defendant in a courtroom in a small American town. A colleague and I had been asked to prepare a sentencing proposal to submit to the court. We were now there, awaiting sentencing by the judge.

The events leading up to this point make a sorry story. When he was sixteen, this young man used a knife to confront a young woman in a dark hallway. In the ensuing scuffle, she lost an eye. Now his fate was to be decided.

Although details are uncertain, something like this seems to have unfolded. The young man, who came from an unhappy—probably abusive—home situation had decided to run away with his girlfriend but lacked the necessary money. He had no record of violence. But television apparently convinced him that if he threatened someone, she or he would hand over money and his problem would be solved.

In choosing a victim, he picked a young woman he sometimes saw around town. On several occasions, he had attempted to talk with her but had been rebuffed. Since he assumed her to be well off, she seemed a logical choice.

So he waited in the hallway of her apartment with a knife in his hand, his face masked. (He claims he had deliberately picked a small knife.) When she entered, he grabbed her from behind. But instead of passively handing over her money as he had expected, the young woman panicked—as most of us would—and began to scream and struggle. The young man's mother later mentioned that he never could stand to have voices raised against him and that he tended to get irrational when that happened. Perhaps this explains his behavior, then, because when she struggled, he too panicked, stabbing her a number of times, including in the eye.

They entered her apartment. Here their stories differ as to whether he held her captive or was attempting to help. He claims that he was taking her for help and that she was cooperating. At the time of arrest, he was reported to have said, "I didn't mean it; I didn't mean it. I didn't want to hurt nobody. Tell her I'm sorry." At any rate, he was arrested as they were leaving the apartment. Eventually he was convicted and now was awaiting sentence.

In the tiny courtroom in this small community, he sat with his attorney at a table facing the judge. Behind him sat his family. In the back row sat the family and relatives of the victim. Scattered through the room were a few interested onlookers and criminal justice professionals.

Before he was sentenced, I presented my sentencing proposal, which called for a limited prison term, supervision, restitution to the victim, restitution to the community, counseling, education, structured living, and employment. He was asked whether he had anything to say.

He talked about his sorrow for what he had done and of his attempt to understand what it meant for the young woman. "I realize," he said, "I have caused a lot of pain. Miss —— lost something she will never get back. I would gladly give her my eye to see through. I am sorry for what I have done, and I ask that I be forgiven. I don't wish to cause [her] family any harm in later years, no matter how long it will be."

Then came time for sentencing. Before pronouncing the sentence, however, the judge methodically enumerated the usual goals of sentences: the need for retribution, the need to isolate offenders from society, the need to rehabilitate, the need to deter. He noted the need for offenders to be held accountable for their actions.

The judge also discussed this young man's intent in committing the crime. He had been charged with armed robbery and assault with intent to kill. The judge appeared to agree with the offender's version, that he did not intend to kill when he undertook the robbery. However, it was the judge's inference that he had formed the intent during the course of the struggle and thus that the charge was both accurate and serious.

Then he pronounced sentence. The young man was given a sentence of twenty to eighty-five years in prison with no possibility of parole or good time before the minimum was served. He would be at least thirty-seven when he emerged. "I trust," the judge admonished this youth as he pronounced this sentence, "that there you will forget the patterns of behavior which led to this violent offense."

That this story is a tragedy can hardly be denied. It is, however, a tragedy that was soon abstracted into a different kind of drama. Instead of a tragic confrontation between two individuals, the legal process and the media transformed it into a *crime* involving a *criminal* and—it is only secondarily remembered—a *victim*. The drama was between two abstractions. The event was mystified and mythologized until the actual experiences and motivations were lost.

Let us begin, therefore, by changing our lenses. Let's demythologize and demystify this all-too-typical tragedy. Let's try to unravel the experience, viewing it as a human tragedy involving real people—people who are in many ways much like us.

2

The Victim

I NEVER MET THIS young woman. I was discouraged from
doing so by the adversarial nature of the legal process, by the
circumstances of my involvement in the case, and by my own
uncertainty about how to proceed. In retrospect, I probably
should have risked the attempt. However, let me try to project,
on the basis of other victims' experiences, something of what
she has gone through.[1]

THE EXPERIENCE

When she entered her hallway and was assaulted by a man
with a knife wearing a mask, she was terrified. Her first reaction was one of shock and disbelief: "This cannot be happening to me." Some victims report that they are paralyzed

---

1 Considerable information about the victim experience is becoming avail-
able. I have especially appreciated Morton Bard and Dawn Sangrey, *The
Crime Victim's Book*, 2nd ed. (New York: Brunner-Mazel, 1986). See also
Shelley Neiderbach, *Invisible Wounds: Crime Victims Speak* (New York:
Hayworth Press, 1986) and Doug Magee, *What Murder Leaves Behind:
The Victim's Family* (New York: Dodd, Mead and Co., 1983). Charlotte
Hullinger, cofounder of Parents of Murdered Children, Inc., has been an
important help. See also Howard Zehr, *Transcending: Reflections of Crime
Victims* (Intercourse, PA: Good Books, 2001).

initially, unable to act. She, however, screamed and struggled. She reported later that she was certain she was going to die.

A common reaction of victims is what psychologists have called *frozen-fear compliance*. Confronted by such a terrifying, overpowering situation, victims of violent crime (like victims of hijackings) frequently seem to cooperate with their oppressor. In some crimes such as rape, this natural psychological reaction may be misinterpreted by courts as willing collaboration. In actuality, however, such compliance is rooted in terror.

Once the initial attack was over, this woman did in fact react in this way. The offender's perspective was that once he realized what he had done, he tried to help her get assistance. In his view, she had cooperated. In reality, however, she was terrified of him, felt completely in his power, and therefore, attempted to cooperate and pacify him in any way she could.

During the initial impact phase, then, her reactions were in common with most victims: she was overwhelmed by feelings of confusion, helplessness, terror, vulnerability. Those feelings stayed with her during the coming weeks, although with less intensity. However, intense new feelings arose: anger, guilt, suspicion, depression, meaninglessness, self-doubt, regret.

During this recoil phase, she struggled to adjust and experienced wide swings in mood. Some days she seemed to be recovering her buoyancy and her optimism, only to be followed by severe depression or rage. She became suspicious of other people, especially strangers, and was easily startled.

She began to have vivid and frightening dreams and fantasies uncharacteristic of her and contrary to her values. She fantasized, for instance, about taking terrible vengeance on the person who did this to her. Since this was in contrast to her values, it brought her anxiety and guilt. When awake, she often replayed what had happened and how she responded, wondering why she reacted the way she did and what she should have done differently.

Like most crime victims, she struggled with feelings of shame and of blame. She asked repeatedly why it happened, why she reacted the way she did, and what she could have done differently, and she was tempted to conclude that it was in some way her fault. If only she had not rebuffed him when he tried to talk with her . . . If only she had not gone out that night . . . Perhaps she was being punished for something she did . . .

She will continue to grapple with feelings of fear as well as a sense of vulnerability and helplessness. Someone else took control, leaving her feeling powerless and vulnerable, and it will be difficult to recover the confidence of again being safe and in control. Accompanying this struggle will be the attempt to regain trust in others, in the world. Someone had violated her and her world, and the sense of being at home with people, with her home, with her neighborhood, with her world, will be difficult to regain.

Most victims experience intense feelings of anger at the person who did this, at others who should have prevented it, at God who allowed or even caused it. This intense anger may contradict the values they profess, increasing their guilt. For a religious person, an experience like this often provokes a crisis of faith. Why did this happen? What did I do to deserve this? How can a loving, just God let this happen? Lack of a satisfying answer can result in a profound crisis of belief.

During the weeks following the attack, this young woman struggled to adjust to her new situation. In part, she was grieving the loss of an eye, the loss of her innocence. She sought ways to deal with intense new feelings of anger, guilt, vulnerability. And she needed to readjust her vision of the world and of herself. She now sees the world as a potentially dangerous place that has betrayed her. No longer can she see it as the comfortable, predictable environment of her past. She sees herself as having been naive, needing to stop being so nice and trusting. Given these new feelings, she is even beginning to adjust her self-image. Although she had previously viewed herself as a caring, loving, person-oriented individual, this self-concept has now been shattered.

What about her friends in all this?

If she had been fortunate, she would have had friends, church members, coworkers, and neighbors willing to seek her out. She needed people who would accept her feelings regardless of whether they are understood, without judgment, and who would listen to her story over and over. She needed friends who would help her not to blame herself for what happened or how she has responded, who would provide support and assistance without taking over for her.[2] Unfortunately, however, her friends tend to avoid the subject. They easily tire of her story, feeling that she needs to put this behind and move on. They admonish her not to be angry and imply in various ways

---

2 Charlotte Hullinger, cofounder of Parents of Murdered Children and herself a victim, has identified four ways that friends tend to respond to victims:

The Rescuer. Fear makes them want quick resolutions. Rather than listen, they make suggestions that encourage dependency. They are uncomfortable with just having victims vent. It is hard for them to see people in pain and to feel helpless, so they want to fix things.

The Hostile Helper. Fear makes them angry. They may want to blame the victim. They speak judgmentally and try to distance themselves from the victim. As they are afraid, they claim it would not have happened to them.

The Helpless Helper. Fear overwhelms them. They feel as bad as or worse than the victim, but they don't really listen. They may make the victim feel so bad that he or she becomes sorry for the helper.

The Positive Helper. This person is aware of and acknowledges fears. She or he faces vulnerability, listens without judgment, and has a sense of timing. Such helpers may say, "You must be terribly upset"; "It takes time"; "You handled it well"; or "It must be awful." In other words, they give victims permission to talk without specifying how they do so.

that she contributed to what happened—that she is somehow to blame. They imply that what happened was in some way God's will. Perhaps she needed to be punished. Perhaps God caused this for some good end. Perhaps God is trying to teach her a lesson. Such suggestions increase her tendency to blame herself and to question her faith.

These reactions by friends and acquaintances are examples of what psychologists have termed *secondary victimization*. When we hear of a crime, when we listen to a victim relate his or her story, we too experience some of the feelings of victimization. Those are painful feelings that we like to avoid. So we avoid the subject and we tend to blame. After all, if we can locate the cause for her troubles in something she did or is, we can distance ourselves from her situation. We can believe that such a thing is not likely to happen to us. That makes us feel more secure.

She therefore had to fight for the right to grieve. Since her close friends—including perhaps a boyfriend—suffered with her, additional strain was caused by the fact that they grieved differently and less apparently. Divorce rates are high among parents of murdered children, for example, in part because partners grieve differently and have different ways of adjusting. If not identified and understood, differences in ways of grieving may drive people apart.

The experience of being a crime victim can be highly intense, touching all areas of life. For this young woman, it affected her sleeping, her appetite, and her health. She turned to drugs and alcohol in order to cope. Medical costs became a significant burden. Her job performance deteriorated. Various experiences and special events continued to bring back painful memories. Had she been married, her marriage might have been strained. Her sexual interest and behavior might have been affected. For crime victims, the aftereffects often are traumatic and far-reaching.

The breadth and intensity of the crime experience is not too difficult to acknowledge in a violent crime like this one, although the full dimensions of the crisis are difficult for non-victims to fathom. What is often overlooked is that victims of offenses that we consider less serious may experience similar reactions. In describing their experiences, victims of burglary often sound much like victims of rape. Victims of vandalism and car theft report many of the same reactions as victims of violent assault, though perhaps in less intense form.

WHY SO TRAUMATIC?

Why such reactions? Why is crime so devastating, so hard to recover from? The reason is that crime is in essence a violation: a violation of the self and a desecration of who we are, of what we believe, and of our private space. Crime is devastating because it upsets two fundamental assumptions on which we base our lives—our belief that the world is an orderly, meaningful place and our belief in personal autonomy. Both assumptions are essential for wholeness.

Most of us assume that the world (or at least the part of the world in which we live) is an orderly, predictable, understandable place. Everything may not happen as we wish, but at least we can provide answers for much of what happens. Generally we know what to expect. How could we live with any sense of security otherwise?

Crime, like cancer, upsets this sense of order and meaning. Consequently, crime victims, like cancer victims, want answers. Why did this happen to me? What could I have done to prevent it? These are only a few of the questions that nag at victims. Answers to such questions are important, because answers restore order and meaning. If we can provide answers to the questions of what and why, the world can make sense again. Without answers, victims tend to blame themselves, others, and God. Blame, in fact, is one important way of providing answers in order to restore meaning and some semblance of wholeness.

But to be whole we also need to have a sense of personal autonomy, of power over our own lives. To be deprived unwillingly of personal power, to be involuntarily in the control of others, is intensely degrading and dehumanizing. Crime destroys this sense of autonomy. Someone else has taken control of our lives, our property, our space. It leaves victims feeling vulnerable, defenseless, out of control, and dehumanized. Here again, self-blame may be a coping mechanism. If we can locate the cause of the crime in something we did, we can determine to avoid that behavior, thus regaining a sense of control.

The woman in our story was not simply the victim of a physical attack, then. She was—and is—the victim of an assault on her very sense of self, on her self-concept as an autonomous individual in a predictable world. The psychological effects may be more serious than the physical loss.

THE RECOVERY PROCESS

To recover, victims need to move from the recoil phase to a reorganization phase. In cases of serious crimes, they need to move from being victims to being survivors. Victims need to progress to the point where the offense and the offender no longer dominate them. However, this is difficult and time consuming. For many people, it may never be fully attained.

What do victims need in order to recover? Any answer to this question is a bit risky. Only a victim can answer authentically, and needs vary from person to person. In general, though, the needs of crime victims include (but are not limited to) the following.

Most obviously, perhaps, victims need compensation for losses. Financial and material losses may present a real financial burden. Moreover, the symbolic value of losses may be as important as or more important than the actual material

losses. In either case, repayment can assist recovery. Full repayment for the material and psychological damage may well
be impossible. But the sense of loss and the resulting need to
have things made right in a material way can be quite acute.

No one can give back an eye to the woman in the preceding story. Restitution for expenses, however, might ease the
burden. At the same time, it may provide a sense of restoration
on a symbolic level.

As important as material losses are, surveys of crime victims find that they usually rate other needs more highly. One
of these is the need for answers, for information. Why me?
Did this person have something personal against me? Is he
or she coming back? What happened to my property? What
could I have done to avoid becoming a victim? Information
must be provided and questions answered.

It can be suggested that to find healing, victims must find
answers to six basic questions:[3]

1. What happened?
2. Why did it happen to me?
3. Why did I act as I did at the time?
4. Why have I acted as I have since that time?
5. What if it happens again?
6. What does this mean for me and for my outlook (my
   faith, my vision of the world, my future)?

Some of these questions can be answered only by the victims
themselves. They must, for example, find their own explanations
for their behavior at the time and since that time. And they must

---

3 Adapted from Charles Finley, "Catastrophes: An Overview of Family
Reactions," in *Stress and the Family, vol. 2: Coping with Catastrophe,* ed.
Charles Finley and Hamilton I. McCubbin (New York: Brunner/Mazel,
1983).

decide how they will respond to similar situations in the future. However, the first two questions have to do with the facts of the offense. What actually happened? Why did it happen to me? Information can be very important to victims, and answers to such questions may provide an entrance on the road to recovery. Without answers to such questions, recovery may be difficult.

In addition to restitution and answers, victims need opportunities to express and validate their emotions: their anger, their fear, their pain. Even though such feelings may be hard for us to hear and may not square with what we would wish them to feel, these feelings are a natural, human response to the violation of crime. Anger, in fact, needs to be recognized as a common stage of suffering and one that cannot simply be short-circuited. The suffering and the pain are part of the offense and need to be expressed and heard. Victims need opportunities and arenas to express their feelings and their suffering but also to tell their stories. They need to have their "truth" heard and validated by others.

Victims also need to be empowered. Their sense of personal autonomy has been stolen from them by an offender, and they need to have this sense of personal power returned to them. This includes a sense of control over their environment. Thus, new locks and other security devices may be important to them, or they may change their lifestyles as a means of reducing risks. Similarly, they need a sense of control or involvement in the resolution of their own cases. They need to feel that they have choices and that these choices are real.

Victims often feel that safety is important. They want assurance that this will not happen again—to them or to others. They want to know that steps are being taken toward this end.

A common thread running throughout may be described as the need for an experience of justice. For some victims, this may take the form of a demand for vengeance. However, a demand for retribution may itself grow out of a victim's failure to have a more positive experience of justice. Indeed, an experience of justice is so basic that without it healing may be well impossible.

An experience of justice for victims has many dimensions, some of which have already been suggested. Victims need assurance that what happened to them was wrong, unfair, undeserved. They need opportunities to speak the truth of what happened to them, including their suffering. They need to be heard and affirmed. People working with women who are victims of domestic violence have summarized these needs in terms such as *truth-telling, breaking the silence, de-privatization,* and *de-minimization.*

As part of this experience of justice, victims need to know that steps are being taken to rectify the wrong and to reduce the opportunities for it to recur. As noted earlier, they may want restitution, not just for the material recovery involved but for the moral statement implied in the recognition that the act was wrongful and in the attempt to make things right.

Justice may be a state of affairs, but it is also an experience. Justice must be experienced as real. Victims are not usually content to be assured that things are being taken care of. They want to be informed and, at least at certain points, to be consulted and involved.

Crime may upset our sense of meaning, which is a basic human need. Consequently the path to recovery involves a search for meaning. Indeed, the six questions that victims must answer in order to recover involve a search for meaning. For crime victims, the need for justice is most basic because, as philosopher and historian Michael Ignatieff has observed, justice provides a framework of meanings that makes sense of experience.[4] All of this leads me to several observations.

---

4 Michael Ignatieff, "Imprisonment and the Need for Justice," an address to the 1987 Canadian Criminal Justice Congress in Toronto. An edited version is printed in *Liaison,* January 1988.

First, victimization can be a highly traumatic experience. It is so because it is a violation of something very basic: our vision of ourselves as autonomous individuals in a meaningful world. It is also a violation of trust in our relationships with others.

Second, this is often true not only for violent crimes such as murder and rape, which most of us view as serious, but also for crimes such as spouse abuse, burglary, vandalism, or car theft—offenses that society often treats as minor.

Third, common patterns of victim response emerge, taking into account variations in personality, situation, and offense. Certain feelings such as fear and anger are nearly universal, for example, and many victims appear to move through identifiable stages of adjustment.

Finally, being victimized by another person generates a series of needs that, if met, can assist in the recovery process. For the unattended victim, however, healing may be very difficult and incomplete.

OUR RESPONSE

It would seem logical, given all this, that victims would be at the center of the justice process with their needs as a major focus. One might suppose that victims would have some say in what charges are brought and that they and their needs might be taken into account in the final disposition of the case. One could at least expect that they would be told when an offender has been identified and would be kept informed as the case moves through the court. In many cases, however, little or none of this happens. Victims have little say as to whether or how the case is prosecuted. Often they are taken into account only if they are needed as witnesses. Rarely are they notified when an offender is apprehended. Only where it is required by law do courts make any regular effort to notify victims of the process of the case through the court or to solicit their input into the final disposition.

This was illustrated graphically by a woman at a seminar I once helped lead. I had spent some time describing the situation of crime victims—their suffering, their needs, their omission from the "justice" process—when a woman near the back stood up and said, "You are right. On one occasion my house was burglarized. On another I was assaulted in a dark street. In neither case was I informed or consulted until the case was through or nearly through the courts. And do you know what? I am the prosecutor! My own staff did not keep me informed." You can imagine, then, what the rest of us can expect.

This realization often comes to victims soon after they report an offense. They are frequently astonished to find that charges can be either pursued or dropped without regard to victims' wishes and that they are provided little information about the case.

Such neglect of victims not only fails to meet their needs but it also compounds the injury. Many speak of a secondary victimization by criminal justice personnel and processes. The question of personal power is central here. Part of the dehumanizing nature of victimization by crime is the way it robs victims of power. Instead of returning power to them by allowing them to participate in the justice process, the legal system compounds the injury again by denying power. Instead of helping, the process hurts.

In the U.S., federal legislation has been passed to help support victim assistance and compensation programs that have begun in many states. Compensation programs allow victims of serious personal crimes who meet a variety of fairly stiff criteria to apply for reimbursement for expenses. Victim assistance programs, in communities where they exist, provide counseling and other resources for victims. England has led in the development of local victim support programs, which use volunteers to provide support and assistance to victims as they proceed through the justice process and seek recovery.[5]

All of this helps, indicating a new and important concern for victims. Unfortunately, though, these efforts remain mere beginnings, veritable drops in the bucket, when compared to the needs. Victims still remain peripheral to the justice process. In the legal process, victims represent footnotes to the crime.

Our failure to take victims seriously leaves a terrible legacy of fear, suspicion, anger, and guilt. It leads to persistent and perhaps growing demands for vengeance. It encourages the building of stereotypes. (How else, after all, is one to make sense of an offender one has not met?) And these stereotypes lead to further distrust, encouraging racism and classism.

Perhaps worst of all, from the point of view of the victim, is the lack of resolution.[6] When victims are unattended and their needs unmet, they often find it difficult to put the experience behind them. Victims often relate their experiences vividly, as if they happened yesterday, when in fact they may have happened years ago. Nothing in their experience has let them really overcome. Instead, the experience and the offender still dominate their lives. The victim is still denied power. And the damage is not limited to individual victims; it is shared by friends and by others who hear about the tragedy. The open wounds result in increased suspicion, fear, anger, and feelings of vulnerability throughout the community. Indeed, they work to undermine a sense of community.

---

5 See National Association of Victim Support Schemes, https://www .victimsupport.org.uk. In the U.S., the National Center for Victims of Crime serves as a clearinghouse for victim services and information: http:// www.victimsofcrime.org.

6 In earlier editions of this book, I used the word *closure* here. This is not a victim-friendly word, and I would never use it today. As Emma Jo Snyder, whose son was murdered, told me, "That one will give you a black eye." Zehr, *Transcending*, 39.

This failure to attend to victims' needs does not mean that we will never mention victims in the legal process or in the news, however. On the contrary, we may invoke their names to do all sorts of things to the offender, regardless of what victims actually want. The reality is that we do almost nothing directly for the victim, in spite of the rhetoric. We do not listen to what they have suffered and what they need. We do not seek to give them back some of what they have lost. We do not let them help to decide how the situation should be resolved. We do not help them to recover. We may not even let them know what has transpired since the offense!

This, then, is the ultimate irony, the ultimate tragedy. Those who have most directly suffered are not to be part of the resolution of the offense. In fact, as we shall see, victims are not even part of our understanding of the problem.

3

The Offender

I HAVE SUGGESTED THAT the wounded victim in our opening story probably has not experienced justice. But what has been happening to the young offender who attacked her?

He has been through an elaborate and lengthy process in which one professional—a lawyer, who is expected to represent his interests—has been pitted against another professional—the prosecutor, who represents the state and its interests. This process is guided by an elaborate labyrinth of rules called *due process*. These are designed to protect both his and society's (but not necessarily the victim's) rights. Through this process, a series of professionals (prosecutor, judge, probation officers, psychiatrists) have helped to decide that he is in fact guilty of the offense as defined by law. This has included a determination not only that he committed a legally defined offense but that he intended to do so. The judge has also determined what should be done with him.

Throughout this process, the offender has been almost a bystander. His primary focus has been on his own situation and future. Almost inevitably he has become preoccupied by the various obstacles, decisions, and stages that need to be faced. Nevertheless, most of the decisions have been made for him by others.

THE PRISON EXPERIENCE

Now he is in prison. While the length of the term commonly assessed in the U.S. may seem unusual in a Canadian or Western European setting, the decision to imprison is not. In fact, prison is the normal response to crime in contemporary Western society. We operate under a presumption of prison. Prison is not a sentence of last resort, which must be justified and rationalized by the judge who imposes it. On the contrary, prison is normative, and judges find it necessary to explain and rationalize a sentence other than prison.

This presumption of prison explains why our incarceration rates are so high. Americans often believe that we are "soft on crime." While it is true that there are individual cases and jurisdictions where offenders may seem to "get off easy," as a nation the reality is quite different. By international standards, we are very harsh. Indeed, we have the highest incarceration rates in the world.[1] This mass incarceration is characterized by huge racial disparities.[2]

Prison is the sentence of first, not last, resort, and this is true not only for violent crimes. Many international observers are surprised to learn that many if not most of the prisoners being held in American prisons are serving sentences for property and drug crimes. American imprisonment rates are high because we consider prison sentences as our norm.

When sentencing the offender, the judge in our case expressed the hope that this young offender would learn nonviolent patterns of behavior while in prison. What, in fact, is he likely to learn?

---

1 Roy Walmsley, "World Prison Population List," 10th ed., *International Centre for Prison Studies*, last modified November 21, 2013, http://www .prisonstudies.org/research-publications?shs_term_node_tid_depth=27.

2 See Michelle Alexander, *The New Jim Crow: Mass Incarceration in the Age of Colorblindness* (New York: New Press, 2010).

By now, this young man may well have become the victim of violence himself. What lesson is he learning? He will learn that conflict is normal, that violence is the great problem solver, that one must be violent in order to survive, and that one responds to frustration with violence. These realities are, after all, normal in the distorted world of prison.

This young man's age and small physical stature make it likely that he will become the victim of not just violence but sexual violence. Rape of young men is frequent in prison, where older, patterned offenders are often mixed in with younger, less experienced men. Such rape may reflect the prolonged sexual deprivation and frustration characteristic of prison life. More often, though, rape becomes a distorted means of asserting power over others by persons denied legitimate forms of power and meaning. Rape in prison is also a vehicle for expressing contempt and for degrading others. This in turn reflects disturbing—but all-too-common—understandings of masculinity and femininity. Given this young man's apparent insecurity, it is likely that his sense of self-worth and manhood will be severely damaged and distorted by this experience.

So much, then, for the judge's hope that patterns of violence will be forgotten. On the contrary, the judge has ordered this offender to live for at least twenty years in an atmosphere that nourishes and teaches violence. Violence may become for him a way of coping, a way of solving problems, a way of communicating.

This offender got in trouble in part because of a poor sense of self-worth, personal autonomy, and personal power. Yet the prison experience will further strip away his sense of worth and autonomy, leaving him with even fewer resources for obtaining a sense of worth and autonomy in legitimate ways.

I am convinced that much crime and violence is a way of asserting personal identity and power. This was expressed well by a friend who spent seventeen years in prison for a series of armed robberies. Finally, through the help of patient church people, he made the transition to society. Bobby had grown up black and poor. His father, a janitor and an alcoholic, felt locked into a world that became a prison with little hope for escape. Crime was, for Bobby, an escape from the prison of personal nothingness. "At least when I had a shotgun in my hand I was somebody!" Bobby told me. How could he respect others when his respect for himself was so poor?

Psychologist Robert Johnson, writing about murderers on death row, has captured well the meaning and roots of violence.

> Their violence is not a specter or disease that afflicts them without rhyme or reason, nor is it merely a convenient vehicle for ugly passions. Rather, their violence is an adaptation to bleak and often brutal lives.... [The violence] of most violent men is ultimately spawned by the hostility and abuse of others, and it feeds on low self-confidence and fractured self-esteem. Paradoxically, their violence is a twisted form of self-defense that serves only to confirm the feelings of weakness and vulnerability that provoke it in the first place. When their violence claims innocent victims, it signals not a triumph of nerve but a loss of control.[3]

Given the poor sense of self-worth and personal autonomy characteristic of so many offenders, petty arguments and conflicts in prison often lead quickly to major violence. An argument over a dollar can easily lead to death.

Our offender may have gotten in trouble because of a poor sense of self-worth and personal power. His offense may have been a distorted attempt to say he was someone and to assert some control over his life and perhaps others. Yet the prison setting will further strip away his sense of power and worth.

---

3 Robert Johnson, "A Life for a Life?" *Justice Quarterly* 1, no. 4 (December 1984): 571.

The entire prison setting is structured to dehumanize. Prisoners are given numbers, standardized clothing, and little or no personal space. They are denied almost all possibilities for personal decision making and power. Indeed, the focus of the entire setting is on obedience, on learning to take orders. In that situation, a person has few choices. He or she can learn to obey, to be submissive. This is the response the prison system encourages, yet it is the response least likely to encourage a successful transition to free society. Our offender got into trouble because of his inability to be self-governing, to take charge of his own life in a legitimate way. Prison will further deprive him of that ability. Thus, it should not be surprising that those who conform to prison rules best are *not* those who make the most successful transition into the community after prison.

A second response when confronted by pressure to conform is to rebel. Many do. In part, such rebellion is an attempt to retain a sense of individuality. As a category, those who rebel seem to make the transition to free society better than those who conform (although rebellion may make release on parole more unlikely). There are exceptions: if the rebellion is too violent or too prolonged, a pattern of rebellion and violence may begin to dominate.

Jack Abbott is a prisoner who has spent most of his life fighting conformity in prison. His book, *In the Belly of the Beast*, is an articulate, insightful look at the world of prison.[4] After years in prison he was released, only to kill again when he perceived that he had been insulted.

A third option is to become devious, to appear to conform while finding ways to retain areas of personal freedom. This leads to another lesson learned in prison: the lesson that manipulation is normal. That is, after all, how one copes in

---

4 Jack Henry Abbott, *In the Belly of the Beast: Letters from Prison* (New York: Random House, 1981).

prison. And it is how prison authorities manage prisoners. How else, after all, can so few authorities manage so many prisoners, given such limited resources? In short, the convict learns to con.

Our offender got into trouble because of his inability to make good choices. The ability to make his own good choices will be further eroded by the prison experience. During his twenty or more years he will have little encouragement or even opportunity to make choices and take responsibility. In fact, what he will learn is dependence. During those years, he will not pay rent, will not have to manage money, will not be primarily responsible for a family. He will be dependent upon the state to take care of him. And when he emerges, he will have few coping skills. How will he learn to keep a job, to save, to budget, to pay bills?

In prison, our offender will absorb a warped ideal of interpersonal relationships. Domination over others will be the goal, whether over a marriage partner, a friend, or a business acquaintance. Caring will be seen as a weakness. And the weak are meant to be preyed upon.

This offender needs to learn that he is someone of worth and that he has the power and responsibility to make good choices. He needs to learn respect for others and their property. He needs to learn to cope peacefully with frustration and conflict. He needs coping skills. Instead, he will be encouraged to turn to violence for personal validation, as a means to cope, and as a way to solve problems. His sense of worth and autonomy will either be weakened or become based on dangerous foundations.

When examined in this context, then, the judge's hope becomes incredibly naive and wrongheaded.

Will prison teach him nonviolent patterns of behavior? Hardly. It is more likely to make him even more violent. Will it protect society from him? For a while, perhaps, but eventually he will come out, and he may be worse for the wear. And while there, he may become a danger to fellow inmates.

Will it deter? Whether his imprisonment will discourage others from committing similar crimes is debatable, but it is unlikely to deter him. Indeed, as I have already suggested, he may be more, not less, likely to commit crimes because of the lack of coping skills and the patterns of behavior he will learn in prison. Moreover, the threat of prison will no longer hold such terror for him since he will know he can survive there. Indeed, after twenty years it will be home, and he will feel insecure outside.

Some prisoners who have spent that long inside commit crimes upon release precisely so they can go back to a place that is familiar. They would rather be where they have the skills to cope than face the uncertainties and dangers of life on the outside. Recently I was a guest at a group meeting in a British day center for ex-offenders. One of the young men participating had been in prison a number of times. "I like being out," he said, "but I'm just as happy inside." The threat of prison can hardly deter such an individual.

Nor is the threat of prison likely to deter people who are poor and marginal, who believe life on the outside to be a kind of prison. To a person in such a situation, a prison sentence is simply to exchange one kind of confinement for another. Yet we reserve prison sentences primarily for the poor and the powerless.

WHAT NEEDS TO HAPPEN?

When sentencing this young man, the judge spoke of the need to hold offenders accountable. Most of us would agree. Offenders do indeed need to be held accountable for their behavior. But what does accountability mean? For this judge, and for most people today, accountability for offenders means that the offender must experience punitive consequences—often prison—whether for deterrence or for punishment. *Making people accountable* means forcing people to "take their medicine"—an odd metaphor for anything as damaging as prison.

This is an extremely limited and abstract understanding of accountability. Without an intrinsic link between the act and the consequences, true accountability is hardly possible. And as long as consequences are decided *for* offenders, accountability will not involve responsibility.

In order to commit offenses and live with their behavior, offenders often construct elaborate rationalizations for their actions, and prison gives them much time and encouragement to do so. They come to believe that what they did was not too serious, that the victim "deserved" it, that everyone is doing it, and that insurance will take care of any losses. They find ways to divert blame from themselves to other people and situations. They also employ stereotypes about victims and potential victims. Unconsciously or even consciously, they work to insulate themselves from the victim. Some burglars even report that they turn photographs toward the wall in homes they burglarize so that they will not have to think of the victims.

Nothing in our criminal justice process ever challenges these misattributions. On the contrary, the process often encourages rationalizations and strengthens stereotypes.[5] The adversarial nature of the process tends to harden stereotypes about victims and about society. The intricate, painful, nonparticipatory nature of the process encourages a tendency to focus on the

---

5 As judge Fred McElrea of New Zealand has often said, a central principle of the Western legal system is "put the state to the proof." That is, it is the state's obligation to prove the charges, so defendants are encouraged by their attorneys to plead not guilty. This tends to reinforce denial of responsibility.

wrongs experienced by the offender, diverting attention from the harm done to the victim. Many, if not most, offenders end up feeling that they have been treated badly (and they may well have!). This in turn helps them focus on their own plight rather than that of the victim. At minimum, because the criminal process is so complex and so offender-oriented, they are caught up entirely in their own legal situations.

Consequently, offenders are rarely encouraged or allowed to see the real human costs of what they have done. What is it really like to have one's home burglarized or car stolen, to experience the fear and questions about who did this and why? What is it like to believe you are going to die and then to lose an eye? What kind of person is the victim? Nothing in an offender's experience with justice addresses those issues. Nothing forces him or her to face up to rationalizations and stereotypes. In the case above, the offender made some attempt to understand what he did, but his understanding is incomplete and will soon be blotted out by his experience of justice and punishment.

Genuine accountability, then, includes an opportunity to understand the human consequences of one's acts and to face up to what one has done and to whom one has done it. But real accountability involves more. Accountability also involves taking responsibility for the results of one's behavior. Offenders must be allowed and encouraged to help decide what will happen to make things right, then to take steps to repair the damage.

Judge Dennis Challeen points out that the problem with most sentences is that although they make offenders accountable (in the sense of taking their punishment), they do not make offenders responsible. Yet a lack of responsibility is what got them into trouble in the first place. When punishment is handed down to responsible people, Challeen argues, they often respond responsibly. When we hand down sanctions to those who are irresponsible, however, it tends to make them more irresponsible.[6]

Some courts have begun to introduce restitution to victims into sentences. This is a step in the right direction. However, the rationale for restitution has often been fuzzy and misplaced. Often it is viewed as a way of punishing the offender rather than a way of making things right to the victim. Also, it is usually an imposed sanction and thus does not encourage offenders' ownership in the outcome. Usually the offender does not participate in the restitution decision and has little or no understanding of the victim's losses. He or she thus is likely to view restitution as one more punitive sanction rather than as a logical attempt to right a wrong and fulfill an obligation to another person. Restitution sentences imposed on offenders as punishment are unlikely to help them be responsible. This is a major reason for poor repayment rates in some restitution programs.

Our offender needs to be held accountable for his behavior in whatever ways he can. This means that he must be encouraged to develop as complete an understanding as possible of what he has done (i.e., what his actions have meant to the other person involved) and to acknowledge his role in it. He must also be allowed and encouraged to make things right to the extent that it is possible to do so. And he should participate in finding ways that this can be done. That is real accountability.

Such accountability may help bring resolution to the victim by meeting some of her needs. It can also help bring resolution to the offender. An understanding of what hurt he has caused may help discourage him from causing such harm in

---

6 Dennis A. Challeen, *Making It Right: A Common Sense Approach to Criminal Justice* (Aberdeen, SD: Melius and Peterson Publishing, 1986).

the future. An opportunity to make things right, to become a productive citizen, can boost his self-esteem and thus encourage lawful behavior.

WHAT WILL HAPPEN?

None of this is likely to happen to our offender during the next twenty years. The result?

He will have no opportunity to confront the stereotypes and rationalizations that have led up to his offense. Indeed, they will be amplified and elaborated upon during his years in prison. He will have no opportunity to build the interpersonal skills and the coping skills that he will need to live successfully on the outside. In fact, he will learn the wrong interpersonal skills and will lose what coping skills he has. He will have no way to face up to what he has done or to make things right.

He will have no way to deal with the guilt that such an offense causes. There is no place in the process where he can be forgiven, where he can feel he has made things right. Imagine the effect on his self-image. His alternatives are few. He can avoid the issue, rationalizing his behavior. He can turn his anger on himself and contemplate suicide. He can turn his anger on others. In any case, he will continue to be defined as an offender long after he has "paid his debt" by taking his punishment. The hatred and violence bred in him in prison may come to replace any sorrow and grief he may have had.

Like the victim, he will have no opportunity for resolution, for putting this behind. The wound will continue to be rubbed raw.

By his actions, our offender has violated another person. He has also violated relationships of trust within a community. Nothing in the process of justice will help him comprehend these dimensions of what he has done.

The offense was committed by a person who himself had been violated. While not excusable on these grounds, his actions grew out of a history of abuse. As a child, he was physically abused. As an adult, he was psychologically and spiritually abused, which wounded his sense of himself and his relationship to the world. Nothing in the process will take that into account. Nothing is likely to start him on the road to wholeness.

4

Some Common Themes

ALTHOUGH I HAVE looked at victim and offender separately, some common themes emerge.

REPENTANCE AND FORGIVENESS

So far, I have analyzed their experiences and their needs primarily in experiential and psychological terms. Let us look briefly at their dilemma in Christian terms.

Both of the young people in the case I have described need to be healed. For genuine healing to take place, at least two preconditions need to be met: repentance and forgiveness.

If healing is to occur, it is helpful for victims to be able to forgive.

From a theological perspective, that seems rather straightforward: We are called to forgive our enemies, those who harm us, because God has forgiven us. We cannot be free as long as we are dominated by enmity. We must follow God's example.

From a practical, experiential point of view, that seems very difficult, perhaps impossible. How can a mother or father forgive a person who has killed their child? How is it possible to move beyond feelings of anger and revenge? How dare someone who has not experienced it even suggest such a thing? Can forgiveness be considered until safety is assured? Is such reassurance possible?

To forgive and be forgiven is not easy and cannot be suggested glibly. Nor should those who cannot find it in themselves to forgive be encouraged to feel an extra burden of guilt. Real forgiveness cannot simply be willed or forced but must come in its own time, with God's help.[1] Forgiveness is a gift. It should not be made into a burden.[2]

It is important to clarify our understanding of forgiveness. Often we think forgiveness means forgetting what happened, writing it off, or perhaps letting the victimizer off the hook easily. But forgiveness does not mean forgetting what happened. This young woman will never—and should never—completely forget her trauma and her loss. She should not be expected to. Nor does forgiveness mean redefining the offense as a nonoffense. It does not mean saying, "It wasn't so bad; it doesn't matter." It was bad, it does matter, and to deny that is to devalue both the experience of suffering and the very humanity of the person responsible.

---

1 I have found Marie Marshall Fortune's work on forgiveness helpful. See, for example, *Sexual Violence: The Unmentionable Sin* (New York: Pilgrim Press, 1983), and "Justice-Making in the Aftermath of Woman-Battering," in *Domestic Violence on Trial*, ed. Daniel Sonkin (New York: Springer Publishers, 1987), 237–48. Cf. Jeffrie G. Murphy and Jean Hampton, *Forgiveness and Mercy* (Cambridge, England: Cambridge University Press, 1988) and Thomas R. Yoder Neufeld, "Forgiveness and the Dangerous Few: The Biblical Basis," address to the Christian Council for Reconciliation, Montreal, Quebec, November 18, 1983.

Morton MacCullum-Paterson has suggested that forgiveness may involve a willingness to give up the intention to inflict vengeance. It may involve a willingness to turn the issue over to God for forgiveness. The root meaning of the word *forgive* in the New Testament, he points out, is to "hand over" or "set aside." See *Toward a Justice That Heals* (Toronto: The United Church Publishing House, 1988), 56.

2 Thanks to Dave Worth for this helpful distinction.

Forgiveness is letting go of the power the offense and the offender have over a person. It means no longer letting that offense and offender dominate. Without this experience of forgiveness, the wounds may fester and the violation may take over our consciousness and our lives. The offense and the offender are in control. Real forgiveness, then, is an act of empowerment and healing. It allows one to move from victim to survivor.

It is possible to move from victim to survivor in other ways. Some victims attempt to do this by "living well," feeling that to live successfully after a tragedy is the best revenge. "I'll show them" is the approach, and it is not without psychological value. But this method of coping still puts the offense and the offender at the center. Forgiveness, on the other hand, allows the experience to become part of one's life story, part of one's biography, in an important way, but without letting it continue to control.

Certain conditions help forgiveness to happen. An expression of responsibility, regret, and repentance on the part of an offender can be a powerful help. An essential condition for most people, however, is support from others and an experience of justice. Prayer is an important part of this healing of memories. A person or group in a pastoral role can hear confession and offer absolution. All of us, and especially our congregations, have a responsibility to encourage an environment where this can happen.

As I suggested earlier, an experience of justice has many dimensions. One of these dimensions is captured in the biblical concept of lament, expressed in some of the psalms. Speaking to the church, theologian Walter Brueggemann has described it well.

The way we move to maturity is to bring all the negativities to full speech. I can see the priest standing by and saying: have you got it all out yet, is there anymore? And I discover that if I get [it] out in structured ways wherein it can be received, I really do walk away new and free. But if we do not practice lament, if we do not practice speech that brings it to the throne of God, I have to sit on it and carry it around with me for the rest of my life. We live in a world of people who are waiting for a chance to speak it into God's Holy Ear. The mystery is that if you say it honestly to God, God is not frightened off, offended, or alienated, but rather God draws nearer.... *Very many people in our repressed culture need constant permission to speak their rage, hatreds, hurts, fears.* People are not likely to sing hymns of praise with the same freedom, power, and energy if they have not been through the full statement of their loss and hurt and grief before they get there. The pastoral task is to authorize people to do the kinds of speech that will make the job possible....

The church's business is not to say something good but to say the truth. Sometimes the only truth is that it hurts. Psalm 88 is a psalm for those times. The only truth that this psalm can muster tonight is that it hurts and you better give the wound air. The next day it may be time for some ointment but not until you've given the wound some air. Psalm 88 does not flinch before the painful truth that there are pieces of life that are unutterable.[3]

The church has a critical responsibility in this process. Unfortunately, too often it has wanted to avoid the pain and dispense with the lament. But at the same time, it has pressured victims to forgive. It has been reluctant to forgive

---

3 From a 1980 workshop on the Psalms presented in Toronto, Ontario. Quoted in "A Reflective Analysis on Reconciliation as It Relates to Criminal Justice," an unpublished discussion paper prepared by a working group of the National Associations Active in Criminal Justice for a May 1987 workshop in Ottawa, Canada.

victims for their natural feelings of anger and hostility toward the offender, toward society, and toward God.

If the victim needs an experience of forgiveness, so also does the offender. How else will he be able to find resolution to his guilt? How else will it be possible for him to move on to new life? How else can he develop a healthy sense of identity and self-worth? How else can he be saved?

Contrary to popular belief, offenders often do feel guilt for what they have done. Yet a sense of guilt can be terribly threatening to one's sense of self-worth and self-identity. One study has concluded that offenders are characterized by tremendous fears and that their greatest fear is of the "zero-state"—that is, personal worthlessness.[4] Consequently, offenders utilize a variety of defensive techniques to avoid guilt and maintain their sense of self-worth.

One method is to develop what Michael Ignatieff has termed "exculpatory strategies" to deflect or deny their guilt.[5] They may argue, for example, that everyone does it, that the victim deserved or could afford the losses, or that they were provoked beyond reason. They may adopt the language of the social and psychological determinism, arguing that "I'm depraved because I'm deprived." Similarly, the tendency of offenders to be obsessed with the injustices that they feel themselves to experience may be a way of insulating themselves from the burdens of guilt.

In order to live with themselves, some offenders even develop elaborate fantasies about who they are and what they did. Some almost become two personalities by drawing a strict line between the guilty person and the other part of themselves.

I'm convinced that guilt is behind much of the anger that offenders express. Guilt that is accepted becomes anger

4 See David Kelley, "Stalking the Criminal Mind: Psychopaths, 'Moral Imbeciles,' and Free Will," *Harpers* (August 1985).

5 Ignatieff, "Imprisonment and the Need for Justice."

at oneself. Guilt that is denied can become anger at others. Either way, such anger can be very destructive.

Some argue that guilt must be relieved through punishment. By accepting one's punishment, the debt is paid and the guilt ended.[6] Whether or not that is true in theory, things do not usually work out that way in reality. If punishment is to relieve guilt, it must be felt to be legitimate and deserved. Such is rarely the case in real life. Furthermore, the idea that the offense is against society and that a debt is owed to society rarely makes sense to offenders. It is too abstract, and their own identification with society is too limited.

We lack rituals that acknowledge that the debt is paid and that the guilt has been ended. As Ignatieff points out, forgiveness would exonerate the debt as well as or better than punishment. However, we assume that we must punish before forgiveness is possible. In practice, we administer punishment in such a way that it damages and feels undeserved, and then we deny opportunities for forgiveness.

New life requires both forgiveness and confession. For offenders to be truly whole, they must confess wrongdoing, admitting their responsibility and acknowledging the harm done. Only then is it possible to repent, to turn one's life around and begin in a new direction. Confession followed by repentance is a key to healing for offenders, but they can also bring healing for victims.

None of this—repentance, confession, and forgiveness by God or by the victim—eliminates the consequences of the offender's actions. Grace is not cheap. Responsibilities to the victim remain. Nevertheless, salvation and freedom are indeed possible.

---

6 James Gilligan, in *Violence: Reflections on a National Epidemic* (New York: Vintage, 1997), argues that punishment tends to relieve guilt but increase shame. Shame, he asserts, is a primary cause of violence.

The road to such salvation, according to many chaplains and prison visitors, lies in the recognition of one's utter sinfulness and worthlessness, because sin is seen as rooted in self-love.[7]

Offenders do often lack a certain moral sense, defined as a preoccupation with their own needs and an ability to empathize with others. However, I have suggested that this preoccupation with self actually is based in a weak self-image, perhaps in self-hate. If that is the case, a precondition for healing may be an awareness that they are loved and of value rather than further confirmation of their worthlessness.

Both victim and offender need to be healed, in short, and this healing requires opportunities for forgiveness, confession, repentance, and reconciliation. Some of this must take place between individuals and their God, their church, and their community. But involved also is the relationship between victim and offender, a relationship that, if it did not exist before the offense, does exist now.

Unfortunately, however, our present system of criminal law encourages none of this. In fact, the system increases hostilities and discourages any possibility of reconciliation. The legal process itself has no real place for repentance and certainly not for forgiveness. Moreover, by its nature it encourages offenders to deny their guilt and to focus on their own situations. It actively seeks to keep victim and offender apart, encouraging them to be adversaries and discouraging them from finding a common understanding of the offense and its resolution.

The latter point was illustrated by a young ex-offender I met years ago. While serving time in prison, he had become a Christian. When he was released by the parole board, he reports that they warned him, "We understand that you

---

7 See Gerald Austin McHugh, *Christian Faith and Criminal Justice: Toward a Christian Response to Crime and Punishment* (New York: Paulist Press, 1978), 172ff.

have become a Christian. That may mean that you want to go back and try to make things right to the victim. If you so much as go near the victim, you will be back here immediately!" An understandable reaction, perhaps, but also a tragedy.

THE ISSUE OF POWER

The issue of personal power and autonomy is central to the phenomena of crime and of justice as they are experienced by both victim and offender.

Denial of victims' autonomy by offenders is in large part what makes being a victim so traumatic. To be whole, we need some sense of being in control of our own lives and destinies. To have that taken away suddenly, arbitrarily, frighteningly, is intensely dehumanizing. Offenders turn victims into objects, into things, robbing them of power over their own lives. This is deeply degrading.

When people are deprived of something as basic as the sense of autonomy, they seek ways to reassert it. Victims need to regain this sense, and they do so in a variety of ways. For some, it is regained simply by overcoming, by living successfully, by becoming survivors. For some, it is done by taking safeguards or otherwise finding ways to make their lives their own again. Some attempt to meet it by demands for revenge and punishment. Some are able to find empowerment through an act of Christian forgiveness. At any rate, the issue of personal power—its deprivation and its reassertion—is fundamental to the victim experience.

This issue is at the heart of the offender experience as well. Many people feel powerless and worthless. In our society, this deprivation of a sense of personal power is experienced by young men as an assault on their masculinity, since masculinity and power are often equated. One way to satisfy this thirst for autonomy and to respond to a sense of being victimized by a society is to find another victim to dominate. Rape in prison is just such a phenomenon. But much crime is a distorted way of asserting one's power and worth, a clumsy way of trying to assert and express oneself.

Do people in our society really have as little power as I have suggested? Certainly that assertion runs contrary to the American myth of rewards for individual ability. This myth suggests that all those with ability who are willing to work hard can make something of themselves. If they do not, the fault is theirs. Moreover, their success is measured in material terms. Power and wealth are the basic measures of success and, thus, of worth. But regardless of whether this myth of individual choice and reward is true—and it is doubtful that this is the case for many—few poor people *believe* it is, at least for them.

I have often thought that the real dividing line between lower and middle-upper classes in our society has less to do with education and wealth per se than it does with the sense of choice, of power. Most of us who grow up among middle- and upper-class families grow up believing that we are basically in control of our own fate. While there may be obstacles, and while luck or providence plays its role, we believe that we do in fact have real choices and some real power to determine our destinies.

Many poor people do not believe this. In their view, what happens to them is due more to chance than to anything they did. If success comes, it is associated more with luck than hard work. If they are arrested for an offense, it has more to do with luck than something they did. Whether or not they do have the power to make real choices, many do not *believe* that they do, and that is what is significant. For some people, then, crime can be a way of asserting a sense of control they feel to be lacking otherwise.

Many people believe that things happen to them rather than that they control their future. This belief has important implications for the idea of deterrence. For deterrence to work, people have to believe that their actions are based on choices that, in turn, affect what happens to them. But Parker Rossman's interviews with young people in conflict with the law in New York provide a different picture.[8]

Every day these young people saw innocent people being arrested. Every day they saw people who were guilty going free. In their mind, there was little relationship between offense and punishment. Rather, they saw punishment like rain. Some days it rains, and some days it doesn't. The rain falls on the just and unjust alike. Most of them expected to experience arrest and punishment during their lives. Like the rest of their future, it was something that just happened under the control of largely irresistible forces.

Many people in our society lack a sense of personal power, and crime can be a way of asserting such power. In that context, our prescription for those who take away another's power in order to assert their own is bizarre: we further rob them of a sense of autonomy. The entire judicial system is designed to do just that by impressing offenders with the power of the state and their own lack of power. They are treated as pawns in the process. Then they are sent to prison, where they are further deprived of a sense of power and worth unless they can derive some from the warped subculture of prison. So they resist "correction" for the same reason victims resist victimization—because they are being denied a sense of autonomy. How can we expect, then, that prisoners will emerge with a sense of worth that does not depend upon dominating others?[9]

---

8 Parker Rossman, *After Punishment What?* (Cleveland, OH: Collins, 1980).

9 Especially helpful on the question of power is Richard Korn, "Crime, Criminal Justice, and Corrections," *University of San Francisco Law Review* (October 1971).

Victims, too, are denied power through the criminal justice process. Their needs are ignored, and they are left out of the process, which only deepens their sense of victimization.

Both victim and offender are denied power in the criminal justice process, with harmful consequences to both. But the one-sidedness of power in the process has other implications as well. A concentration of power can intoxicate individuals, making them act as if they are above the law. This concentration of power, combined with differences in education and social status, often discourages people in key roles from identifying with the powerless, whether victim or offender. They are often unwilling to listen to perspectives other than their own. The centralization of power in prosecutor and judge can intensify the problem.

In short, crime may be a way for offenders to assert power in order to gain a sense of personal worth. In their crime, however, they rob victims of their sense of personal power. For victims to regain wholeness, this sense of autonomy must be returned. For offenders to be whole, they must develop a sense of autonomy that is not based on overpowering others. Yet the criminal justice process compounds the problem, robbing both victim and offender of a legitimate sense of power while concentrating power dangerously in the hands of a few.

Now let's explore the parallels between victim and offender experiences in somewhat different terms.

Judge Challeen has noted that one characteristic of many of the offenders who appear before him is that, by society's standards, they are losers.[10] People who see themselves as losers are more likely than others to assert their identities through crime. They are also less likely to be deterred by the fear of

---

10 Dennis A. Challeen, *Making It Right* (Aberdeen, SD: Milieus and Peterson Publishing, 1986), 21ff. and 43ff.

consequences. Deterrence, Challeen concludes, works least for those who need it the most—those who are losing, who have the least to lose, who are least likely to be concerned about the effects of apprehension and punishment.

Turning to victims, Norwegian criminologist Nils Christie has pointed out that victimization in itself is not "a thing."[11] Rather, it has to do with participants' interpretations of situations. Given the same experience, some people might define themselves as victims. Others might define themselves as losers. Still others might interpret themselves as victors. Just how a victim interprets the situation depends upon a number of factors. If such people can identify that they have been wronged and can identify how they were wronged and by whom, they may be likely to identify themselves as victims. On the other hand, some are used to losing, to being victims. If they cannot clearly identify how they have been wronged and by whom, they may interpret the same experience as another loss, more evidence that they are losers.

Both Christie and sociologists Richard Sennett and Jonathan Cobb have suggested that our society tends to encourage people at the bottom to see themselves as losers rather than as victims.[12] Working-class children tend to see their defeats not as evidence of the social constraints upon them but as personal failures. Poor people especially, therefore, often develop self-definitions of themselves as losers.

People who identify themselves as losers may commit crimes as a way of asserting and empowering themselves. However, because they are used to believing that they do not have the power to determine their futures and that what happens to them "just happens," they are unlikely to be deterred

11 Nils Christie, "The Ideal Victim" (unpublished lecture, 33rd International Course in Criminology, Vancouver, BC).

12 Jonathan Cobb and Richard Sennett, *The Hidden Injuries of Class*, reprint ed. (1977; New York: W. W. Norton and Company, 1993).

by the threat of punishment. The result? The creation of another class of victims: crime victims.

Some of these victims will identify themselves as crime victims, but some will not. Persons who are used to misfortune and who experience crime daily are likely to see themselves as losers, to view life as being beyond their control, and to see crime as one more misfortune. The victimization simply confirms their plight. From this group may come more offenders. The cycle is repeated.[13]

THE MYSTIFICATION OF CRIME

The case of the young man who robbed and wounded a young woman received considerable attention in its community. Like most such cases, however, the events and the people involved were transformed by the legal process and by media coverage.

The wounded young man who committed this injury became a *criminal* and was thus dealt with as an abstraction and in stereotypes. The young woman who was injured became a *victim*, but her needs probably received relatively little attention. The events became a *crime*, and the *crime* was described and dealt with in symbolic and legal terms foreign to the people actually involved. The whole process was mystified and mythologized and thus became a useful tool in the service of the media and the political process.

Crime is prominent in media coverage. Studies have found that it is so in part because it sells. People are drawn to the sensational. But coverage *is* prominent also because it is "easy news." Unlike much other news, news about crime is simple to obtain. The reporter simply needs to stay in contact with the police and the prosecutor. But this news is often obtained uncritically. Crime news is often accepted from official sources

13 For more on the victim/perpetrator cycle, see Carolyn Yoder, *The Little Book of Trauma Healing* (Intercourse, PA: Good Books, 2005).

without question and without independent verification. To maintain access to such news sources requires that report-ers remain on good terms with police and prosecutor, and this does not encourage objectivity. Consequently, crime news is viewed through the eyes of the legal process and its professionals. Such news is not only one-sided but tends to encourage crime to be abstracted and mystified.

Crime is also an important tool for politicians. Crime can be an important beating stick. A position on crime is one crucial way to position oneself in our society. Are you tough-minded, realistic? Or are you soft, idealistic? A statement about crime is a way to take sides, as we frequently see in U.S. presidential elections.

Again, however, the harms and events behind what we call crime get lost. The process is mystified and mythologized until it is larger than—and distant from—life. In that process, we all become more fearful.

All of this has an impact on our sense of community. We have several options when faced with *crime*. We can draw to-gether defensively, against the "enemy." A sense of community may be increased, but it is a defensive, exclusive, threatened community. Alternately, we can retire to fortified homes, be-coming distrustful of others. The sense of community, already weak, becomes further eroded.

The issue of how we respond to wrongdoing, then, has im-portant implications for our future.

Part II

The Justice Paradigm

5

Retributive Justice

THROUGHOUT THE CRIMINAL justice process, the wounds and needs of both the victim and the offender are neglected. Worse yet, injuries may be compounded.

Throughout this process, the phenomenon of crime becomes larger than life. Crime is mystified and mythologized, creating a symbol that is easily manipulated by politicians and the press.

Many have introduced attempts to reform this process over the past several centuries. The conclusion of some that nothing works or that no good has come of these reform efforts is inaccurate. Nevertheless, many if not most have gone astray. They have had all sorts of unintended consequences. Reform efforts have been used for purposes much different from those originally envisioned. Prisons themselves were originally promoted as a humane alternative to corporal and capital punishment. Incarceration was to meet society's need for punishment and protection while encouraging reformation of offenders. Within a few years of their introduction, prisons became places of horror, and the prison reform movement was born.

Recognition of the inadequacies and misuse of prison soon led to a search for alternatives to prison.[1] Numerous alternatives have been introduced, but their history has not been encouraging. Frequently they have served as alternatives to other alternatives, not as alternatives to prison. Too often they have been alternatives to taking no formal action. Prison populations have continued to grow while alternatives expanded as well, increasing the total number of people under the control and supervision of the state. The net of control and intervention has widened, but without discernible effects on crime and without meeting essential needs of victim or offender.

Why is this true? Why are the actual needs of those involved in crime—whether transgressed or transgressor—so irrelevant in the "justice" process? Why are changes intended as reforms so often unsuccessful at altering this pattern? The answers lie in our shared understandings of what crime and justice are all about. Unless we address these fundamental definitions and assumptions, real change will be unlikely.

Are there, in fact, commonly shared assumptions about what crime and justice are all about? On the surface, we find considerable diversity, even among criminal justice professionals. Judges, for example, show tremendous variety in their perceptions about what outcomes are appropriate and why. This is a major reason behind the serious lack of uniformity in sentences. The diversity of philosophy and opinion has been highlighted by researchers who have given judges identical case histories and then asked them to indicate what their sentences would be. The range in outcomes is breathtaking. Each

---

1 A considerable literature on the history and effects of "alternatives" has emerged. See, for example, David T. Rothman, *Conscience and Convenience: The Asylum and Its Alternatives in Progressive America* (Boston: Little, Brown, and Co., 1980) and M. Kay Harris, "Strategies, Values, and the Emerging Generation of Alternatives to Incarceration," *New York University Review of Law and Social Change* 12, no. 1 (1983–84): 141–70.

judge, each prosecutor, and each probation officer operates according to his or her own understandings of what is appropriate, which can vary markedly.

So understandings of what should be done about crime vary. In the U.S., people frequently use the words *liberal* and *conservative* as a way of making sense of this diversity. We expect conservatives to demand quick, sure, and stiff punishment, to decry the rules that protect offenders' rights, and to emphasize offenders' choices to offend while downplaying their circumstances. We expect liberals to be more concerned with offenders' rights and circumstances. We assume that liberals and conservatives have quite different approaches to crime and justice.[2]

Yet the two "opposites" may not actually differ from each other very much. On closer analysis, we find that most of us share assumptions and understandings that transcend liberal and conservative labels. Some of these assumptions are embodied in criminal law. Some are not. It is important to understand what they are.

When we identify something as a crime, a number of basic assumptions shape our responses. We assume that

1.   Guilt must be assigned.

2.   The guilty must get their "just deserts."

3.   Just deserts require the infliction of pain.

4.   Justice is measured by the process.

5.   The breaking of the law defines the offense.

Let's look at these assumptions in more detail.

---

2 Liberal and conservative approaches are helpfully explored in Elliott Currie, *Confronting Crime: An American Dilemma* (New York: Pantheon Books, 1985). See also Nils Christie, "Crime, Pain, and Death" in *New Perspectives on Crime and Justice,* no. 1 (Akron, PA: Mennonite Central Committee, 1984).

GUILT MUST BE ASSIGNED

The question of guilt is the hub of the entire criminal justice process. Establishing guilt is the central activity, and everything moves toward or flows from that event.

Because this event is so important and the consequences so profound, elaborate rules govern this event. Once guilt has been established, concern about procedural safeguards and rights diminishes.

The centrality of guilt means that the actual outcome of the case receives less attention. Legal training concentrates on rules and processes related to guilt, and law students receive little training in sentence negotiation or design. Consequently, few judges and even fewer lawyers have much training about appropriate outcomes of criminal cases.

Our preoccupation with blame-fixing means that we tend to be oriented toward the past. What happened? Who did it? These questions take precedence over what to do to solve the problems that the offense created (or out of which the offense arose). Legal professionals spend little time on what can be done to prevent a recurrence of future problems.

The concept of guilt guiding the justice process is a narrow, highly technical one that is primarily objective or descriptive in nature. Did the accused person commit the act as described by law? Did he or she intend to do it? Was the act contrary to law? Legal guilt asks simply whether the person charged in fact committed the act and, if so, whether he or she is liable under the law.

In the legal system, offenses and questions of guilt are framed in terms much different from how the victim and the offender actually experience them. The legal charge may seem to bear little relationship to the actual offense, and the language of guilt and innocence may seem to have little connection to what actually happened. As several defenders of the system acknowledged recently, "legal guilt, not factual guilt . . . is the foundation of the criminal justice process."[3]

This is soon brought home to a defendant. He may be charged with something that sounds quite different from what he actually did. The charges may be the result of negotiation between his attorney and the prosecutor. Even if he committed an offense, he may not be legally guilty and may be advised to plead "not guilty." Thus, he may come to believe that he is in fact not guilty. Even if he is legally guilty, his attorney will likely tell him to plead "not guilty" at some stage. In legal terms, "not guilty" is the way one says, "I want a trial," or "I need more time." All of this tends to obscure the experiential and moral reality of guilt and innocence.

Legally, the question of guilt is an either-or question. Degrees of severity of the offense may vary, but in the end there are no degrees of guilt. One is guilty or not guilty. Someone must win, and someone must lose. Nils Christie identifies the implications well: we view courts as teaching and upholding social norms, but in fact they teach the hidden message that people can be evaluated in simplistic dichotomies.[4]

Although the jurist's concept of guilt is technical and descriptive, an offender may have contact with professionals whose perspective is what theologian Tom Yoder Neufeld has called "prescriptive." This concept of guilt or responsibility concerns itself with explaining why the offense happened, focusing on causality and predictability, usually in social and psychological terms.[5]

3 Donald R. Ranish and David Shichor, "The Victim's Role in the Penal Process: Recent Developments in California," *Federal Probation* XLIX, no. 1 (March 1985): 55.

4 Nils Christie, *Limits to Pain* (Oslo, Norway: Universitetsforlaget, 1981), 45.

5 This discussion of guilt draws heavily upon Tom Yoder Neufeld, *Guilt and Humanness: The Significance of Guilt for the Humanization of the Judicial-Correctional System* (Kingston, ON: Queen's Theological College, 1982). See

The psychologist, for instance, may approach the concept of guilt in terms that are neither legal nor moral. In fact, she may avoid the concept altogether. Rather, she will look at what psychological factors led to this event, perhaps viewing the behavior as evidence of illness or serious dysfunction. Meanwhile, the sociologist will focus on patterns and causes in terms of social forces in the family, the community, and the larger society. While the jurist will treat the offender as an autonomous individual making more or less conscious choices, social and behavioral scientists will view the offender at least in part as responding to a variety of larger forces. This perspective raises questions about the extent to which the offender is personally responsible and perhaps about the extent to which he is an offender rather than a victim.

While specialists such as jurists and social scientists will consider the issue of guilt in their own ways, a third perspective will color most people's thinking—including that of many criminal justice officials. This concept is a more moralistic or *ascriptive* one. In the popular view, guilt is not merely a description of behavior but a statement of a moral quality. Guilt says something about the quality of the person who did this and has a sticky, indelible quality. Guilt adheres to a person more or less permanently, with few known solvents. It often becomes a primary, definitional characteristic of a person. A person found guilty of theft becomes a thief, an offender. A person who spends time in prison becomes an ex-prisoner, an ex-offender, an ex-con. This becomes part of his or her identity and is difficult to remove.

The young offender in the case I described earlier will forever be affected and defined by that offense, no matter what

---

also Gerald Austin McHugh, *Christian Faith and Criminal Justice* (Mahwah, NJ: Paulist Press, 1978), chapter 7; and Patrick Kerans, *Punishment vs. Reconciliation: Retributive Justice and Social Justice in the Light of Social Ethics* (Kingston, ON: Queen's Theological College, 1982).

good qualities he has or may develop. The fact that he has of-fended will define his job possibilities, his career potential, and the rest of his life. His guilt, not his other qualities, is likely to be decisive. Nothing in the criminal justice process will al-low him to overcome that—not even if he repays his "debt to society" by serving his time.

The legal concept of guilt, then, is highly technical and re-moved from real-life experience. However, many concepts of guilt operate in a specific case, which can be very confusing to an offender. His lawyer will talk to him about guilt in techni-cal terms, and the process may encourage him to deny his guilt unless he is legally guilty or has no other choice. Meanwhile, he may see a psychological evaluator or therapist who will help him to understand his behavior in psychological terms, possibly muting his sense of personal responsibility. In addi-tion, he may bump into a chaplain who will talk of moral guilt but also of mercy, grace, and forgiveness. This chaplain may suggest that his guilt is real, not merely technical, but that resolution is possible. Then there will be other people, such as prison guards, who reflect a popular concept of guilt, which suggests that not only is his guilt real but it is hard to get rid of. He is, in fact, "bad."

What does *guilt* actually mean? How can one who has of-fended make sense of it? Is he or she actually an offender or a victim? Is he really guilty? What is he guilty of? Is it possible to put it behind and start over? As Neufeld has pointed out, of-fenders are constantly confronted with the terminology of guilt, but they are denied the language and clarity of meaning to make sense of it. Moreover, mechanisms for resolution are lacking.

The legal and popular concepts of guilt that govern our responses to crime are confusing and even contradictory, but they have this in common: they are highly individualistic. Western law and values often are predicated on a belief in the individual as a free moral agent. If someone commits a crime, she has done so willfully. Punishment is thus deserved because it is freely chosen. Individuals are personally and individually accountable. Guilt is individual.

The basic assumption of human freedom and of personal accountability is important. Simple determinism is clearly inadequate. Still, there are problems with the forms our assumptions about freedom and responsibility take in Western culture.

Much evidence suggests that offenders often do not act freely or at least do not perceive themselves as capable of free action. As I suggested in the previous chapter, many people in our society do not see themselves as free agents, in charge of their own lives. Instead, they see themselves as shaped by almost irresistible forces—whether socioeconomic or providential. Ideas of human freedom and thus responsibility necessarily take on a different hue in such a context.

The atomistic understanding of guilt and responsibility also fails to take into account the context of behavior. Although each of us is responsible for the choices we make, the social and psychological context in which we find ourselves certainly influences our actual and potential choices. The social, economic, political, and psychological context of behavior is indeed important, but our individualistic concept of guilt ignores the context.

The motivation to do wrong is much more complex than our individualistic approach acknowledges. The apostle Paul certainly recognized the complexity of responsibility for wrongdoing. While he assumed that human beings make choices and are responsible for their behavior, he acknowledged that the simple image of a person as a totally free agent does not do justice to the pervasiveness and power of evil. In his letter to the Romans, Paul agonized over the power of evil in his own life, telling of his own tendency to do what he should not. And he suggested that there is a difference between actual and potential freedom, seeing freedom as a gift, not something intrinsic in an individual (see Romans 7). Wrongdoing can be a pattern, shaped by a variety of forces, some of which are the result of choices and some which are not. Such patterns can be difficult to break.

With our individualistic concepts of guilt and freedom, we assume that the individual is free to make choices and has anticipated the consequences of those choices. We assume that the person has modified his or her behavior to take this into account. This assumption ignores the question of whether individuals believe themselves to have this freedom. It assumes that they have the ability to anticipate long-range consequences. Furthermore, it expects them to make a connection between behavior and consequence. Moreover, it ignores the nature of wrongdoing as a complex pattern. Finally, it ignores the social, economic, and psychological context in which actions occur. Consequently, justice for offenders can be conducted without reference to social justice and without threatening the status quo. Punishment can be justly deserved, regardless of whether the social setting is just.

Perhaps this view of guilt and responsibility is inevitable in an individualistic, competitive culture that defines worth in terms of material and social success and that defines success and failure in purely individual terms. Persons are judged in terms of their access to wealth and power. Those who fail to measure up are held individually responsible. They have not only lost; they are losers. The same is true for guilt. *Guilt* is defined as an individual failing. The context of an individual's behavior is ignored. Offenders have had various choices and, having accepted the wrong ones, are labeled as guilty.[6]

To summarize, then, the fixing of blame is central to our understanding of justice. The administration of justice is a kind

---

6 An important discussion of these issues may be found in Philip Zimbardo, *The Lucifer Effect: Understanding How Good People Turn Evil* (New York: Random House, 2008).

of theater in which issues of guilt and innocence predominate. The trial or guilty plea forms the dramatic center, with the sentence as a denouement. As a result, justice is preoccupied with the past to the detriment of the future.

The legal concept of guilt that guides the justice process is highly technical, abstracted from experience. This makes it easier for offenders to avoid accepting personal responsibility for their behavior. It also frustrates victims, who find it difficult to match the legal description of the event with their own experience. Both victim and offender are forced to speak the language of the system, to define their reality in its terms instead of their own.

Because guilt is narrowly defined, centering on individual behavior, it allows us to ignore the social and economic roots and contexts of crime. We thus attempt to create justice by leaving out many of the relevant variables. And since guilt is viewed in either-or terms, it encourages a simplistic view of the world that tends to see things as good and bad, them and us. Justice becomes a drama of guilt, a morality play that allows us to make simple sense of the world.

But the legal concept of guilt operates alongside several other concepts. This fact in itself causes confusion for participants and may assist offenders in denying responsibility for action. Some of these assumptions—such as the indelible quality of guilt—have serious, long-term consequences for offenders.

Offenders need to be held accountable for what they have done. One dimension of accountability is taking ownership for wrongdoing. Our concepts of guilt, however, at best fail to encourage such accountability and at worse make it more difficult. The lack of a process for resolving guilt encourages the use of *exculpatory strategies,* such as rationalization and stereotypes, as a way of shielding oneself from the heavy burden of this guilt. Alternately, offenders may be encouraged to fulfill the prophecy inherent in the label.

While the process focuses on questions of the defendant's guilt and responsibility, it tends to disperse responsibility for outcomes and to deny questions of collective responsibility for offenses. Key decision-makers (lawyers, prosecutors, judges, probation officers) are encouraged to see themselves as carrying out the law, doing their duty. They are encouraged to see that responsibility for the outcome of a case belongs to the system. This means that those who "make" justice can deny personal responsibility for outcomes. They are also discouraged from acknowledging what they have in common with offenders as people.

Renate Mohr, in a paper on Canadian criminal law, has said it well:

> How is it that we *do* punishing? It is done in a way that no single person can be held responsible for the deprivation of liberty of another person. The criminal justice system . . . was craftily designed as a series of discreet, self-contained compartments. He who lays the charge, he who bargains the charge, he who pronounces the sentence, and he who administers that sentence are all different people who have little or no contact with each other or the accused person. We have a special word for sealing the judge's compartment. Having completed their job of imposing the punishment, they become "functus." That means they need not, indeed ought not . . . concern themselves any further with the pains of the punishment they have imposed on another human being. And so the process ensures that violence may be done to others on a daily basis without any one person having to take responsibility.[7]

7 Renate M. Mohr, "A Feminist's Analysis of the Objectives and Alternatives Re: Punishment" (unpublished paper, Conference on Feminist Perspectives on Criminal Law Reform, Ottawa, Canada, 1987).

THE GUILTY MUST GET THEIR "JUST DESERTS," AND JUST DESERTS REQUIRE THE INFLICTION OF PAIN

Once guilt has been established, a second assumption comes into play. We assume that offenders must receive their "just deserts." Offenders must get what is coming to them. Justice must settle the score, tit for tat. Crime creates a moral debt, which must be repaid, and justice is a process of righting the balance. It is as if there is a metaphysical balance in the universe that has been upset and that must be corrected.

This concept of justice tends to focus on abstractions rather than the harm done. It assumes that what is needed to settle the score in each case is knowable and attainable. And it assumes that what is needed to right the balance, to pay the debt, is punishment. Criminal justice officials see their job as meting out appropriate levels of punishment. Offenders are encouraged to believe that by taking their punishment, they are paying their debt to society.

On closer examination, offenders find it hard to feel they are actually "paying their debt" in this way. The "repayment" is terribly abstract, and there is no public resolution when the debt has been paid. The repayment does little good for the community. In fact, it actually costs the community money. To say to the offender, in effect, "You have harmed someone so we will even things up by harming you too," merely adds to the amount of harm in the world.

Guilt and punishment are the twin fulcrums of the justice system. People must suffer for the suffering they have caused. Only the infliction of pain will right the balance.

We must be honest in our use of language. When we speak about punishment, we are speaking about inflicting pain intended as pain. Nils Christie has helped us to see that penal law is in fact "pain law," because it is an elaborate mechanism for administering "just" doses of pain.[8]

Usually we attempt to hide this reality. Our culture tries to avoid the reality of pain. We have tried to banish death from our consciousness, so we give it over to professionals. We also call it by other names: we "pass away" rather than die.[9]

The unease with delivering pain is complicated by a taboo against revenge as a motive. This in turn heightens the need to deny the nature and motives of what we are doing. We do not like pain and revenge and certainly do not want to be thought of as inflicting it, so we hide and obscure it. Nevertheless, that is what we do when we do "justice." We inflict pain in response to crime.

So we give punishment over to professionals, to be carried out beyond our sight. We obscure its reality with a variety of rationales and terms. We talk of "correctional centers" rather than prisons and of "correctional officers" rather than guards.

We devise a variety of rationales for delivering pain. At some times we have done it in the name of treatment, as a means of rehabilitation. Often we do it to prevent crime, to deter this offender ("individual deterrence") as well as to discourage other potential offenders ("general deterrence") by the fear of similar consequences. We administer pain in the name of deterrence, in fact, despite substantial questions about whether such deterrence actually works. We administer pain in the name of deterrence despite questions about the morality of administering pain to one person for the purposes of *possibly* deterring another. We administer pain even though it may have little relevance to what the victim needs or to the problems involved in the offense. We administer pain, observes John Lampen of Northern Ireland, because we've been

---

8 Christie, *Limits to Pain.*
9 Christie, "Crime, Pain, and Death."

educated to believe that humiliation and suffering are what justice is about and that evil must be held in check by harshness rather than by love or understanding.[10]

Ironically, this focus on inflicting pain can interfere with the first focus, the establishment of guilt. Because of the threat of punishment, offenders are reluctant to admit the truth. Because the punitive consequences are so serious, elaborate safeguards of offenders' right are needed, and these can make it difficult to get at truth. Judges and jurors too may become less likely to convict when the potential punishment is seen as very severe.

The assumptions of just deserts and the imposition of pain mean that offenders are caught up in a tit-for-tat world. This in turn tends to confirm the outlook and life experiences of many offenders. Wrongs must be repaid by wrong, and those who offend deserve vengeance. Many crimes are committed by people "punishing" their family, the neighbors, or their acquaintances.

Studies of capital punishment have failed to find evidence that the death penalty deters. Some evidence shows that the example of the death penalty actually causes some people to kill.[11] Apparently, the message some potential offenders receive is not that killing is wrong but that those who wrong us deserve to die. The message that offenders must get their due, and that what they are due is punishment, may teach a lesson quite different than what we intend.

The threat to inflict pain on those who disobey has long been recognized as the basis of modern law. The essence of the state is often identified by political scientists as the "legitimate"

---

10 John Lampen, *Mending Hurts* (London: Quaker Home Service, 1987), 61, 67ff.

11 For example, William J. Bowers and Glenn L Pierce, "Deterrence or Brutalization: What Is the Effect of Executions?" *Crime and Delinquency* 26, no. 4 (October 1980): 453–84.

monopoly on violence. As political philosopher J. W. Mohr has noted, the institutions and methods of law are thus part of the cycle of violence rather than a solution to it.[12]

JUSTICE IS MEASURED BY THE PROCESS

The primary goal of our justice process is the determination of guilt and, once that is determined, the infliction of pain. Following a direction set by ancient Roman law, however, *justice* is defined by the process more than by the outcome.[13] Procedure overshadows substance. Have the right rules and processes been followed? If so, justice was done.

The appeals process in the U.S. illustrates this well. Only in specialized circumstances can outcomes of trials be appealed on the basis of the outcome or on the basis of the facts. Rather, appeals usually center on whether correct procedures have been followed. An appeals court does not examine the original evidence in itself.

Several characteristics of this process need to be noted.

The process is adversarial. It assumes—and encourages—a conflict of interest between parties. Through the regulated conflict of opposing interests, the truth will eventually come out and the interests of the parties will be safeguarded. It assumes irreconcilable interests and then goes a long way to ensure that they are. Adversarial justice tends to become a self-fulfilling prophecy.

Jerold Auerbach, in his history of dispute resolution in the U.S., has eloquently pointed out that this is also a supremely

---

12 J. W. Mohr, "Causes of Violence: A Socio-Legal Perspective" (unpublished paper, John Howard Society conference, Violence in Contemporary Canadian Society, Ottawa, Canada, June 1986).

13 In 1993 the U.S. Supreme Court actually ruled that correct procedures can justify execution even if a death row inmate offers new evidence of innocence. On this and other issues, Herman Bianchi's work has been helpful; see Bianchi, *Justice as Sanctuary* (Eugene, OR: Wipf and Stock, 2010).

individualistic, competitive model. It not only grows out of, but helps to promote, a fragmented, competitive society.[14]

There are strengths to this model, but it is at heart a battle model, a regulated duel. It is no accident, therefore, that politicians and law enforcement so often use the language of "war on crime."

Liberals and conservatives in the U.S. may differ on where they put the emphasis, but both assume justice to be a conflict guided by rules. Conservatives, expressing what has been termed a "crime control" orientation, have tended to give more priority to fighting crime (note the language!) than to the rights of the accused. Liberals, on the other hand, have emphasized the centrality of individual rights—a "due process" model. Both, however, assume that justice involves a battle between hostile parties, regulated by rules.

In this emphasis on rules and process, priority is given to equity of treatment as a test of justice. The intention is that defendants be treated equally. Two characteristics of this emphasis on equity should be noted. First, the emphasis is more upon intent than upon actual outcome. In practice, even approximate equity in outcome is rarely achieved, as is illustrated by racial disparities in prison and death row populations. These outcomes are difficult to challenge, however, as long as one cannot show there was an intent to treat defendants inequitably.

Justice is imaged as a blindfolded goddess holding a balance. The focus is on equity of process, not of circumstances. The criminal justice process claims to ignore social, economic, and political differences, attempting to treat all offenders as if they were equal before the law. Since the process aims to treat unequals equally, existing social and political inequities are ignored and maintained. Paradoxically, justice may thus maintain inequities in the name of equity.

14 Jerold S. Auerbach, *Justice Without Law?* (New York: Oxford University Press, 1983), 138ff.

The justice process, ringed about as it must be with complex rules, requires dependence upon proxy professionals who represent offender and the state. This, in turn, removes the process of justice from the individuals and the communities that are affected. Victim and offender become bystanders, nonparticipants in their own cases. A huge bureaucracy with vested interests of its own is born. Our society's tendency to look to professionals to solve our problems is encouraged.

We tend, then, to define justice as procedures for a battle or game.[15] We emphasize the intent to treat people equally in the process, without regard to equity of circumstances and with less concern for equity of outcome. We find ourselves dependent upon proxy professionals in this complex process.

THE BREAKING OF THE LAW DEFINES THE OFFENSE

In our society, *justice* is defined as applying the law. *Crime* is defined as lawbreaking.

Instead of concentrating on the actual harm done or on what victim and offender have experienced, we focus on the act of breaking the law. The act of breaking a law, not the damage or conflict, defines the offense and triggers the justice process.

The emphasis on lawbreaking is what allows both the offense and guilt to be defined in purely legal terms. As I noted earlier, moral and social issues become not only secondary but often irrelevant. The context of the action is not considered except to the extent that it has legal implications. As Christie has rightly pointed out: "Training in law is training in simplifications. It is a trained incapacity to look at all values in a situation, and instead to select only the legally relevant ones,

---

15 See also John Griffiths, "Ideology in Criminal Procedure or a Third 'Model' of the Criminal Process," *The Yale Law Journal* 79, no. 3 (January 1970): 359–415.

that is, those defined by the high priests within the system to be the relevant ones."[16]

Social, moral, and personal factors are relevant only insofar as they are legally defined as relevant. Questions of social justice are rarely relevant. The "criminal act" is of decisive significance, and it is narrowly and technically defined.

WHO IS THE VICTIM?

I have tried to outline five assumptions that we make about crime and justice. We assume that: (1) Crime is essentially *lawbreaking*; (2) when a law is broken, justice involves establishing *guilt*; (3) so that *just deserts* can be meted out; (4) by inflicting *pain*; (5) through a *conflict* in which *rules* and intentions are placed above outcomes.

These assumptions and their implications help to explain some of our failures, but there remains still another essential element: our identification of the victim.

In criminal law, crime is defined as an offense against the state. The state, not the individual, is defined as victim. The state—and only the state—may respond.

Since the state is the victim, criminal law pits offenders against the state. In practice, this means one proxy professional representing the offender (defense attorney) is pitted against another professional representing the state (prosecutor), with still another professional (judge) acting as referee and arbiter.

Because the power of the state is so vast and civil liberties implications are so profound, complex safeguards for the procedures are essential. Because the state is so impersonal and abstract, forgiveness and mercy are nearly impossible to achieve.

Since the state is defined as victim, it is not surprising that victims are so consistently left out of the process and that

---

16 Christie, *Limits to Pain*, 57.

their needs and wishes are so little heeded. Why should their needs be recognized? They are not even part of the equation of crime. Victims are mere footnotes to the criminal justice process, legally necessary only if needed as witnesses.

Victim compensation and assistance programs have become popular in recent years. And indeed they should be. Nevertheless, they cannot be expected to have a major and lasting impact until we reexamine our definition of crime. As long as victims are not intrinsic elements in the definition of crime, we must expect them to be more pawns than participants.

The justice process does not seek reconciliation between victim and offender because the relationship between victim and offender is not seen as an important problem. Indeed, how could their feelings toward one another be taken seriously if both are not part of the equation?

The sixth assumption we make, therefore, is perhaps most important: that *the state is the real victim.* The implications of that assumption are profound.

Crime is an offense against the state. Justice consists of establishing blame and administering pain in a battle guided by rules. The process is assumed to be the responsibility—indeed, a monopoly—of the state.

Until we begin to question these assumptions, the changes we introduce may make little difference. Ours is essentially a retributive[17] model of justice, and that model is at the root of many of our problems.

---

17 Cautions about the term *retributive* are discussed in chapter 10.

6

Justice as Paradigm

DURING THE PAST century, we have become a bit more modest than we once were about what we know with certainty. We are less sure that what we think we know about the universe accurately portrays an objective reality outside of ourselves.

Historical and cross-cultural perspectives have helped us to see how much our view of the world is shaped by the particular lens through which we view it. Modern psychology has revealed hidden motivations for what we do and think and has demonstrated that there are complex and overlapping layers of conscious and subconscious reality. As a result, we have to acknowledge that what we think we know as reality is often more complex and problematic than it appears on the surface.

At one time, the physical sciences seemed to promise certainty about the nature and structure of reality. In the twenty-first century, however, scientists are less confident that their pictures of reality actually mirror the physical universe. Many are also less insistent than they once were that their methods can be applied with equal value to all areas of reality. Although scientists were initially quite immodest, claiming certainty and promising answers, today the sciences tend to confirm certain limits to our understandings of reality. They are realizing that what they work with are models, or paradigms, rather than photographic reproductions of reality.

THE IMPORTANCE OF PARADIGMS

Before the seventeenth century, Western understandings of the world were governed by the Ptolemaic worldview. Everyone knew that the earth—and humankind—was at the center of the physical universe. The planets spun around this nucleus embedded in concentric glass globes. This image of the cosmos meshed with Aristotelian physics, which explained motion in terms of purpose and the "nature" of things. Theology and physics thus supported each other.

People generally agreed that this worldview presented an accurate picture of the universe. Anything that did not fit into this perspective seemed nonsensical. As strange as this model may seem to us today, to the medieval and early Renaissance mind, it was common sense.

The seventeenth-century scientific revolution created a whole new picture of the world, and this perspective has shaped our understandings into the present age. The new framework, shaped by such pioneers as Copernicus and Newton, puts the sun at the center and recognizes the earth as one of the planets. This separates theology from physics. Newton's physics, which made this sun-centered cosmos seem workable, posits a rational, mechanistic universe that obeys knowable, rational laws. It assumes that regularities exist and that one can discover and quantify such phenomenon. It implies that one can explain such events in terms of cause and effect. Thus, the past can be seen as a complete cause or explanation of the present. Moreover, the present shapes the future (but the future cannot shape the present).

The universe is therefore predictable, assuming that one can discover the correct factors. One basic rationality exists for the world, and with this rationality one can understand the world.

The Newtonian or "scientific" approach works well to explain and predict much of what happens in the visible, physical world. For years, it was believed to represent an accurate picture of the structure of the world, applicable to the psychological as well as the physical world. It has formed our common sense.

Today we are learning, however, that there are definite limits to this understanding. These limits exist not only in areas such as psychology but even in the physical world itself.

The Newtonian picture does work for bodies of "normal" size moving at "normal" speeds—the see and touch world. However, scientists have found that when things get tiny or begin to move very fast, Newtonian science no longer works. Similarly, in the realm of genetics Newtonian assumptions often break down. In these situations, probability begins to take the place of laws and predictability. The future becomes hard to predict in cause-and-effect terms. In outer space at high velocity, "commonsense" concepts of time and space become inadequate as they become more plastic and intermixed. In this world, Einsteinian physics begins to take the place of Newtonian. One must begin to use a different picture of the world.

In *Einstein's Space and Van Gogh's Sky*, Lawrence Leshan and Henry Margenau, a physicist and a psychologist, have shown us that the traditional scientific worldview is also inadequate in art, psychology, and spirituality.[1] Here other dynamics are at work, and we must use other ways of knowing. Human beings, for example, are able to project into the future

---

1 Lawrence Leshan and Henry Margenau, *Einstein's Space and Van Gogh's Sky: Physical Reality and Beyond* (New York: Collier Books, 1982). This represents a significant advance in paradigm theory. The present chapter owes much to their work.

and to shape their behavior accordingly. Here the future can indeed affect the present. Ideas of cause and effect must be tempered with the concept of purpose. Rational, mechanistic "laws" cannot be assumed. We must use other descriptions of reality. The limits of traditional science in the domain of psychology are nicely captured in the First Law of Animal Psychology: "If an animal of known, stable genetic background is raised in a carefully controlled laboratory environment, and administered a precisely measured stimulus, the animal will act as it damn well pleases."[2]

Leshan and Margenau clarify and expand what philosophers of science have been saying for some time. Our definitions of reality in a particular culture and era are ways of constructing reality. They are in fact models, paradigms. They will work to explain and influence in some situations, but they may not in others. They are pictures of reality shaped by our particular needs and assumptions, and they may be quite incomplete.

Paradigms shape our approach, not only to the physical but also to the social, psychological, and philosophical world. They provide the lens through which we understand phenomena. They determine how we solve problems. They shape what we "know" to be possible and impossible. Our paradigms form our common sense, and things that fall outside the paradigm seem absurd.

Our paradigms are particular ways of constructing reality, and our retributive understanding of justice is one such construct. The retributive paradigm of justice is one particular way of organizing reality. That paradigm shapes how we define problems and what we recognize as appropriate solutions. It is common sense.

---

2 Leshan and Margenau, *Einstein's Space*, 150.

However, it is in fact a paradigm. Like all paradigms, it has certain strengths. Like all paradigms, it is also a trap.

Christie has captured well the importance of paradigms in shaping our expectations: "A warrior wears armor, a lover, flowers. They are equipped according to expectations of what is to happen, and their equipment increases chances that their expectations will prove right."[3]

So also with the institution of penal law.

APPLYING THE PARADIGM

Interestingly enough, we apply the retributive paradigm only in very limited situations. Many conflicts and harms occur every day, but most are handled informally or extralegally. Only a tiny minority ever enter the legal process. In other words, the legal system is only one of many ways to settle disputes and wrongs, and it is rarely used.

Of those few that do enter the legal system, however, most are channeled through civil law. In civil procedures, person is pitted against person rather than against the state. The state plays the role of referee and arbiter. Whether or not to use the process is usually at the discretion of the people involved. And they can drop out of the process if and when they find a resolution.

Because the focus is on settlement rather than loss of liberty or life, civil procedures are less strictly regulated than criminal ones. For the same reason, the definition and criteria of guilt are looser. In fact, at stake are questions of liability and obligation rather than guilt, and degrees of responsibility are possible. Consequently, outcomes are less likely to be seen in dichotomous, win-lose terms than in criminal cases. Unlike criminal cases, civil cases usually result in some form of compensation.

3 Christie, "Images of Man in Modern Penal Law," *Contemporary Crises: Law, Crime and Social Policy* 10, no. 1 (1986): 95.

Only a small fraction of disputes ever enter the specialized processes of criminal law. Once they do, however, a completely different set of assumptions and understandings takes over. Here the retributive paradigm reigns.

The proportion of disputes and harms that are criminalizable is quite small, then, and only a fraction of these are, in fact, criminalized.[4] The selection of situations to define as criminal and then to actually process as criminal is actually quite variable and arbitrary.

Definitions of *crimes* vary through time and space, often in rather arbitrary ways. We define many harms by individuals as crimes, for example, but ignore serious harms—often affecting many people—that are committed by corporations.

Of those acts that are criminal, only a fraction become criminal cases. Again, the selection can be quite arbitrary. Factors such as status, race, and the ethnicity of the victim and offender play a part, for example. So do the priorities and workloads of prosecutor, the police, and the court system.

What is important is that we recognize what we call crime as the tip of a pyramid of harms and conflicts. Only some of those situations and behaviors are designated as potentially criminalizable. Only a smaller fraction are actually criminalized. We handle most of our wrongs and conflicts in different ways.

Once we decide to criminalize a certain event or behavior, we begin to define reality quite differently, in ways that may not correspond to the experience of the participants. The retributive paradigm creates its own reality. *Now* the offense is

---

4 Louk H. C. Hulsman has argued this in a number of settings. See "Critical Criminology and the Concept of Crime," *Contemporary Crises: Law, Crime and Social Policy* 10, no. 1 (1986): 63–80. See also John R. Bled, Hans van Mastrigt, and Niels A. Uildriks, eds., *The Criminal Justice System as a Social Problem: An Abolitionist Perspective* (Rotterdam, Netherlands: Erasmus University, 1987).

against the state, which determines the response. Punishment, not resolution or settlement, is seen as the appropriate outcome. Responsibility becomes absolute, defined in terms of guilt rather than liability. Outcomes are imposed with little participation by victim or offender. The retributive paradigm takes over, shaping our perceptions of what can and should be done.

PARADIGMS CHANGE

Our understandings of what is possible and impossible are based on our constructions of reality. These constructs can and do change.

Thomas Kuhn, in an influential book entitled *The Structure of Scientific Revolutions*, has suggested that changes in scientific outlook come about through a series of paradigm shifts.[5]

One model or paradigm replaces another, thus causing a revolution in the way we view and understand the world. This pattern of changes suggests a possible pattern for paradigm changes in general.

The Ptolemaic paradigm, which shaped Western understandings until the seventeenth century, seemed to fit observed phenomena. If you lie on your back at night and use the North Star as a point of reference, the stars and planets appear to be in a circular globe with the earth at the center. Also, they do appear to revolve. It made sense to think of the cosmos as a series of concentric "crystalline spheres" with the earth at the center.

The earth-centered universe fit philosophic and theological assumptions as well. Humankind represented the pinnacle of God's creation, and it was only logical that their dwelling would be at the center of the universe.

---

5 Thomas Kuhn, *The Structure of Scientific Revolutions*, 50th anniv. ed. (1970; Chicago: University of Chicago Press, 2012).

A number of phenomena did not fit this pattern. As telescopes were invented and the skies explored, this number grew. Comets seemed to move through the areas where glass globes were supposed to be, for example. Calculated distances seemed incorrect. And planets seemed to move backward at certain points in their orbit.

This latter phenomenon, called retrograde motion, was troubling, since it was difficult to see how this could happen if the planets were embedded in glass globes. Scientists decided that the planets must move in small orbits within the larger orbit. They called this phenomenon *epicycles*. As they observed more and more retrograde motion, the number of epicycles grew phenomenally.

The dysfunctions in the Ptolemaic understanding multiplied in the early seventeenth century. At the same time, a series of new discoveries and theories emerged. Kepler published his laws. Galileo suggested laws of motion. Through the lens of the telescope he developed, he began to observe the skies. Brahe began systematically to record movement in the heavens. Increasing numbers of phenomena simply did not fit the expectations of the paradigm.

Nevertheless, it was difficult to junk the Ptolemaic understanding. After all, it was common sense. It had been for centuries. And it was linked closely with many philosophical and theological understandings. To jettison this paradigm would be revolutionary and frightening. So scientists used a multitude of epicycles to patch it together, and considerable pressure was put on the innovators to withdraw their claims.

By the early seventeenth century, however, more and more phenomena did not fit. At the same time, scientists were making new discoveries. Isaac Newton fit the pieces together in a paradigm that was so compelling, so sensible, that it could not be avoided. Newtonian physics allowed Copernicus's universe to work, making possible the new paradigm.

Kuhn suggests that by implication we can find in this scientific revolution a pattern for intellectual revolutions. He suggests that the way we understand phenomena is governed by a particular model, a particular paradigm. This governing paradigm seems to fit most phenomena, and various exceptions are made for those phenomena that do not fit.

Over time dysfunctions begin to develop as more and more phenomena do not fit the paradigm. However, we keep trying to rescue the model by inventing epicycles—reform—that piece it together. Eventually, though, the sense of dysfunction becomes so great that the model breaks down and is replaced by another. This cannot happen, however, before a new "physics" is developed. That is, a variety of building blocks must be in place before a new synthesis is possible and a new common sense emerges.

In an interesting article several years ago, Randy Barnett suggested that the history of our justice paradigm shows some of the symptoms of paradigm change.[6] As with the seventeenth-century scientific revolution, for example, the paradigm has long been recognized as having certain inadequacies and dysfunctions. A series of "epicycles" has been used to patch it together, but the sense of dysfunction is becoming too great to allow easy remedies.

In early applications of the retributive model, punishment was severe. There were no safeguards against abuse and no relationship between the severity of the offense and the punishment inflicted. The idea of proportionate punishment was an Enlightenment invention that made punishment more rational and palatable. The idea was that if punishment can be made to fit the crime and thus be less arbitrary, less at the whim of those in authority, punishment would make more sense.

---

6 Randy Barnett, "Restitution: A Paradigm of Criminal Justice" in *Perspectives on Crime Victims*, ed. Burt Calaway and Joe Hudson (St. Louis, MO: C. V. Mosby Co., 1981), 245–61.

Prisons became popular as a way to apply proportionate punishment. Prison sentences can be measured in lengths of time and graded to fit the crime. They can be seen as scientific and logical. In an age when science and rationality were so important, proportionate punishment was a sensible way to shore up the punishment paradigm. Prison terms became a way to apply the concept "scientifically."

Other epicycles have been constructed. Rehabilitation, for example, governed sentencing schemes during the first half of the twentieth century. It brought a new rationale for punishment. In the 1960s, however, rehabilitation was discredited and the discretionary, indeterminate sentences that were part of that "treatment" model were abandoned. That epicycle was replaced by the just deserts philosophy, which underlies the mandatory and determinate sentencing laws popular today.

The search for alternatives to prison represents still another attempt to patch up the paradigm. Instead of seeking alternatives to punishment, the alternatives movement offers alternative *punishments*. By offering new ways to punish that are less expensive and more attractive than prison, proponents are able to prop up the paradigm. However, because it is only an epicycle, it does not question fundamental assumptions about punishment. It has thus failed to have impact on the very problems (e.g., prison crowding) that it was designed to address.

Community service orders have become a popular sanction, for example. When introduced, they promised to take prison-bound offenders, relieving prison crowding. In actuality, they have usually provided a new form of punishing offenders who might not have been punished. Today, electronic monitoring of offenders claims new possibilities for punishment and control.

Victim compensation and assistance may be viewed as another such epicycle. In the U.S., proposals for such efforts tend to be based on claims of victims' rights. In England, arguments are more likely to focus on their needs and welfare. Both approaches seek to remedy a problem in the existing paradigm, but neither questions basic assumptions about the state's and the victim's role in justice. They recognize a legitimate problem but not the root source of the problem.

The sense of dysfunction and crisis is widespread. At the same time, many people are groping for a new "physics" for understanding and responding to the situations we call crime. Perhaps the ground is being prepared for a shift in paradigm.

The source of many of our failures, I am arguing, lies in the lens through which we view crime and justice, and that lens is a particular construction of reality, a paradigm. It is not the only possible paradigm. In the following chapters, I will summarize some historical and biblical understandings. These suggest that our retributive paradigm is relatively recent and that other paradigms are conceivable. They also suggest some building blocks for an alternative vision.

Part III

Roots and Signposts

7

Community Justice:
The Historical Alternative

OFFENDERS HAVE VIOLATED the state's laws. They must be punished. The state must take charge. All of this seems so natural and inevitable. Surely this retributive paradigm must have been with us for a long time. Surely it must represent a definite improvement over what went before. Surely it is what must be.

The retributive model of justice is not the only way we have envisioned justice in the West. In fact, other models of justice have predominated throughout most of our history. Only within the past several centuries has the retributive paradigm come to monopolize our vision.

Nor does the victory of this paradigm necessarily represent improvement. A common historical fallacy is to interpret history as progress. We view recent developments as almost inevitable improvements over the past. But the present is not inevitably inherent in the past, nor does it always represent progress.

Historical interpretation has tended to focus on two developments in the history of "criminal justice": the rise of public justice at the expense of private justice and an increasing dependence on prison as punishment. That both developments occurred in some form is not in doubt. However, recent historical work raises questions about the pattern and meaning of these developments.

Usually we think of the past as dominated by *private justice*. Private justice is characterized as private vengeance, often uncontrolled and brutal. Modern *public justice*, in contrast, is controlled justice: more humane, more balanced, less punitive. We assume that prisons are less punitive and more enlightened than what went before. In this view, we have become more civilized and rational in dispensing justice and punishment.

Reality is more complex than this conventional picture would imply. "Private" justice was not necessarily private and did not necessarily involve vengeance. "Private" settlements were not necessarily more punitive, less restrained, or less enlightened than state-dispensed justice. On the contrary, public justice may actually be more punitive in focus and may offer a narrower range of possible outcomes. Vengeance, while it certainly could occur prior to state-based justice, was only one of a much richer set of options. So-called private justice certainly had deficiencies, but the picture is not as simple as we usually assume.[1]

---

1 In addition to works cited in this chapter, the following resources were particularly helpful: George Calhoun, *The Growth of Criminal Law in Ancient Greece* (Berkeley: University of California Press, 1927); Michael Ignatieff, *A Just Measure of Pain: The Penitentiary in the Industrial Revolution, 1750–1850* (New York: Pantheon Press, 1978); Stanley Cohen and Andrew Scull, eds., *Social Control and the State* (New York: St. Martin's Press, 1983); John H. Langbein, "The Historical Origins of the Sanction of Imprisonment for Serious Crime," *Journal of Legal Studies* 5 (1976); Langbein, *Prosecuting Crime in the Renaissance, England, Germany and France* (Cambridge, MA: Harvard University Press, 1974); Alfred Soman, "Deviance and Criminal Justice in Western Europe, 1300–1800: An Essay in Structure," *Criminal Justice History: An International Annual* 1 (1980): 3–28; Pieter Spierenburg, *The Spectacle of Suffering: Executions and the Evolution of Repression* (Cambridge: Cambridge University Press, 1984).

COMMUNITY JUSTICE

The history of the West encompasses considerable diversity of structures and customs. Not surprisingly, local practices of justice varied in time and locale. Yet broad similarities existed in the overall understandings of what was involved in crime and justice in the premodern world. To some extent these similarities reflected common traditions. Greco-Roman and Germanic tribal culture, for example, shaped in part the medieval worldview. Shared experiences and needs also led to similarities in understandings.

Until well into the modern era, crime was viewed primarily in an interpersonal context. Most crime essentially represented a wrong toward or a conflict between people. As in "civil" conflicts, what mattered in the majority of offenses was the actual harm done, not the violation of laws or an abstract social or moral order. Such wrongs created obligations and liabilities, which had to be made right in some way. The feud was one way of resolving such situations, but so were negotiation, restitution, and reconciliation. Victim and offender, as well as kin and community, played vital roles in this process.

Since crime created obligations, a typical outcome of the justice process was some sort of settlement. Restitution and compensation agreements were commonplace, even for offenses to the person. Laws and customs frequently specified a range of appropriate compensations for both property and personal offenses. These included formulas for converting personal injury to material compensation. Our concepts of guilt and punishment may represent a transformation (and a perversion, perhaps) of this principle of exchange. The Greek *pune* refers to an exchange of money for harm done and may be the origin of the word for *punishment*. Similarly, *guilt* may derive from the Anglo-Saxon *geldan*, which, like the German word

Geld, refers to payment.[2] Offenses created liabilities. Justice demanded some steps to make losses right.

The offender and the victim (or a representative of the victim in the case of murder) settled most disputes and wrongs—including those we call criminal—outside of courts. They did this within the context of their kin and community. Church and community leaders often played central roles in negotiating or arbitrating settlements, registering agreements once they were made. The administration of justice was primarily a mediating and negotiating process rather than a process of applying rules and imposing decisions.

Reflecting this understanding of the church's role, a French Reformed church elder in 1681 urged the church to "work diligently to reconcile any quarrels which may be known to members of the consistory."[3] Such quarrels included offenses we would call crime. The elders thus decided to make a list of conflicts, urge disputants to settle, and suspend from Eucharist those who did not come to agreement. The French acts of accommodation represented such agreements, which were registered before a notary.[4]

As the preceding suggests, this approach to justice may be better termed *community justice* than *private justice.* Justice was private only in the sense that it was not state justice. Both the harm done and the resulting justice process were clearly placed in a community context. Wrongs were often viewed collectively. When an individual was wronged, the family and community felt it as a wrong also. And family and community

2 J. W. Mohr, "Criminal Justice and Christian Responsibility: The Secularization of Criminal law," (unpublished paper, Mennonite Central Committee Canada annual meeting, Abbotsford, BC, January 22, 1981).

3 Soman, "Deviance and Criminal Justice," 18.

4 Bruce Lenman and Geoffrey Parker, "The State, the Community and the Criminal Law in Early Modern Europe," in *Crime and the Law: The Social History of Crime in Western Europe since 1500,* ed. V. A. C. Gatrell, Bruce Lenman, and Geoffrey Parker (London: Europa Publications, 1979), 19ff.

were involved in the resolution in substantial ways. They might generate pressure for a settlement or serve as arbiters and mediators. They might be called upon to witness or even help enforce agreements.

Community justice placed a high premium on negotiated, extrajudicial settlements, usually involving compensation. Nevertheless, two alternative approaches existed. Both tended to be choices of last resort, chosen either as a means of forcing negotiation or growing out of the failure of negotiation. Thus both represented a kind of failure, although their existence may have helped to ensure the working of the norm.

THE RETRIBUTIVE OPTION

Vengeance represented one of these alternatives. This option was resorted to less often than is commonly thought for reasons that are obvious. Vengeance was dangerous. It often led to reciprocal violence and blood feuds. In societies characterized by small, close-knit communities, emphasis of necessity had to be on maintaining relationships. Here negotiation and compensation made much more sense than violence.

The possibility of vengeance certainly existed, but use of it was limited, and its roles and meanings were often different from what we assume.

One limit on vengeance, which in turn confirms the importance of negotiated justice, was the existence of sanctuaries.[5] Throughout the medieval period until at least the French Revolution, western Europe was dotted with a variety of safe areas independent of other laws and authorities. Those who were accused of wrongdoing could run to these areas in order

---

5 On sanctuaries see Herman Bianchi, *Justice as Sanctuary: Toward a New System of Crime Control* (Bloomington: Indiana University Press, 1994); Michael R. Weisser, *Crime and Punishment in Early Modern Europe* (Atlantic Highlands, NJ: Humanities Press, 1979), 54; Paul Rock, "Law, Order and Power in the Late Seventeenth- and Early Eighteenth-Century England," in *Social Control and the State*, ed. Cohen and Scull, 191–221.

to escape private vengeance or even local authorities. Many of these were not long-term havens but places of safety that allowed tempers to cool while negotiations went on. Some sanctuaries specified the length of time the accused could remain. But while there, offenders were to be safe.

Dutch criminologist Herman Bianchi has suggested another possible role for such sanctuaries. He and his coworkers have found that pilgrims traveling to do penance stopped at such sanctuaries. These pilgrims appear to have been making their pilgrimage as a penance for a crime. This suggests that both penance and compensation may have been seen as appropriate responses to certain offenses.

While on a sabbatical leave in the English city of Winchester, I discovered the House of Godbegot. This building, now a clothing store, is a remnant of the Manor of Godbegot, which was bequeathed by Queen Emma in 1052 to the church. It was given complete rights to be self-governing, including the right of "excluding all other officers from the place." Surviving court records from the manor suggest that it served as a sanctuary for offenders until it was dissolved by Henry VIII in the sixteenth century.

Court records indicate that on several occasions people entered the sanctuary and apprehended offenders. But they also show that this was considered a violation of the sanctuary. A thirteenth-century statute in Winchester specified that one could not belong to both Winchester and the manor without paying a fine. The exception, significantly, was for those there "for felony." Both of these examples suggest the manor's role as a sanctuary for offenders.

Vengeance was also limited by a mixture of law and custom. For example, in medieval Europe the feud was not considered legitimate unless negotiations had been offered and refused. The well-known Old Testament formula, "an eye for an eye," was the kind of formula that helped to regulate private vengeance throughout much of Western history.

"An eye for an eye" could of course be taken literally, and such vengeance could be brutal. However, in societies unregulated by formal legal codes and procedures, these formulas were not commands, but limitations on violence: "Do this much, but only this much." Responses were to be in proportion to the wrong and were not to escalate the conflict.

Moreover, persons have often understood these formulas as equations for determining compensation: "the value of an eye for the value of an eye." Settlements in money or property were quite common in our history, even in cases of serious violence. Such codes provided principles for determining compensation.

Even when "an eye for an eye" was taken literally, it was viewed as compensation. When someone dies or is hurt in a communally organized society, the balance of power between tribes, clans, or other groups is upset. Balance may need to be restored by evening out numbers. The formulaic violence was intended as much to balance power as to exact revenge.

Then as now, victims needed to be morally vindicated. They demanded public recognition that they had been wronged and public acknowledgment by offenders of their responsibility. Compensation was one way of achieving this vindication, but retribution sometimes provided a certain moral compensation as well. Sometimes the threat of retribution also served to encourage offenders to take such public responsibility.

The threat of retribution certainly existed, but it may have been a means as much as an end in itself. Moreover, the meaning and functions of retribution often reflected a compensatory vision. The system rested first of all on the necessity of compensating victims and repairing relationships. This usually necessitated negotiations toward a settlement that would acknowledge the offender's responsibility and liabilities.

Throughout most of our history there have been exceptions to this ideal of restitutive justice for certain kinds of crime. Early theocratic societies considered a limited number of offenses to have religious dimensions requiring special, "abnormal" responses. Certain sex offenses, for example, were especially heinous because they offended the deity. These brought collective guilt upon the whole society. In order to demonstrate society's condemnation of such behavior and thus avoid sharing in the guilt, a symbolic cleansing was necessary. Such offenses were few and carefully proscribed by law and custom, however, and did not set the norm for most "criminal" offense.

In the early modern period in Europe a limited number of offenses were seen as a challenge to the moral and political order, thus requiring the application of violent responses. These included witchcraft, incest, sodomy, and certain types of particularly heinous homicides.

THE JUDICIAL OPTION

Vengeance was one alternative to the ideal of negotiated, restitutive justice. Appeal to established courts was another. Like vengeance, however, this option was usually a last resort when negotiations failed or in those situations where law or custom required it. It was chosen as a means of encouraging negotiated settlements. To the modern mind, members of this society were remarkably reluctant to use the formal machinery of justice.

During the Middle Ages in western continental Europe, for example, a variety of official courts existed. Some of these were state or royal courts. Others were operated by ecclesiastical, municipal, or seigneurial authorities. Even state courts, however, tended to operate within the context and principles of community justice.

Medieval courts were accusatorial in nature. Except in a few types of offenses (e.g., those against the person of the crown), even royal courts could not initiate prosecution without a request by the victim or the family of the victim. Without an accuser, there could be no case. There were no public prosecutors and few legal grounds for independent prosecution by the state except for an offense in which the crown itself was the actual victim.

Once someone initiated prosecution, the court's role was to see that the parties cooperated. It was to equalize power relationships insofar as it was possible and generally to regulate the conflict. The courts thus served as a kind of referee. If the parties involved came to an agreement, they were free to terminate the case at any time. The state had no legal authority to continue prosecution without an accuser. Initiative was in the hands of those involved.

Persons usually turned to the courts only to pressure the other party to acknowledge responsibility and to settle. Extrajudicial forms of community justice were preferred well into the modern era. This reluctance to use the judicial option was based on a variety of factors. Preference for negotiated settlements was one. However, local resistance to the claims of central authorities was a major factor as well. So was the financial cost that prosecution could entail. Also, medieval courts often assumed a reciprocity of risk. If the accuser failed to make his case successfully, he might be subject to the consequences intended for the accused. An accuser would of necessity want to have a strong case before proceeding. Finally, royal courts often had the option of imposing a fine as an outcome. Since the money went to the authority operating the court, it did the victim little good.

The accusatorial model that shaped court structures and procedures thus operated in the context of community justice, which in turn placed a high premium on compensation and on participant initiative. Accusatorial courts confirmed the centrality of community justice.

AN ASSESSMENT

Premodern justice is conventionally portrayed as vengeful and barbaric, in contrast to the more rational and humane approach of modern justice. Clearly that picture is too simplistic and too grim. Nevertheless, it would be equally wrong to wax nostalgic for a golden age that has been lost. Community justice had serious deficiencies. Methods for establishing guilt in contested cases were arbitrary and inaccurate, lacking safeguards. This form of justice worked most satisfactorily among equals. Where offenders were subordinate, justice could be summary and brutal.

Community justice could also put a heavy load on victims, since the pursuing of cases depended upon their initiative and perhaps even their resources. Penalties for offenses considered especially heinous could be barbaric.

Yet negotiated, compensatory settlements that guided community justice represent an alternative understanding of crime and justice that is important. Traditional concepts of justice recognized that harm had been done to people, that the people involved had to be central to a resolution, and that reparation of harm was critical. Community justice placed a high premium on maintaining relationships, on reconciliation. Thus, the paradigm of community justice may have reflected the reality of crime better than does our own more "enlightened" paradigm.

Traditional justice is often characterized as punitive justice. Yet punishment was only one of many possible outcomes and often represented a failure of the ideal. Community justice offered a wider range of outcomes than does our contemporary retributive paradigm. At minimum, we must revise our assessment of traditional justice to reflect its possibilities for retribution *and* reconciliation.

THE LEGAL REVOLUTION

No system of criminal law as we understand it existed in medieval Europe. No written body of law identified certain acts as crimes and prescribed certain punishments. Cases were not normally handled by legal professionals. Political and judicial authorities did have a recognized role, but it was quite limited. A variety of courts existed, but on the whole they functioned within the assumptions and parameters of community justice. They were used with considerable reluctance.

In the eleventh and twelfth centuries, however, a series of changes began which for the next several centuries lay the basis for a drastically new approach to crime and justice. These changes took centuries to mature and were fiercely resisted by many. The new model of justice was not victorious until the nineteenth century. Nevertheless, this metamorphosis, although protracted and often overlooked by historians, constituted what legal historian Harold J. Berman has termed a legal revolution.[6]

Earlier political authorities had felt constrained to shape law within the framework of customary understandings and practices. In the later medieval period, they began to claim the right to make new law and to abrogate old. Formal, written law codes incorporating new principles began to replace custom. By the eighteenth and nineteenth centuries, a special

---

6 Harold J. Berman, *Law and Revolution: The Formation of the Western Legal Tradition* (Cambridge, MA: Harvard University Press, 1983), and "The Religious Foundations of Western Law," *The Catholic University of America Law Review* 24, no. 3 (Spring 1975): 490–508. Berman's pioneering work is extremely important. Other important sources on early modern justice and the legal revolution are A. Esmein, *A History of Continental Criminal Procedures* (Boston: Little, Brown, and Co., 1913), and Weisser, *Crime and Punishment.*

body of codified law had been developed to cover certain harms and disputes called crimes.

New arguments and procedures began to open the possibility of state intervention and initiative in certain types of cases. On the European continent, prosecutors representing the state began to appear. In England, justices of the peace came to represent the state in limited ways. Courts began to move from their reactive, umpiring role to claim ownership of certain types of cases. They began to take the initiative in beginning procedures and compiling evidence in such cases.

In continental Europe, the style of courts changed from accusatorial to inquisitorial. Here the court was responsible for bringing charges, compiling facts, and determining the outcome—often in secret. In England, an accusatorial framework was maintained due to the role of the jury and the retention of at least the form of private prosecution. Here, too, agents of the state took the place of citizens as the guiding force in criminal cases.

In such cases, the nature of the outcomes began to change. Punishment began to take precedence over settlements. Fines—which went to the state's coffers—began to replace restitution to victims. Torture came to be not simply an acceptable penalty but a forensic tool for finding truth. The actual victim's stake in all this decreased.

This process did not happen by a sudden, direct state takeover of large categories of cases. Instead, representatives of the state gradually insinuated themselves into the accusatorial process. Starting as an investigator, for instance, the state eventually became accuser. By 1498, French law recognized that the king or the king's procurator was a party to every action. Arguing first that it had a right to participate in cases, the state eventually claimed ownership.

State lawyers used a variety of legal devices and arguments, some new and some old, to justify state involvement. Accusatorial procedures had recognized that the ordinary way for cases to be initiated was by victims or their relatives. Some jurisdictions had left room for certain extraordinary prosecutions by the court or state in limited situations. In fourteenth-century France, for example, there were several ways that a court might take cognizance of an offense. The ordinary way was by accusation brought by accuser. However, in the case of *present misdeed* (if the offender was caught in the act) or by *common report* (when the offense and offender were commonly known), the court could intervene without a direct accuser. Also, some provision was made for initiating a case by *denunciation*. Here there would be accusers, but they remained in the background, playing only a minimal role. As is so often the case, procedures intended as extraordinary in the long run became ordinary.[7]

The use of such legal devices was combined with new arguments. The crown began to claim that it was keeper of the peace. From that it was a short step to the claim that, when the peace was violated, the state was victim. That the role and claims of individual victims would be lost in this process is not surprising.

THE ROLE OF CANON LAW

Not incidentally, the development of this new legal system with central authorities occurred within the context of an overall struggle for power. This struggle for hegemony occurred both *within* and *between* religious and secular structures. It profoundly affected the way justice came to be done. The development of canon law—the law of the Catholic Church—was a critical part of these struggles.

---

7 See Esmein, *A History*, 121ff.

During the first Christian centuries, the church was decentralized. Gradually, several competing power centers emerged, each claiming certain authority. Also, problems of internal discipline arose within the church. A primary concern of the papacy during the medieval years, therefore, was to consolidate its authority within the church. At the same time, the papacy was engaged in a struggle to claim authority equal to or above secular political authorities.

Centralizing secular authorities were beginning to emerge during this time, however, and with similar needs. They too needed to consolidate their power within their realms by finding ways to subordinate other power centers, including the church.

Both religious and secular authorities, therefore, sought new arguments and devices to help them consolidate their authority. Law from the late Roman Empire provided just such an instrument, first for the church and then for the state.

During the Republican era of Roman history, crime had remained primarily a private or community affair, with the state having only a limited role. As the empire emerged, however, a tradition of law developed that recognized an expanded role for the state in creating law and administering justice.

This law was largely lost after the sixth century, although it may not have been entirely forgotten. The rediscovery of Justinian's Code by the West in the late eleventh century may not have been an accident. Supporters of the pope and perhaps supporters of secular authorities as well may have been searching for some time. Once rediscovered in the eleventh century, Roman law created the basis for canon law, which became the fundamental law of the church. Later its outlines were adopted by secular powers throughout all of western continental Europe. It influenced English law to some extent as well.

Berman has examined this law and its adaptation. He notes that Roman law was a radical departure from customary practices. What was adopted was an autonomous body of law from a civilization remote in time and culture. This law introduced important new elements.

Roman law was formal, rational, codified law based on logic and fundamental principles. Instead of being based on custom and history, this law stood alone. Therefore, it provided central authorities with possibilities and methods for inventing new law and voiding old laws. Also, Roman law assumed a central authority and thus provided a basis for "legitimate" initiation of action by central authority. Part of the attraction of Roman law, then, was the important role it gave to central authorities.

Roman law was written law, based on principles that were independent of specific customs. It had an accompanying method for testing and developing law (i.e., scholasticism). Roman law, therefore, could not only be systematized and expanded but could also be studied and taught transnationally by professionals. This universal character helps explain its appeal and almost immediate spread to universities throughout most of western Europe.

From the base of Roman law, the church built the elaborate structure of canon law, the first modern legal system. This was a revolutionary development. It provided the papacy with an important weapon in its struggle for supremacy, both within the church and in its relationship to secular political authorities.

By providing for prosecution by a central authority, it established a basis for attacking both heresy and clerical abuse within the church. The most extreme expression of this new approach was the Inquisition, in which representatives of the pope ferreted out heretics and tortured them, both to obtain evidence and to settle accounts.

No longer was the individual the primary victim. In the Inquisition, it was a whole moral order that was the victim, and the central authority was its guardian. Wrongs were no longer simple harms requiring redress. They were sins.

As this implies, canon law did not only represent the introduction of systematic, formal law and an enlarged role for central authorities. It also implied a wholly different concept of crime and justice. Justice became a matter of applying rules, establishing guilt, and fixing penalties. Early Christian practice had focused on acceptance and forgiveness of wrongdoing, emphasizing the necessity of reconciliation and redemption.[8] Canon law and the parallel theology that developed began to identify crime as a collective wrong against a moral or metaphysical order. Crime was a sin, not just against a person but against God, and it was the church's business to purge the world of this transgression. From this it was a short step to the assumptions that the social order is willed by God and that crime is also a sin against this social order. The church (and later the state) must therefore enforce that order. Not surprisingly, focus shifted from settlements between participants to punishment by established authorities.[9]

Canon law and its accompanying theology formalized concepts of free will and personal responsibility. This helped to lay a basis for a rationale of punishment. Imprisonment became a means of punishing wayward monastics, which led to the widespread use of imprisonment as punishment beginning in the eighteenth and nineteenth centuries.

---

8 Gerald Austin McHugh, *Christian Faith and Criminal Justice: Toward a Christian Response to Crime and Punishment* (New York: Paulist Press, 1978), 14ff.

9 This kind of reasoning was not totally new, of course. The medieval trial by ordeal was based on related concepts. Medieval thought related behavior and nature. Because certain offenses were contrary to God and nature, nature could be expected to reject the criminal. An evil person tossed into water would float, since the water, being pure, would reject him or her. An innocent person was expected to sink—a dubious victory if one could not swim.

Canon law introduced important new principles. These in turn were adopted and adapted by political authorities, serving as an important model for secular legal systems from England to Poland and Hungary.

The example of canon law is by no means a complete explanation for the development of a state-centered, retributive understanding of justice. England was less influenced by canon law than was the continent. While it did not develop an inquisitorial justice system, nevertheless it did develop a system of criminal law with the state as a guiding force. Given trends in society and the needs of emerging nation-states, justice may well have gone in a similar direction without the example of canon law. However, the pattern provided by this adaptation of Roman law did provide important techniques and concepts for use by political authorities in consolidating their positions.

The role of Christian theology in all this is uncertain. Some historians have argued that theological concepts of guilt and moral responsibility played a causative role, helping to create new concepts of crime, justice, and power that the state came to embody. Others have argued that the development of modern justice was based on the political needs of emerging nation-states or on socioeconomic processes. Theology then followed, providing justification for these new forms. That there are links between theology and these developments is clear, however.[10]

---

10 Recent research has explored and clarified the ways in which the developing legal system and emerging biblical interpretation interacted, contributing to a punitive theology, worldview, and legal system in the West. See Timothy Gorringe, *God's Just Vengeance: Crime, Violence and the Rhetoric of Salvation* (Cambridge: Cambridge University Press, 1996); and T. Richard Snyder, *The Protestant Ethic and the Spirit of Punishment* (Grand Rapids, MI: Wm. H. Eerdmans Publishing, 2001).

STATE JUSTICE VICTORIOUS

Historians Bruce Lenman and Geoffrey Parker have suggested that Western history may be viewed as a dialectic between two basic models of law or justice: community and state.[11] State justice reared its head early. Elements of it may be seen in the Babylonian Code of Hammurabi or in Solon's law reforms in ancient Greece. However, only in the past several centuries has true state justice become victorious, monopolizing our views about crime.

Community justice at its best represented negotiated, restitutive justice. Its sense is captured in *frith*, the Germanic tribal word for peace implying a horizontal, agreed-upon peace. State justice, however, is the king's peace. It is vertical, hierarchical, imposed, punitive.[12]

While community and state justice may seem to be opposing concepts, it is more accurate to see them as poles on a continuum, with many variations in between.[13] On one pole is pure community justice involving negotiated settlements between the parties concerned. Justice becomes a bit more formal when other parties, perhaps appointed by political authorities, are involved as arbitrators or notaries. Accusatorial courts are even more formal, specifying a role for the state. At the end of the scale lies the true state court with state initiation, state discretion, state control, and the state as victim.

Community justice, as it operated in early modern Europe, contained elements of state justice. Perhaps the mix, the symbiotic relationship, between the two forms of justice allowed community justice to work. Perhaps the threat of state justice

---

11 Lenman and Parker, "The State, the Community and the Criminal Law." Lenman and Parker's thesis provides part of the framework for this chapter.

12 Bianchi, *Justice as Sanctuary*, chapter 6, 13ff.

13 See also Herman Diederiks, "Patterns of Criminality and Law Enforcement during the Ancient Regime: The Dutch Case," *Criminal Justice History: An International Annual* 1 (1980): 157–74.

oiled the works of community justice. Perhaps the ability to choose arenas of settlement was important. As true state justice emerged victorious, however, understandings of what was appropriate and possible changed. Community justice was no longer an option for most events we call crimes.

By the end of the sixteenth century, the cornerstones of state justice were in place in Europe. New legal codes in France, Germany, and England enlarged the public dimensions of certain offenses and gave to the state a larger role. Criminal codes began to specify wrongs and emphasize punishment. Some of these punishments were overwhelmingly severe, including torture and death. Economic sanctions also remained a possibility in many cases.

The sixteenth-century Protestant Reformation may have encouraged this trend toward punitive sanctions administered by the state.[14] Luther actively endorsed the state as God's agent in administering punishment. Calvinism tended to emphasize images of God as a punitive judge. It also gave the state an important role in enforcing the moral order.

State justice represented the wave of the future, but it was not yet dominant and could not claim a monopoly. The eighteenth-century Enlightenment and French Revolution were required before state justice could make such a radical claim.[15] By the eighteenth century, the state had come to claim absolute power, which it exercised in exceedingly arbitrary and abusive ways. Almost unimaginable forms of torture and punishment were commonplace—not only for duly-convicted

---

14 See T. Richard Snyder, *The Protestant Ethic and the Spirit of Punishment* (Grand Rapids, MI: Eerdmans, 2001).

15 In addition to sources cited previously, see Michael Ignatieff, "State, Civil Society, and Total Institutions: A Critique of Recent Social Histories of Punishment," in *Social Control and the State*, ed. Cohen and Scull, 75–105; and Jacques Ellul, *The Theological Foundation of Law* (New York: Seabury Press, 1969).

criminals but for suspects and political enemies. The crown claimed to be above the law, and the law was a crazy maze of custom and principle, logic and arbitrariness, special interests and public concerns.

The reformers of the Enlightenment sought to place law above governments and to provide law with a rational foundation. Deeply critical of tradition and religion, which they saw as superstitious and illogical, they embraced a secular form of law based on natural law and rational principle.

In this process, Enlightenment thinkers began to formulate new conceptions of society and the state based on an implied social contract. Laws should reflect the will of larger society, they said, and governments should articulate and administer such laws. This is not to say that they saw ordinary people making political decisions. Most Enlightenment thinkers were decidedly not democrats! But they did begin to articulate a concept of government as representing the interests of society at large instead of special interest groups or the royal family.

Faced with the abuse of power by a state claiming to be absolute, eighteenth-century reformers could have attacked the assumptions of a centralized state. They did not. Instead, they not only assumed a powerful state but provided a basis for an enlarged power rooted in a new logic and a new accountability. The new logic consisted of a social contract and a new accountability to wider elements of the population and to law.

Cesare Beccaria's *On Crime and Punishment,* first published in 1764 and often cited as the foundation of modern penal law, was in part an expression of this Enlightenment approach. Beccaria assumed that law should be rationally rooted in the will of the entire community. He said it should be equally applied to all, and it should be administered in a rational way *by the state.*

Beccaria posited that people decide their behavior on the basis of expectations about the pain and pleasure that will result from their choices. Law should administer rational and limited doses of pain, therefore, taking into account the amount of pain needed to outweigh the pleasure to be derived from the offense. The pain that is administered, however, should be proportionate to the wrong that has been done.

Beccaria's book provided a useful weapon with which to attack abuses by the state and traditional law. Rather than question the central role of the state in the business of justice, however, it provided a new legitimacy. Moreover, although understood by many as enshrining a fully rational, utilitarian, concept of law, in fact it retained strong punitive and even retributionist elements.[16]

The French Revolution, which began in 1789 and extended into the next century, drew on Enlightenment roots but had a dynamic of its own. It too attacked custom and privilege, seeking to replace it with a rationalized concept of law and a new concept of the state. Like the Enlightenment, it embodied more, not less, ambitious concepts of power for the state.

The new criminal codes adopted by the revolutionary and Napoleonic governments illustrated these tendencies. They gave to the state strong prosecutorial powers. These codes were also quite punitive but with a more rational and equitable focus.

Eighteenth- and early nineteenth-century developments, therefore, were important in the formulation of the modern form of retributive justice. The state was provided with a new legitimacy as well as new mechanisms for exercising power. Law was given a new sanctity, making lawbreaking more reprehensible and consequences more "deserving."

---

16 See David B. Young, "Let Us Content Ourselves with Praising the Work While Drawing the Veil Over Its Principles: Eighteenth-Century Reactions to Beccaria's *On Crime and Punishment*," *Justice Quarterly* 1, no. 2 (June 1984): 155–69.

Enlightenment thought and post-Enlightenment practice increased the tendency to define offenses in terms of law-breaking rather than actual harms. To the extent that harms were important, emphasis was increasingly upon public rather than private dimensions. If the state represented the will and interests of the public, it was easier to justify defining the state as victim and giving up to the state a monopoly on intervention. Most importantly, the Enlightenment provided a new physics of pain.

Enlightenment and French Revolution thinkers did not question the idea that when wrongs occur, pain should be administered. Instead, they offered new justifications. They instituted more rational guidelines for administering pain. And they introduced new mechanisms for applying punishment.

The primary instrument for applying pain came to be the prison. The reasons for the introduction of imprisonment as a criminal sanction during this era are many. However, part of the attraction of prison was that one could grade terms according to the offense. Prisons made it possible to calibrate punishments in units of time, providing an appearance of rationality and even science in the application of pain.

Prisons also matched well with evolving sensibilities and needs. Publicity and physical suffering had characterized punishments during the old regime. Absolutist regimes had used brutal, public punishments as a way of making visible their power. New, more popularly based governments had less need for public displays of power as a basis for legitimacy. Moreover, people were becoming less comfortable with pain and death. Ways of handling death and illness changed, reflecting a need to hide or even deny these hard aspects of life.[17]

In that context, prisons provided a way to administer pain in private.

---

17 Spierenburg, *Spectacle of Suffering*, chapter 6.

As the technology for imposing pain changed, so did the scope of what was intended. Early-modern forms of punishment punished the body, often in brutal ways. Modern uses of prison sought, as French historian Michel Foucault has noted, to reach the soul.[18] American Quakers who championed the prison did so with the expectation of encouraging repentance and conversion.[19] Later justifications claimed prisons as a laboratory for changing behaviors and thought patterns, for reshaping personality. A wonderful variety of reasons have been invented for using prisons to administer what Christie has called "pain with a purpose."

The roots of formal, state-centered justice go back many centuries, but state justice met considerable resistance. Only in the last century did it emerge victorious. The American experience is a case in point.[20] Portrayals of American justice often emphasize the early development of legal, public forms of justice, locating the origin of formal, public prosecution in the prerevolutionary period. Recent studies, however, have found that public prosecutors had only limited roles. They had little discretion to initiate or drop criminal cases until the middle of the nineteenth century or even later. Instead, other forms of justice (including mediation, arbitration, and civil court procedures) were popular and persisted long after state justice was victorious. Restitution was a popular form of settlement, at least for property harms, and victims had important roles.

---

18 Michel Foucault, *Discipline and Punish: The Birth of the Prison* (New York, Pantheon Press, 1977). See also Ignatieff, *A Just Measure of Pain*, and "State, Civil Society."

19 The year 1990 marked the two-hundredth anniversary of the first modern prison: the Walnut Street Jail.

20 See Josephine Gittler, "Expanding the Role of the Victim in a Criminal Action: An Overview of Issues and Problems," *Pepperdine Law Review* 11 (1984): 117–82; and Allen Steinburg, "From Private Prosecution to Plea Bargaining: Criminal Prosecution, the District Attorney, and American Legal History," *Crime and Delinquency* 311, no. 4 (October 1984): 568–92.

Eventually state justice was victorious. The establishment of public prosecutors with broad discretionary powers, combined with the spread of penitentiaries, were an important part of this process in the U.S. The result is that today, as Jerold Auerbach has so eloquently said, "Law is our national religion; lawyers constitute our priesthood; the courtroom is our cathedral, where contemporary passion plays are enacted."[21]

DIMENSIONS OF THE LEGAL REVOLUTION

The victory of state justice was long in coming. But as Berman has documented, it represented nothing less than a legal revolution of profound implications. The dimensions of this revolution in the way we do justice and think about justice may be summarized as follows.

First, at the core of this revolution was a movement from private or community justice to public justice. This movement began with the opening of possibilities for state-initiated prosecution. Eventually the state claimed partnership, then ownership, until finally, for harms and conflicts termed crimes, the state had a monopoly on justice.

In that process, the victim of crime was redefined, with the state becoming the legal victim. Victims were abstracted, and individuals became peripheral to the problem or the solution.

Second, concurrent with this process, justice came increasingly to be based on formal law rather than custom or convenience. Justice came to be equated with written law as interpreted and managed by professionals. Increasingly the test of justice was the process used.

Certain harms and conflicts came to be defined as different from others, activating criminal procedures in which the state was predominant. Others were left to civil law, where participants maintained considerable discretion and power.

---

21 Jerold S. Auerbach, *Justice Without Law?* (New York: Oxford University Press, 1983), 9.

Third, vengeance was one possible outcome of community justice. The state took over that option, decreasing the availability of other possibilities. Punishment became normative. Resolution and settlements became unusual and even illegal. Since punishment rather than restitution was normative, individual victims' standing in cases was reduced.

Interestingly, the church never mounted any serious criticism of this process. Concerned to control private vengeance and quick to acknowledge a role for the state, it provided active support.

As punishment became normal, new forms of punishment arose. Punishment also changed in symbolic meaning.

In the premodern world, the revenge motive clearly played a role when punishment was sought. At least as important to the idea of punishment, however, was vindication of the victim. Punishments were largely public. In imposing punishments, a symbolic statement of the moral rightness of the victim was implied.

In theocratic societies, punishment also involved a symbolic cleansing function that cleared the community of the pollution created by crime. Punishment demonstrated that society did not condone such actions, thus helping to maintain a sense of boundaries and self-identity for the community.

Newly emerging governments were often highly personalized in the royal family and were concerned to secure their positions. Public, brutal punishment served as a symbol of the power of the state, a way of asserting and dramatizing its power. Justice in these circumstances was often no more than a theater of guilt and vindication that demonstrated the awesome power of central authorities.[22] That symbolic role helps

---

22 See also Spierenburg, *Spectacle*, 200ff.; Mark A. Sargent, review of Foucault in *New England Journal on Prison Law* (Spring 1979): 235–40; Heinz Steinert, "Beyond Crime and Punishment," *Contemporary Crises: Law, Crime and Social Policy* 10, no. 1 (1986): 25; and Horace Bleackley and John Lofland, *State Executions Viewed Historically and Sociologically* (Montclair, NJ: Patterson Smith, 1977).

explain the severity of many punishments. They were meant to demonstrate the power of the state and the consequences of opposing it. Punishment had to strike terror. This role as symbol of state power also helps explain public resistance to some forms of punishment. The hangman was a particularly loathsome figure in many European communities, in part because he represented state-imposed justice.[23]

Today punishment is usually justified in pragmatic, utilitarian terms—as deterrence, as incapacitation, as rehabilitation. Behind it remain important symbolic functions, however, which may retain elements of earlier forms of punishment. As I observe punishment being imposed, I often suspect a need to dramatize the power of the state and the law over the individual.

Fourth, with changing concepts of justice came new understandings of crime and the criminal. Instead of an individual wrong or conflict, certain behaviors became collective harms and social or moral heresies. Crimes were now a violation of both a social and supernatural order. The public dimensions were elevated above the private. This provided important justification for the state to enforce the social and moral order. Justice came to be seen as a righting of a balance, a metaphysical balancing of abstractions.

A PARADIGM SHIFT

The legal revolution, as I have already suggested, involved a shift in paradigms in ways of constructing and understanding reality. What underlay such a shift? A variety of answers can be and have been suggested.

Leshan and Margenau note that new paradigms emerge as an attempt to solve a society or culture's most pressing problems.[24] The scientific paradigm, they argue, emerged as an at-

---

23 See Spierenburg, *The Spectacle of Suffering*, chapter 2 and 200ff.

24 Lawrence Leshan and Henry Margenau, *Einstein's Space and Van Gogh's Sky: Physical Reality and Beyond* (New York: Collier Books, 1982).

tempt to solve Western society's most desperate problem in the late Middle Ages. This was the problem focused by catastrophes such as the Black Death. Society was faced with a pressing need to control its environment and, therefore, developed a paradigm adequate to do that. As other problems emerged, however, the paradigm was found to be inadequate, and new paradigms had to emerge.

What, then, was the problem that the retributive paradigm attempted to solve? Some explanations have centered on the growing complexity and anonymity of society as populations grew, cities emerged, and society became industrialized. Perhaps traditional methods of solving problems worked less well without a basis in community.

Others have noted the need by society, or at least the upper levels of society, to control unrest. They have sought to reduce class conflict and to find ways to maintain order without disrupting patterns of social and political inequality.

A common interpretation points to the need to control private vengeance. In this view, vengeance was out of control, and only by giving the state a "legitimate monopoly on violence" could vengeance be controlled. Representatives of the state often advanced this argument. Historians have questioned, however, whether vengeance was as uncontrolled or the alternatives as limited as this explanation would suggest.

Part of the answer to our question may lie in the needs of emerging states to monopolize and exercise power. What was the problem which the retributive paradigm sought to solve? Perhaps it was the need of the state to legitimate and consolidate its power. The modern state is, in sociologist Lewis Coser's terms, a "greedy institution."[25]

At any rate, the paradigm shifted. But inadequacies in the new paradigm soon became apparent, and a variety of

25 Lewis A. Coser, *Greedy Institutions* (New York: Free Press, 1974).

epicycles and modifications were introduced. Today the sense of dysfunction is high. Is another paradigm possible? If so, can it draw on elements of the past? The Christian tradition suggests some possibilities.

8

Covenant Justice:
The Biblical Alternative

OUR PAST PROVIDES one model that demonstrates a different way: community justice. There is another model, which to Christians is still more important: biblical justice.

That biblical justice should offer a sharp contrast to a retributive justice model may come as a shock. After all, the place in our society where the Bible seems to be cited most frequently is in just this arena. "Eye for eye, tooth for tooth," (Leviticus 24:20; Exodus 21:24). What could be clearer than that the Bible mandates just deserts in the form of punishment for crime?

But there is more to "an eye for an eye" than meets the eye. On closer examination, this principle of *lex talionis* does not mean what most people take it to mean. Moreover, it most decidedly is not the overriding theme, the paradigm, of biblical justice.

WHAT DOES THE BIBLE SAY?

What does the Bible have to say about subjects such as crime and justice? Obviously it has many things to say. Not everything makes equal sense to us, given the age and situation we live in. Some passages even seem mutually contradictory on the surface.

Take, for example, the following examples of legal statements, all drawn from the Old Testament Torah.

Anyone who injures their neighbor is to be injured in the same manner: fracture for fracture, eye for eye, tooth for tooth. The one who has inflicted the injury must suffer the same injury (Leviticus 24:19-20).

Do not seek revenge or bear a grudge against anyone among your people, but love your neighbor as yourself. I am the LORD. Keep my decrees. Do not mate different kinds of animals. Do not plant your field with two kinds of seed. Do not wear clothing woven of two kinds of material (Leviticus 19:18-19).

If someone has a stubborn and rebellious son who does not obey his father and mother and will not listen to them when they discipline him, his father and mother shall take hold of him and bring him to the elders at the gate of his town. They shall say to the elders, "This son of ours is stubborn and rebellious. He will not obey us. He is a glutton and a drunkard." Then all the men of his town are to stone him to death. You must purge the evil from among you. All Israel will hear of it and be afraid (Deuteronomy 21:18-21).

When they sin in any of these ways and realize their guilt, they must return what they have stolen or taken by extortion, or what was entrusted to them, or the lost property they found, or whatever it was they swore falsely about. They must make restitution in full, add a fifth of the value to it and give it all to the owner on the day they present their guilt offering (Leviticus 6:4-5).

Do not plow with an ox and a donkey yoked together (Deuteronomy 22:10).

Anyone who blasphemes the name of the LORD is to be put to death. The entire assembly must stone them. Whether foreigner or native-born, when they blaspheme the Name they are to be put to death (Leviticus 24:16).

Some passages seem to emphasize retribution. Others seem restorative. Some "make sense" to a twenty-first-century mind. Others seem completely foreign or even barbaric. Obviously, we cannot follow all of them. How do we choose which to use? How do we get an accurate picture?[1]

One approach that may reduce the number of interpretive problems is to limit ourselves to the New Testament, the most recent of biblical material. This method has merit since Christ himself made it clear that the new covenant superseded the old.[2]

Clearly the New Testament must be our primary standard. But to ignore the Old Testament is to cut ourselves off from a wealth of material, much of which provided the background and roots of the New Testament. To understand more fully the dimensions of justice and God's intent for humankind, we must take seriously the Old Testament. We cannot ignore the Old Testament if for no other reason than that it is cited so often in our society.

---

1 For discussions of approaches to biblical interpretation, see Willard M. Swartley, *Slavery, Sabbath, War, and Women: Case Issues in Biblical Interpretation* (Scottdale, PA: Herald Press, 1983), chapter 5; and Perry Yoder, *Toward Understanding the Bible* (Newton, KS: Faith & Life Press, 1978).

2 An important exploration of the New Testament is Christopher Marshall, *Beyond Retribution: A New Testament Vision for Justice, Crime and Punishment* (Grand Rapids, MI: Eerdmans, 2001). See also Marshall, *Compassionate Justice: An Interdisciplinary Dialogue with Two Gospel Parables on Law, Crime, and Restorative Justice* (Portland, OR: Cascade Books, 2012).

When looking at the Bible, and especially the Old Testament, we must first remember that we are reading literature from another world. This world is far from us not only in time and in geography but in philosophy, political systems, and social structure. As one would expect, laws took a much different form. They had much different purposes and were administered quite differently from laws in our own day.[3] Even underlying assumptions about subjects such as guilt and responsibility were different than ours, and these affected concepts of law and justice.

Guilt, for instance, was collective and so was responsibility. Because of this, certain types of crimes were felt to contaminate the entire society. To relieve such guilt, collective, ceremonial expiation was necessary, and the responses suggested in the Old Testament for certain offenses thus have a sacrificial character that seems foreign to us.

All of this may make the law codes in Leviticus or Deuteronomy look rather strange to us. As the preceding selection suggests, topics of concern that to us seem appropriate in a legal code (such as murder and theft) are mixed in with topics that do not (such as regulations about agriculture, food, clothing, marriage, worship). Some offenses and responses clearly have religious and cultic dimensions while others appear more straightforward.

Because our worlds are so different, it can be quite problematic to apply biblical—particularly Old Testament—legal and judicial prescriptions to our own situations. Certainly it is not adequate simply to pick a law selectively and to plug it in to our own situation. Nor is it accurate to take isolated

---

3 Helpful introductions to Old Testament law include Hans Jochen Boecker, *Law and the Administration of Justice in the Old Testament and Ancient East* (Minneapolis: Augsburg Publishing House, 1980); Dale Patrick, *Old Testament Law* (Atlanta: John Knox Press, 1985); and Millard Lind's work, cited later.

concepts and to graft them on to other philosophic bases. As we shall see, that approach has, in fact, led to a perversion of important biblical ideas. Rather, we must attempt to understand underlying principles and intentions, then to move from them to concepts such as law and justice. As Christ suggested, we must grasp the spirit, not just the letter, of the law. Only after that can we begin to understand individual biblical laws to make contemporary applications.

These basic perspectives and directions are what we must try to unravel here. This is not the place for a detailed analysis of the function, form, content, and administration of Hebrew law. My approach, rather, will be to sketch what appear to be underlying directions, then to look at concepts of justice and law given those directions. Finally, I will try to draw some conclusions about the meaning of crime and justice that have application today.

Two foundational concepts are essential if we are to begin to unravel biblical thinking about law and justice (or, for that matter, anything else): shalom and covenant. It is here that we must start.

SHALOM: A UNIFYING VISION

An essential theme of the biblical message, expressed in both the Old and New Testaments, resides in the Hebrew word *shalom*. (In New Testament Greek, the comparable word is *eirene*.) Shalom is not a peripheral theme, nor is it simply one among many themes. Shalom is a basic core belief around which many other important beliefs are organized. Shalom encapsulates God's basic intention, God's vision, for humankind. Consequently, we must understand salvation, atonement, forgiveness, and justice from their roots in shalom.

The usual translation of shalom, "peace," captures one aspect of the concept but does not adequately convey all the connotations of the word. Shalom refers to a condition of "all rightness," of things being as they should be, in various dimensions. Old Testament scholar Perry Yoder's authoritative study found that shalom, as used in the Bible, has three basic dimensions of meaning.[4]

Contrary to common assumptions, shalom usually refers to material or physical conditions or circumstances. God's intent is for humanity to live in physical well-being. At a minimum, this means a situation where things are all right. At some points, however, it seems to point to more, to prosperity and abundance. At any rate, the visions of the future, articulated so graphically by the prophets, include health and material prosperity and an absence of physical threats such as illness, poverty, and war.

A second dimension of shalom has to do with social relationships. God intends for people to live in right relationship with one another and with God. To live in shalom means that people live in peace, without enmity (but not necessarily without conflict!).

The Bible makes it clear that this includes living in just economic and political relationship with one another. Over and over the Bible makes it clear that oppression and injustice are contrary to shalom, that they do not represent right relationships, and that they must not be allowed to exist. Shalom depends on right relationships between people, and this means the removal of oppression. Marked divisions in material conditions and in power that result in the impoverishment and oppression of some cannot coexist with shalom, for shalom means the well-being of all in a society. When that is lacking, shalom cannot exist.

A third application or dimension of shalom in its biblical use applies to the moral or ethical realm. According to Yoder,

4 Perry B. Yoder, *Shalom: The Bible's Word for Salvation, Justice, and Peace* (Newton, KS: Faith & Life Press, 1987). This chapter draws heavily upon Yoder's discussion of shalom, justice, law, and covenant.

shalom here refers to a "straightforwardness." The concept functions in two ways in this application. It refers to honesty or absence of deceit in dealing with one another and to a condition of blamelessness (i.e., being without guilt or fault). Shalom involves a condition of honesty, of moral integrity. This dimension of shalom, while important, is the one mentioned least often in the Bible.

Shalom defines how God intends things to be. God intends people to live in a condition of "all rightness" in the material world; in interpersonal, social, and political relationships; and in personal character. There can be no shalom when things are not as they ought to be, and the absence of shalom is at the heart of the criticisms the Old Testament prophets leveled at God's people. The vision of shalom also shapes hopes and promises for the future.

While the fuller implications of shalom are beyond our scope here, this vision of shalom underlies the meaning of other central pillars of biblical faith. The shalom vision also helps us understand God's actions and God's promises throughout the biblical story.

The shalom theme undergirds Old Testament thought, but it is also central in the New Testament. New Testament writers used *eirene*, like shalom, to define God's good news for humanity.[5] Like shalom, *eirene* refers to peace between people and God and between people themselves on a variety of levels.

Christ's life, teaching, and death show a pattern for such living. They transform divine-human relationships, but they also transform relationships between people. In Yoder's words, "Jesus came so that things might be as they ought to be both among people and between people and God and even in nature."[6]

---

5 Yoder, *Shalom*, 19–21.
6 Ibid., 21.

Thus, reconciliation is an important theme in the New Testament, but the state of "all rightness" that God intends continues to have the material and physical dimensions that it had in the Old Testament.

COVENANT: BASIS FOR SHALOM

The basis and primary model of shalom in the Bible is the concept of covenant.[7] Part of what differentiated the Israelites so sharply from their contemporaries in the ancient Near East was the belief that God had made a covenant with people. This concept of covenant profoundly shaped concepts of law, of justice, of social order, of faith, of hope. Laws that were similar to—and perhaps in some cases borrowed from—those of surrounding societies were radically transformed by this covenant.

In the biblical milieu, a covenant was a binding agreement made between two parties. Covenants assumed a personal relationship between parties and implied certain reciprocal responsibilities and commitments. Biblical faith assumes a covenant between God and people, a covenant based on God's righteous acts of salvation. The central act of salvation in the Old Testament was an act of liberation, the exodus from Egypt. This act of salvation was performed because of God's love, not because it was earned or deserved.

Although the exodus was definitional, the Old Testament story is one of repeated deliverance, repeated acts of salvation. The prophets understood these repeated acts of deliverance to be part of God's commitment stated in God's covenant to

7 In addition to Yoder's work (e.g., 75–82), I have depended heavily upon Millard Lind's discussions of covenant and law. See Lind, "Law in the Old Testament" in *The Bible and Law*, ed. Willard M. Swartley, Occasional Papers No. 3 of the Council of Mennonite Seminaries (Elkhart, IN: Institute of Mennonite Studies, 1983); and Lind, *The Transformation of Justice: From Moses to Jesus*, Issue No. 5 of *New Perspectives on Crime and Justice: Occasional Papers* (Akron, PA: Mennonite Central Committee, 1986).

God's people. Even though God's people frequently fell down on their end of the responsibilities implied in the covenant, the prophets maintained that God had remained faithful to the original promise.

The people occasionally renewed their covenant with God, and the result created conditions for shalom since the relationship was now right. Covenant, therefore, provided both the basis for and a model of shalom.

But a covenant implies mutual responsibilities. Concepts of law and justice provided ways for people to understand or work toward shalom by heeding these responsibilities.

In the Old Testament, the fundamental act of liberation that provided the paradigm of covenant and the basis for the shalom vision was the exodus from slavery in Egypt. The new act of liberation represented by the life, death, and resurrection of Christ formed the basis for a "new" covenant, a new way of living together. The New Testament, perhaps better understood as the new covenant, grew out of previous understandings and continues the concepts of shalom and covenant, but in a renewed form. A new day in relationships between God and humanity—and between persons—has been born. However, as in the Old Testament, the basis for this covenant is God's act of salvation and liberation. This act by God provides us a way of living together in shalom that involves mutual responsibilities between God and people and among people.

The covenant of the Old Testament was based on a central act of salvation and liberation. This covenant created the basis for a new society, one different from others, with operating principles of its own, and which would work toward shalom. The covenant of the New Testament too is based on a foundational act of salvation and liberation. It likewise creates the basis for a new community, with its own operating principles, which will provide the basis for God's work of shalom in this world. Covenant continues to be foundational.

SHALOM AND COVENANT AS TRANSFORMING FORCES

Shalom and covenant were transforming forces in the development of ideas of law and justice in biblical society. As it developed, Hebrew society encountered many of the same needs and pressures as did other ancient Near Eastern societies. Like the Babylonian ruler Hammurabi, for instance, Hebrew leadership faced the need to standardize and unify in the face of growth, urbanization, and specialization. Legal and judicial tools used in this process sometimes had common forms or even common roots in Israel and in other Near Eastern kingdoms. However, Hebrew ideas of law and justice were radically different in substance from those of Hammurabi. They were different because they were transformed by shalom and covenant.

Old Testament scholar Millard Lind has written that Hammurabi's law was state law. It was hierarchical, imposed, punitive, rooted clearly in a distant and all-powerful king.[8] Hebrew law, on the other hand, assumed that God was the source of all authority, above even kings. This God was personal, faithful, and concerned about the underdog and about the human condition generally. These qualities were embedded in the vision of shalom and the belief in covenant. Taken together, they transformed justice and law. As a result, covenant justice stood in marked contrast to state law.

The concept of transformation is important but has another dimension as well. God works within the limits of an age, within the limits of understanding and vision. Human understandings are always incomplete and, as Christ reminds us (see Mark 10:5), allowances are made for this. Yet God pushes the limits, seeking to expand our understandings and

8 Lind, *Transformation of Justice*, 3.

insights. Consequently, human understandings continued to develop throughout the biblical story, throughout history. As part of this process, Christ built upon, but often transformed, old covenant understandings. Concepts of shalom and covenant were transforming forces, shaping ideas of law and justice, but they in turn were transformed as well.

The concept of transformation, therefore, makes sense in several dimensions. Lind has helpfully termed this multi-dimensional process "the transformation of justice from Moses to Jesus."

COVENANT JUSTICE

As the shalom concept implies, the question of justice is not marginal to the Bible. Justice is not an "elective" we can choose to ignore.[9] Justice has to do with shalom relationships and thus is fundamental to what God is about, to who God is, and to what we are to be. In fact, justice serves as a measuring stick to test for shalom!

It is no surprise, then, that the topic of justice recurs frequently in the Bible. Nor should we be surprised that when the prophets condemned Israel for straying from their God, they made it clear that injustice was the problem as much as failure to worship as they ought.

No single Hebrew word directly translates as "justice," but two words often translated into English in this way are *sedeqah* and *mishpat*.[10] Neither carries with it quite what we mean in English by justice, but both have to do with righteousness, right-ordering, and making things right. To do justice is to make things right, and the history of God's covenant relationship with Israel is a model, a promise, and a call. The norm

---

9 In addition to works cited, see Matthew Fox, *A Spirituality Named Compassion and the Healing of the Global Village, Humpty Dumpty and Us* (Minneapolis: Winston Press, 1979).

10 For example, in Micah 6:1-8. See Lind, *Transformation*, 1; see also n. 13.

for justice, then, arises from Yahweh's relationship with Israel. Biblical justice is rooted in a vision of shalom, modeled by God's definitional acts of salvation in God's covenant relationship with God's people. The way God responds to wrongdoing provides an important window into God's justice.

What then are the qualities of God's justice?

Following Greek and Roman cues, we tend to divide justice into areas such as *social justice*, sometimes called *distributive justice*, and *criminal justice* or *retributive justice*. When we talk about wrongs having to do with the distribution of wealth and power, we call these questions of social justice. When we talk about wrongs legally defined as crimes, we categorize this as the realm of retributive justice.

Distributive justice we understand to be difficult to attain, a distant goal. In the meantime, however, we actively pursue retributive justice. We assume, that is, that one can separate the areas of justice and deal with them in different ways.

Biblical justice is more holistic. It sees both spheres as part of the same whole. Injustice of any kind, in any sphere, is contrary to shalom. The acts of the one who oppresses are as serious as those of the one who assaults or robs. Both are contrary to shalom. Justice is not separable.

Our fields of retributive and distributive justice, though governed by different operating rules, both assume that justice has to do with the fair distribution of rewards. Both have to do with seeing that people get what they deserve. Thus, both retributive and distributive justice are based on the principle of reciprocity, of just deserts. This often suggests a kind of abstract, moral order where imbalances must be righted. It also implies that justice must be deserved or earned. Distributive justice, for example, assumes that on some level people have to earn what they get. Likewise, a central concern of retributive justice is making sure people receive the punishment they deserve.

The Bible recognizes some place for this tit-for-tat justice, but its emphasis is elsewhere. Tit-for-tat justice must be tempered by shalom justice, and shalom justice, like God's salvation, concerns itself with need, not merit.

The ultimate rejection of legalistic, tit-for-tat justice appears throughout the biblical story. It appears in the many places where consequences mandated or recognized in the law are not carried out. Although Cain may have deserved the death penalty for committing murder, God rejects this penalty. When Hosea's wife commits a capital sin, she is spared. The woman who had committed adultery deserved to die by contemporary standards, but Jesus rejects the penalty. This rejection of just deserts is demonstrated also in Christ's story of the workers in the vineyard. Workers who began at noon are paid the same generous amount as those who began in the morning, contrary to the expectations of tit-for-tat justice.

Above all, this rejection of just deserts is demonstrated by God's own actions, actions designed to model shalom justice. Confronted by repeated wrongdoing, God did not give up on Israel.

We tend to assume that love and mercy are different from or opposite to justice. A judge pronounces a sentence. Then, as an act of mercy, she may mitigate the penalty. Biblical justice, however, grows out of love. Such justice is in fact an act of love that seeks to make things right. Love and justice are not opposites, nor are they in conflict. Instead, love provides for a justice that seeks first to make right.

It is worth noting here that Western concepts of romantic and emotional love complicate our understanding of love as a source for action. Biblical concepts of love do not rule out how we feel. Certainly, Christ makes it clear that feelings of hate are as serious as actions. Yet love is not defined as a mushy emotion. Love is, rather, a conscious act of looking after the good of another. When the Bible talks of love, the words usually connote action and volition more than feelings.

Biblical justice seeks to make things right, and the emphasis is upon liberation. God seeks to make things right by liberating those who are oppressed materially, socially, and emotionally. Justice is an act of liberation. This liberation does not happen because it is merited but because it is needed.

Our image of justice, borrowed from the Romans but put in legal form by the French Revolution, is of a blindfolded woman neutrally balancing a scales. Justice is treating people as equals, without partiality. But is it really just to treat unequals equally? Does this not perpetuate inequality? Biblical justice seeks to make things right, and this often means liberation for the unequal. Thus, biblical justice shows a clear partiality toward those who are oppressed and impoverished. It is clearly on the side of the poor, recognizing their needs and disadvantages. Biblical justice is open-eyed, with hands outstretched to those in need.

Since biblical justice seeks to make things better, justice is not designed to maintain the status quo. Indeed, its intent is to shake up the status quo, to improve, to move toward shalom. The move toward shalom is not necessarily good news to everyone. In fact, it is downright bad news to the oppressor. This too stands in contrast to the justice that—by working to maintain "order"—works in fact to maintain the present order, the status quo, even when it is unjust.

The test of justice in the biblical view is not whether the right rules are applied in the right way. Justice is tested by the outcome. The tree is tested by its fruit.[11] It is the substance, not the procedure, that defines justice. And how should things come out? The litmus test is how the poor and oppressed are affected.

---

11 See also Herman Bianchi, *A Biblical Vision of Justice,* Issue No. 2 of *New Perspectives on Crime and Justice: Occasional Papers* (Akron, PA: Mennonite Central Committee, 1984), 7.

The actual administration of justice in biblical times, although necessarily an imperfect reflection of this ideal, nevertheless often embodied the assumptions of covenant justice.[12] When wrongs were done, ordinary people went to the city gates to seek justice in a "legal assembly" in which citizens participated. The focus of this court, sometimes called an "organization of reconciliation," was not to satisfy some abstract concept of justice but to find a solution. The word for judgment here can be translated *settlement*. Restitution and compensation were common outcomes. The passage from Leviticus 6 quoted earlier in this chapter was characteristic in that it called for replacement of loss, plus additional compensation. In Exodus 18, Moses established a system of judges. His aim was not to identify winners and losers but to ensure that "all these people [would] go home satisfied" (i.e., in shalom; v. 23).

Given this emphasis, it should be no surprise that the words for "paying back" (*shillum*) and for "recompense" (*shillem*) have the same root word as shalom. Restitution was a way of seeking to make things right. Recompense, sometimes translated *retribution* but implying satisfaction rather than revenge, provided vindication. Both had to do with restoring shalom.[13]

---

12 See Boecker, *Law and the Administration of Justice*, 31ff.

13 See Dan W. Van Ness, *Crime and Its Victims* (Downers Grove, IL: InterVarsity Press, 1986), 120; and Van Ness, "Pursing a Restorative Vision of Justice," in *Justice: The Restorative Vision*, Issue No. 7 of *New Perspectives on Crime and Justice: Occasional Papers* (Akron, PA: Mennonite Central Committee, 1989), 18.

Millard Lind has suggested the following definitions:

Shillum: Requittal, retribution, reward (Hosea 9:7; Micah 7:3).

Shillem: Recompense (Deuteronomy 32:35).

Shalom: The well-being that arises out of the covenant relationship.

Mishpat: The social expression of God's righteousness; the norm for behavior that arises out of the divine-human relationships, and the inter-human relationships based thereupon.

Sedeqah: As a synonym of *mishpat*, it may be translated *justice*. Where it differs, *mishpat* may refer to applied justice, while *sedeqah* is an attribute of God's character as sovereign leader. Often it may be translated *salvation* or

Offenses were understood to be wrongs against people and against shalom, and the justice process involved a process of settlement. This is the model in Micah 6. The people of Israel had violated God's intent, violating covenant. God's grievances are stated in a form that was probably characteristic of contemporary lawsuits. Through the prophet Micah, God's grievances—and the consequences of such wrongs—are presented in graphic form. Then comes the ultimate outcome. In spite of this, God will not give up. Micah 7:18 demonstrates God's justice: "Who is a God like you, who pardons sin and forgives the transgression. . . . You do not stay angry forever but delight to show mercy."

As this example suggests, retribution is one theme in the Old Testament. Usually, however, punishment by God appeared in the context of shalom. Punishment was not—as it usually is for us—the end of justice. It was often aimed at restoration or at breaking the power of the oppressor (i.e., at vindicating the oppressed). And this shalom context served to limit its retributive potential.

Likewise, punishment was often understood to occur in a context of love and community. That is, punishment was accompanied by renewal of the covenant. This meant that punishment could be viewed as fair, as deserved. It also kept open the possibility of eventual reconciliation and restoration rather than perpetual alienation. It was thus restorative rather than destructive. Punishment was not the end. The concept of shalom thus tempered the operation of retributive justice.

Biblical justice decidedly was not a forensic inquiry into wrongdoing to establish guilt and decide what punishment

---

victory. When used of humans, it may refer to moral conduct, those human acts that are a remembrance of Yahweh's deeds and teaching.

Eirene: Harmony and concord between nations and individuals; security and well-being that arises out of the covenant relationship (see shalom).

was merited. Rather, biblical justice was an attempt to right wrongs, to find solutions that would bring about well-being.

COVENANT LAW

The focus of biblical justice was on substance much more than legality. Wrongdoing was not defined primarily as non-conformity to rules, to laws. Justice was not the right application of rules.

This may seem somewhat problematic to us. We tend to see in laws the safeguard of both justice and order. We, therefore, see offending as breaking the law, and we see justice as applying the law. The Bible does neither.

The Ten Commandments, the most famous (though not necessarily the most characteristic) of biblical laws, provide one window into the nature and function of law. We tend to interpret such law from the perspective of our own law so we see them primarily as imperatives, prohibitions: "You must do this or else." But this collection of laws can be read in the future indicative. The Ten Commandments, like much biblical law, are like invitations or promises: "If you are really living as you should be, this is what life will be like. You will not kill. You will not steal . . ." The Ten Commandments—and indeed the whole Torah—are intended as a pattern for living in covenant, in shalom.[14]

The Torah is thus a pattern for living in shalom under the old covenant. We misunderstand if we see it primarily as a set of imperatives, of rules that must not be broken. It is a promise, an invitation, an example of what life should be like.

If the Torah offers a pattern for living in community under the old covenant, the Sermon on the Mount provides a pattern for living under the new covenant. Again, we misread this set of teachings if we see it primarily as rules, as imperatives

---

14 Herman Bianchi, *A Biblical Vision*, 5–7. See also his discussion of *Torah* and of *sedeqah* here.

and prohibitions. Like the Torah, it is an invitation, a pattern for shalom. Both are less rules than a glimpse of what life will be like when we are really living in shalom.

Biblical law is thus intended to provide a direction: "This is the direction in which you should move." *Torah* translates as "teaching" and may include both story and directive or *halaka*: "the way to walk." Given our understanding of the rigidity and finality of law, we are often amazed at the way the Israelites questioned and debated the law. But laws were to be used in teaching moral principle. Moreover, they were starting points for discussion, for people were supposed to talk about the law. Martin Buber, in his German translation of the Bible, perhaps captures best the spirit of biblical law when he calls them "wise indications." They set a direction and in doing so establish principles, but they are meant to be discussed.

Biblical law was intended as a means, not an end in itself. The best law was unwritten law, and it was the spirit, not the letter, of the law that mattered. This was the original focus of the Torah, but in time it became rigidified. And it was this legalism, this rigidity, that Christ so objected to. This perspective also helps to explain why so often the spirit, not the letter, of the law seems to be carried out in the Old Testament. As Christ pointed out in his comments about the Sabbath, law was made for people, not people for the law. The intent was that "wise indications" be internalized, that the thrust of the law be followed.

The Bible contains many detailed statements of law on a wide variety of topics. We tend to understand these laws from the perspective of our own laws, so we interpret them as codes. In fact, however, many of these represent past judicial decisions, offered as a guideline for finding principles that might apply in other situations. Again, they are wise indications more than rules for conduct. They provided principles for use in settling disputes, not bases for establishing guilt and meting out punishment.

Law was intended as a means, not an end. It was an instrument for building shalom, for building relationships that are all right. Its characteristic purpose was not to punish but to redeem, to make things right.

The law codes of ancient Israel's contemporaries combined elements of community law and state law.[15] Ultimately, however, laws such as Hammurabi's code, like today's law codes, were impersonal and based on the coercive power of the state. The covenant basis of biblical law, however, meant that obedience was to be in response to God's liberating acts, not to governmental coercion. Moreover, both law and political authorities were subject to God. Neither had independent standing. Law was not autonomous, and neither the formulation nor the administration of law was to be centered in the state. Although Israel adopted a form of kingship, laws were never reoriented to center on this, so the administration of law remained primarily a matter for local courts and clan.

The form of biblical law reflects its basis in covenant and its focus on redemption. Biblical law commonly begins by a statement of what God has done, then moves to proper response. That is, statements of law often begin with what is known as the "motive clause." God has performed an act of liberation salvation; *therefore*, this is the proper response. The Deuteronomic law on slaves, for example, is coupled with this motive clause: "Remember that you were slaves in Egypt. That is why I command you to do this" (Deuteronomy 24:22).

Similarly, the Ten Commandments follow a reminder of God's act of liberation (see Deuteronomy 5:15). This motive

---

15 This discussion of law draws primarily from Lind, Yoder, Boecker, and Patrick. However, see also John E. Toews, "Some Theses Toward a Theology of Law in the New Testament," in *The Bible and Law*, ed. Willard M. Swartley, 43–64.

clause is characteristic of much Old Testament law, but the same *therefore* pattern is used by Paul in the New Testament.[16]

The motive clause—the *therefore* pattern—is directly rooted in the covenant concept, and in this form the law itself became a restatement of covenant. The law is based on God's acts of saving liberation, performed out of love and not because they are deserved. Since God has done this for us, here is how we should respond. The pattern, then, is grace followed by law. The form of the law states not only our responsibility but the reasons for it: God's redemptive acts.

The real story of the Bible, from the Old Testament into the New, is this: God does not give up. It is precisely in this way that we are to imitate God, to be "perfect": in indiscriminate love, in love that is undeserved, in forgiveness, in mercy.

The phrase "eye for an eye" is commonly taken to summarize the retributive, tit-for-tat nature of biblical law. However, the phrase only occurs three times in the Old Testament. In the New Testament, Christ specifically rejects it. "You have heard that it was said, 'Eye for an eye, and tooth for tooth.' But I tell you, do good to those who harm you" (summary of Matthew 5:38-39). Was he in fact directly contradicting Old Testament law?

"Eye for an eye" was a law of proportion intended to limit rather than encourage revenge. It limited destructive vengeance. In fact, this legal principle laid the basis for restitution, providing a principle of proportionality in response to wrongdoing.

So the focus of "eye for an eye" was not on retribution but on limit and proportion. But there is more. In the covenant context, with its focus on liberation, this common principle also established equity.

---

16 See especially Deuteronomy 12–28 and Leviticus 17–26. For short discussions of the motive clause pattern, see Lind, "Law in the Old Testament," 17ff., and Yoder, *Shalom*, 71ff.

Leviticus 24 is one of three places where this phrase occurs. The "eye for an eye" principle is poetically stated in several versions. Immediately following this appears the admonition that there must be one standard for all, for the stranger as well as the native. Strangers were often the dispossessed, the oppressed. God frequently reminded the people of Israel that they were once strangers and that it was God's own act of salvation that rescued them. In turn, they should take care of the stranger among them. A guidepost like "eye for an eye," then, established the idea that all should be treated alike.

The motive for vengeance exists and is recognized in the Old Testament, but biblical law early sought to establish limits. One such limit was the *lex talionis*, the guideline of proportionality.[17] Another was the cities of refuge. Deuteronomy 19 mandates the establishment of sanctuaries where those who committed unintentional homicide could run and be safe while feelings cooled and negotiations were conducted.

THE BIBLICAL PARADIGM

All of this suggests that the paradigm of biblical justice, including Old Testament justice, is not to be found in retribution. The key is not in "eye for an eye" but in the motive clause. God's own response to wrongdoing is normative.

When confronted by wrongdoing, God is described in human terms as being angry, full of wrath. The roots of words translated "wrath" and "anger" (*aph, anaph, naqam*) have graphic connotations including heat, snorting, and deep breathing. God becomes angry and is sometimes understood to punish.[18]

---

17 See Patrick, *Old Testament* Law, chapter 4; Roland de Vaux, *Ancient Israel* (New York, McGraw-Hill, 1961), 149; Boecker, *Law,* 171ff.

18 See Virginia Mackey, *Punishment in the Scripture and Tradition of Judaism, Christianity and Islam* (New York: National Interreligious Task Force on Criminal Justice, 1983). See also C. F. D. Motile, "Punishment

Here again, however, we must be careful in translation. Students of Hebrew report that several root words often translated "retribution" and "punishment" may mean "to restrain, to teach, to make right." The concept of punishment may be present, but often with different connotations than that of our English word.[19] Moreover, Paul reminds us in Romans 12:19, quoting the Scriptures, that such punishment is God's business, not ours.

These connotations help to make sense of what seems to be a contradiction between the descriptions of God as punisher and God as slow to anger and overflowing in lovingkindness (e.g., Exodus 34:6; Numbers 14:18). God punishes, but God is also faithful. Israel repeatedly does wrong, and God becomes angry, but God does not give up. God moves, in other words, through wrath to restoration. That retribution is subordinate to shalom tempers and limits retributive justice.[20]

This character of God's justice is demonstrated dramatically in passages such as Leviticus 26 and Deuteronomy 4. The people of Israel receive graphic descriptions of the horrible consequences of wrongdoing. Terrible things will happen. Yet the passages end by promising that God will not give up. God will not destroy them. God is faithful and compassionate.

In the New Testament, Christ's focus is even more clearly on restorative responses to wrongdoing. This presents no

---

and Retribution: An Attempt to Delimit Their Scope in New Testament Thought," *Suensk Eregetisk Arssbok,* 30 (1966): 21–36; James B. Lindsey Jr., "Vengeance,"in *The Interpreter's Dictionary of the Bible,* supplementary volume (Nashville: Abingdon, 1976), 932–33. On God's wrath, Mort MacCallum-Paterson's writing has been most helpful. See, for example, "Blood Cries: Lament, Wrath and the Mercy of God," *Touchstone* (May 1987): 14–25; and *Toward a Justice That Heals: The Church's Response to Crime* (Toronto: United Church Publishing House, 1988).

19 Bianchi, *A Biblical Vision,* 1–2. See also Motile, "Punishment and Retribution."

20 Yoder, *Shalom,* 36.

radical break from the Old Testament direction, no rejection of the overall thrust of the old covenant. Rather, it provides an unfolding of understanding, a continued transformation of justice.

The Bible begins with the story of a murder. The Bible recognizes here that unlimited retaliation is a normal, human response. Genesis 4 portrays the "law of Lamech" as seventy times seven, almost without end.[21]

But soon revenge is limited. In the case of Cain, the first story of a murder, the "normal" response of death is not applied. And in Leviticus we find "eye for an eye," the principle of limit, of proportionality.

Included is still another limit: love your neighbor. Do not take vengeance on your brother or sister. Vern Redekop has provided a helpful translation of Leviticus 19:17-18: "Do not let your mind be filled with hatred toward your brother or sister. Confront your associate, making a strong case to him or her. Don't let yourself get carried away with a wrong course of action (sin). Do not take vengeance and don't maintain angry feelings against the people in your community. Love your neighbor as yourself. I am your Lord."[22]

Shalom is possible only if we look out for the welfare of one another, even in wrongdoing.

Christ continues this theme, deepening and broadening its application. The story of the good Samaritan points out that our neighbor is not simply one of our own kind. We have responsibilities beyond our own people. We are, in fact, to do good even to those who harm us. Not unlimited retaliation, the law of Lamech. Not limited retaliation, the law of *talion*.

---

21 Clarence Jordan has outlined in several places this movement from unlimited retaliation to unlimited love. See, e.g., *Sermon on the Mount*, rev. ed. (Valley Forge, PA: Judson Press, 1973), 63ff.

22 Vern Redekop, "Update," Church Council on Justice and Corrections Canada (Spring 1985).

Instead, unlimited love. It is no accident, perhaps, that he extends this to seventy times seven, a number almost beyond imagination. From unlimited retaliation to unlimited love—we have come full circle.

The God who saves, freeing from oppression regardless of merit, is limited in wrath but unlimited in love (in the poetic language of Deuteronomy 7:9, "to a thousand generations"). It is God's unlimited love, not God's wrath, that we are told to imitate. The motive clause is also a model clause.[23]

The motive clause, not *lex talionis*, captures the essence of covenant justice. Restoration, not retribution, is the paradigm.

In chapter 2, I sketched a number of assumptions on which our present retributive model of justice is based. How then do these assumptions measure up to a biblical yardstick? The following chart compares biblical and contemporary assumptions about justice.

Contemporary Justice	Biblical Justice
Justice divided into areas, each with different rules	Justice seen as integrated whole
Administration of justice as an inquiry into guilt	Administration of justice as a search for solutions
Justice tested by rules, procedures	Justice defined by outcome, substance
Focus on infliction of pain	Focus on making right
Punishment as an end	Punishment in context of redemption, shalom
Rewards based on just deserts, deserved	Justice based on need, undeserved
Justice opposed to mercy	Justice based on mercy and love

---

23 Lind, *Transformation*, 5ff.

Justice neutral, claiming to treat all equally	Justice both fair and partial
Justice as maintenance of the status quo	Justice as active, progressive, seeking to transform status quo
Focus on guilt and abstract principles	Focus on harm done
Wrong as a violation of rules	Wrong as violation of people, relationships, shalom
Guilt as unforgivable	Guilt as forgivable, though an obligation exists
Differentiation between offenders and others	Recognition that we are offenders
Individual solely responsible; social and political contexts unimportant	Individual responsibility, but in holistic context
Action as free choice	Action as choice, but with recognition of the power of evil
Law as prohibition	Law as "wise indicator," teacher, point for discussion
Focus on letter of law	Spirit of law as most important
The state as victim	People, shalom, as victim
Justice serves to divide	Justice aims at bringing together

Our system of justice is above all a system for making decisions about guilt. Consequently, it focuses on the past. Biblical justice seeks first to solve problems, to find solutions, to make things right, looking toward the future.

Today's justice seeks to administer to each his or her just deserts, to make sure that people get what they "deserve." Biblical justice responds on the basis of need, often returning good for evil. Biblical justice responds because shalom is lacking, not because justice is deserved.

Our first—and often only—response after guilt has been established is to deliver pain as punishment. Once delivered, the process of justice has ended. When punishment occurs in covenant justice, however, it is not usually the end but the means toward ultimate restoration. Moreover, punishment is primarily God's business. The primary focus of biblical justice is to make things right, to build shalom, by acting in aid of those in need.

Today the test of justice often is whether the proper procedures have been followed. Biblical or *sedeqah* justice is measured by the substance, by the outcome, by its fruits. Does the outcome work to make things right? Are things being made right for the poor and the least powerful, the least "deserving"? Biblical justice focuses on right relationships, not right rules.

Our legal system defines offenses as violations of rules, of laws. We define the state as the victim. In biblical terms, however, wrongdoing is not a contravention of rules but a violation of right relationships. People and relationships, not rules or governments or even a moral order, are the victims.

The assumptions of biblical justice are thus quite different than our own. But a biblical critique of modern justice goes beyond the assumptions I outlined in chapter 2. Biblical justice does not allow us to divorce questions of crime from questions of poverty and power. Justice is a whole. It cannot be fragmented. Corporations that commit fraud or harm people through destruction of the environment are as responsible for their actions as are those individuals who commit murder. Moreover, the social context of crime must be considered. One cannot separate criminal acts or actors from the social situation that lies behind them. Unjust laws of whatever kind must be challenged.

Contemporary justice seeks to be neutral and impartial. It seeks to treat people equally. It sees as its primary focus the maintenance of order. Because of this, and because it can separate questions of criminal justice from social justice, the order that it tends to maintain is the present order, the status quo. All too often, therefore, modern law is a conservative force. Biblical justice, on the other hand, is an active, progressive force seeking to transform the present order toward one that is more just. In doing so, it looks out especially for the poor and the weak.

Contemporary justice puts the state and its coercive power at the center, as source, guardian, and enforcer of law. Biblical justice puts people and relationships at the center, subjecting both law and government to God.

Biblical justice, then, provides an alternate paradigm that critically challenges our own state-centered, retributive approach.

A HISTORICAL SHORT CIRCUIT

Contrary to common assumptions, then, biblical justice is primarily restorative rather than retributive. If this is true, how did such a misconception develop? How was the restorative theme overwhelmed by the retributive?

Some have argued that such misconceptions developed as the result of a "historical short circuit" arising from the mix of biblical with Greco-Roman ideas.[24] Concepts such as the law of *talion*, which had a specific meaning in the context of covenant and shalom, were taken from their context and grafted onto a more punitive and abstract Greco-Roman philosophy. Ideas of retribution and penalty lost their grounding in shalom and became ends in themselves apart from any restorative context or purpose. Greco-Roman interests in abstract principles and ideals led to an abstraction of concepts of justice and just deserts that were contrary to the spirit of biblical law. Thus, the original focus was lost and perverted

24 For example, Herman Bianchi, *Justice as Sanctuary*. See also Timothy Gorringe, *God's Just Vengeance*.

while some of the old forms were retained. Consequently, the new hybrid perspectives appeared to have biblical roots.

With that done, people began to look back at the Bible through this lens, interpreting and translating passages from that perspective. Working from a retributive mindset that emphasized rigid laws, guilt, punishment, and condemnation, it was easy to find in the Bible such themes. It was also then easy to overlook the larger, more important, story of restoration.

Our understanding of a central biblical event, the atonement, may be a case in point. Perry Yoder explains that the Bible itself offers no developed theory of atonement (i.e., of Christ's death).[25] Rather, it offers a series of images, metaphors, and insights that theologians have used to construct various explanations.

A central question for many people has been why Christ died, why one person's death could "atone" for the sins of others. The theories that developed in answer to this question tend to interpret the rest of the Bible from the viewpoint of Roman ideas of justice.

Some atonement theories, for instance, see God as an angry judge who needs to be appeased. People are guilty sinners and have offended God. They deserve punishment since punishment is normative and there is no way to make restitution. God cannot simply forgive because that would represent the failure of retributive justice. A debt is owed, and Jesus offered himself as a substitute. The context of this approach, then, is clearly retributive rather than shalom justice.

The usual translation and use of Romans 5:1-11 illustrates this perspective. The opening words of this passage are about peace and justice, but training and translation has obscured this dimension.[26] They are usually translated, "Therefore, since

---

25 Yoder, *Shalom*, 53–70.

26 See Lois Barrett, "The Gospel of Peace," MCC *Peace Section Newsletter* 18, no. 2 (March–April, 1988), 1–8.

we are *justified* by faith, we have peace with God" (RSV). Most Protestants have focused on *justification*, interpreting it as an act by which God proclaims us innocent even though we are not. A judicial proceeding, a legal fiction, is at the heart of atonement, and it required God's action, not ours. Lois Barrett notes that a more faithful translation of the passage might be, "Therefore, since we come into right relationship through faith (or faithfulness) . . ." The Old Testament background from which Paul worked was that of covenant justice. The atonement takes on new dimensions in that light.

Thus, a grounding in shalom presents a different view of atonement, one that brings into harmony Christ's life and death and the larger scope of biblical history. Christ's life is an attempt to move humanity toward shalom, toward the kingdom of God. This brought him in conflict with established authorities, resulting in his death. But Christ arose, and the resurrection is a sign: a sign that suffering love is victorious over evil, a sign that good will triumph in the long run. Christ's life provides a model of shalom living.

His death and resurrection are harbingers of future liberation, a sign that shalom is possible.

Drawing upon the sacrificial symbolism of the old covenant, a new covenant is affirmed. Characteristic of covenant justice, God offers forgiveness—not because we have earned it or deserve it but because God loves us. The slate can in fact be wiped clean.

Whether the thrust of the Bible is on retribution or restoration is not a marginal issue. The question is at the heart of our understandings about the nature of God and about the nature of God's actions in history. It is not an issue that Christians can avoid.

9

VORP and Beyond: Emerging Practices

On MAY 28, 1974, two young men from Elmira, Ontario, pleaded guilty to vandalizing twenty-two properties.[1] No one could have guessed that their cases would lead to a movement with international dimensions.

Several days earlier, a group of Christians had met to talk about a Christian response to shoplifting. The Elmira case had been widely publicized and so came up in the discussion. Probation officer Mark Yantzi, whose responsibility it was to prepare the presentence report in the case, was present. "Wouldn't it be neat," he dreamed, "for these offenders to meet the victims?" Knowing it was impossible, Mark dropped the idea.

---

1 John Bender recounts this story in *Peace Section Newsletter* 16, no. 1 (January–February, 1986), 1–5. So also does Dean Peachey, "The Kitchener Experiment," *Mediation and Criminal Justice: Victims, Offenders and Community,* ed. Martin Wright and Burt Calaway (London: Sage Publications, 1989), 14–26.

VICTIM-OFFENDER RECONCILIATION PROGRAMS /
VICTIM-OFFENDER CONFERENCING

But Dave Worth, coordinator of Voluntary Service workers for Mennonite Central Committee (MCC) in Kitchener, Ontario, would not let the idea go.[2] Frustrated with the usual process and interested in making peacemaking practical, he announced, "I am ready for a pie-in-the-sky idea." Mark, also a Mennonite, had originally been placed in the probation department through a cooperative arrangement with MCC. His mandate was to help explore community-oriented alternatives. He was open to new ideas, but he had doubts. "Do I want to risk my reputation in suggesting a negotiated settlement between the victim and these offenders that has no basis in law?" he wondered. Mark decided to take a chance, and so he proposed to the judge that the offenders meet with and pay back the victims.

The judge's first response was predictable: "That can't be done." To Mark and Dave's surprise, however, when the time for sentencing arrived, face-to-face meetings between victim and offender to work out restitution were exactly what the judge ordered. Accompanied by their probation officers or the volunteer coordinator, the two boys visited the homes of all but the two victims who had moved. Restitution was negotiated, and within months repayment had been made. From this beginning, the victim-offender reconciliation movement was born in Canada. In the U.S., the movement came to birth through a project started in Elkhart, Indiana, in 1977–78.

In the Elmira case, the approach was simplistic. "We were pretty brutal," Mark remembers. "We walked up to the door. They [the boys] knocked. We stood back with our note pads."

---

2 Mennonite Central Committee, a worldwide ministry of Anabaptist churches, shares God's love and compassion for all in the name of Christ by responding to basic human needs and working for peace and justice. For more information, go to www.mcc.org or www.mcccanada.ca.

Fortunately, both the approach and the underlying philosophy have been much refined since that time.

This original program, and many that followed, used the name Victim-Offender Reconciliation Programs (VORP). Few programs today use that language, because the term *reconciliation* is misleading and often off-putting. More common today is Victim-Offender Dialogue or Victim-Offender Conferencing (VOC).

Although approaches and names vary, today there are hundreds of such programs in many countries working with criminal cases. In addition, the model has been adapted for uses in schools and other contexts.

THE VOC CONCEPT

In its "classic" form as pioneered in Kitchener, Ontario, and Elkhart, Indiana, VOC is based in an independent organization outside the criminal justice system. But it works in cooperation with this system. The VOC process consists of a face-to-face encounter between victim and offender in cases that have entered the criminal justice process and in which the offender has admitted the offense. In these meetings, emphasis is upon three elements: facts, feelings, and agreements. The meeting is facilitated and chaired by a trained mediator, preferably a community volunteer.

Third-party facilitators or mediators play an extremely important role in this process, but they are trained not to impose their own interpretations or solutions. Meetings are conducted in an atmosphere that provides some structure yet allows participants rather than facilitators to determine outcomes. Both parties are encouraged to tell their stories. Both get a chance to ask questions, to discover from the other just what happened. They also talk about the impact and implications of this experience. When they have done this, they decide together what will be done about it. Once they come to agreement, they sign

a written contract. Often this takes the form of financial restitution, but that is not the only possibility.

Offenders may agree to work for victims. Sometimes victims ask that offenders work for the community instead, and
offenders may sign a community service agreement. Or they
may agree to a certain behavior. If the incident involved people
who knew one another previously, such an agreement might
specify how they will behave to one another in the future.

These encounters can be important experiences for both
victims and offenders. Victims receive a unique opportunity
to "get the facts" and to ask the questions that bother them.
They can also talk about what the offense meant to them *and*
to the one who did it. Since they are able to meet the actual
person involved, stereotypes are challenged and fears are often
reduced. Not only do they receive an opportunity to be repaid
for losses, but they also have input into what that repayment
will be. Thus VOC provides opportunity for expression of
feelings, exchange of information, and recovery of losses while
leaving victims with a sense of empowerment.

Offenders receive an opportunity to put a real face to those
they have harmed. They learn firsthand the consequences of
their actions. Stereotypes and rationalizations are confronted
directly. In this way—and by being encouraged to take responsibility for making things right—they are held directly
accountable for what they have done. They are provided opportunity to bring emotional resolution to the offense by
actions to make things right and, if they wish to do so, by expressing remorse or seeking forgiveness. Because they are real
participants rather than bystanders, they too can experience
empowerment.

Victim-offender encounters to discuss the offense and its
resolution are the heart of the VOC process, but important
work goes on before and after such meetings. Victim and

offender are contacted separately first. This provides them with an opportunity to express their feelings and needs and to decide whether they wish to participate. If they choose to do so, a meeting is arranged. After the meeting, there is follow-up to do. A staff person must monitor contracts, making sure they are fulfilled, and do some troubleshooting if they break down. Some programs are also instituting final victim-offender meetings to bring resolution to the case after agreements have been fulfilled.

Most VOC cases are referred by courts, although there are exceptions. Some programs receive referrals from the police or prosecutor. Sometimes victims or offenders initiate contact. Cases may be handled as a diversion from prosecution, but in its "classic" form in the U.S., the program takes most referrals from the court, with the agreement becoming the sentence or part of it. For court-referred cases, offenders often go on probation while their contract is being fulfilled.

Earlier, the majority of cases handled by VOCs in the U.S. and Canada were property cases, with burglaries a common offense. Burglary is a good case for the VOC process. While the judicial system often treats burglary as fairly minor, victims experience burglary much like a violent personal attack. A meeting with an offender provides an opportunity to vent feelings, to find out what really happened, and to meet the actual person. (Why my house? What if I had been home? What happened to the property that was of such sentimental value?) Fears are often reduced and stereotypes modified. Because there are material losses, discussions about restitution provide a concrete focus for the meeting.

Today, nonproperty crimes are handled as well. Indeed, half the states in the U.S. now have programs or protocols for dialogue in cases of severe violence when the person who caused the harm is in prison and the person harmed requests such a meeting. Such cases, of course, require special precautions. Many of these explicitly aim to provide opportunities for healing rather than affecting the outcome of the case.[3] Some research suggests that the more serious the offense, the more impactful the encounter is likely to be.

WHAT HAVE WE LEARNED?

Most research findings have been encouraging. Not all referrals result in conferences, for a variety of reasons, but when they do, nearly all meetings result in an agreement.[4] Studies have found high satisfaction rates by participants and reduced fear and trauma on the part of victims. Most studies have also found reduced recidivism on the part of offenders.[5] Moreover, unlike nonmediated restitution contracts, most of these agreements are fulfilled—the figure is normally above 80 or even 90 percent.

Victims give a variety of reasons for participating, but going into the process many note the importance of restitution. After the VOC experience, however, other benefits loom larger for them. In a study of burglaries in Minneapolis, for example, victims reported that the most important benefit was

3 On mediation in serious violence, see, for example, Mark S. Umbreit, *Mediating Interpersonal Conflicts: A Pathway to Peace* (West Concord, MN: CPI Publishing, 1995), 148ff.

4 Research since 1990 confirms the findings summarized here. See, for example, Mark S. Umbreit, *Victim Meets Offender: The Impact of Restorative Justice and Mediation* (Monsey, NY: Criminal Justice Press, 1994); "Victim and Offender Mediation: International Perspectives on Theory, Research, and Practice," Harry Mika (ed.), *Mediation Quarterly* 12, no. 3 (special issue, Spring 1995); and Lawrence Sherman and Heather Strang, *Restorative Justice: The Evidence* (London: Smith Institute, 2007), http://www .restorativejustice.org/10fulltext/restorative-justice-the-evidence.

5 See, for example, the 2007 meta-analysis by Lawrence Sherman and Heather Strang. This study has some limitations in the recidivism data due to the type of programs that were included, but it is especially illuminating concerning victims; see http://www.restorativejustice.org/10fulltext /restorative-justice-the-evidence

meeting the offender. Sometimes this allayed fears, reduced stereotypes, or gave them a chance to see to it that the offender got help. But they also noted the importance of telling what happened and getting answers.[6]

Overall, a sense of participation was the strongest theme in this study. VOC appears to make possible some of the preconditions for healing: empowerment, truth-telling, answering of questions, recovery of losses, even a sense of reassurance. It also provides victims with a chance to feel that they are "doing something" to perhaps help change the offender's behavior, a theme that research has found to be perhaps surprisingly important to victims.

Offenders, too, apparently find satisfaction in participating. All offenders in one study in the U.S. Midwest and 91 percent of offenders in a study in Langley, British Columbia, said that, if they had it to do over, they would go through VOC again.[7] Offenders expressed an increased awareness of victims as people, and attitudinal change was measurable in some cases. Nevertheless, they found the experience difficult and talked of it as being tough punishment. Often offenders listed meeting the victim as both the best and the worst part of the process.

VOC practitioners tend to think that VOC does encourage behavioral changes in offenders but question whether this concern should be central. VOC is important because it addresses the distrust, fear, and hostility between victims and offenders and meets some important victim and offender needs that are normally unmet. VOC recognizes the obligations created by

6 Mark S. Umbreit and Mike Schumacher, *Victim Understanding of Fairness: Burglary Victims in Victim Offender Mediation* (Minneapolis: Minnesota Citizens Council on Crime and Justice, 1988).

7 Robert B. Coates and John Gehm, *Victim Meets Offender: An Evaluation of Victim-Offender Reconciliation Programs* (Michigan City, IN: PACT Institute of Justice, 1985); and Andrew Gibson, "Victim-Offender Reconciliation Program: Research Project, Langley, B.C.," Simon Fraser University, 1986.

crime and that even if VOC had no impact on behavior, making things right would be the right thing to do.

But is VOC justice? In the midwestern study, victims and offenders were asked what justice meant and whether they had experienced it. Almost 80 percent of both victims and offenders who had gone through VOC believed that justice had been served in their cases. Definitions of justice varied, but common themes were "making things right" (a biblical concept!), holding offenders accountable, and "fairness and equity in settling disputes." "To make things right," in fact, was the leading reason given by offenders for participating in the Langley, B.C., program. In the Minneapolis study of burglaries, the more traditional idea of justice as punishment through imprisonment was the least frequent concern expressed by victims who participated.

The Minneapolis study was small and preliminary, but one of its findings was particularly hopeful. Victims who went through VOC were *twice* as likely to feel that they had been treated fairly by the criminal justice process. Apparently VOC does indeed provide an experience of justice.

Another purpose of punishment is specific deterrence. Do people repeat their offenses? A growing body of evidence suggests that restitution, including VOC, has an impact on recidivism as great as or greater than other sanctions.

Both victims and the general public will support the use of restitution. A variety of studies show that the public approves of reparative sanctions and that members of the public, as well as victims, support moves toward noncustodial sanctions that include restitution. Moreover, programs such as VOC can provide information to victims about their cases and give them a sense of participation. Studies show these to be important victim concerns.

GOALS ARE IMPORTANT

A VOC approach clearly has the potential to address a number of needs. However, the movement as a whole has been challenged to be clear about its values and goals. Is the primary goal to be an alternative? To reform offenders? To help victims? To involve the community? To punish offenders? The goals that VOC chooses to pursue make a great deal of difference in how it operates in practice.

In fact, the movement has been reminded that its goals are sometimes unclear and that some of these goals may be mutually contradictory. Programs need to choose one overriding goal and to be clear about the implications of this decision for its other goals and its operations.

If a primary purpose is to reform offenders or to mitigate their punishment, VOC programs may easily come to neglect victims' needs and perspectives, even if VOC claims to take victims seriously. This criticism emerged early on from evaluations of some British programs.[8] If VOC programs seek primarily to provide an alternative to prison, they will concentrate primarily upon serious, prison-bound cases—to the neglect of more "minor" cases that may have serious implications for victim and offender or their relationships. Clarity about and priorities among goals are important.

A decision to make one goal primary does not mean that other potential benefits do not exist or should not be pursued but simply that they are secondary. VOC practitioners believe, for example, that the personal accountability that VOC offers can change offenders' attitudes and behavior. Yet this is not the primary goal. The process is worth doing even if attitudes and behaviors are not changed. An offense harms a person and

---

8 The British Home Office has sponsored extensive quantitative and qualitative research on the VOC or "reparations" projects there. I am indebted to Tony Marshall—who oversaw this research for the Home Office—for summaries of the results.

creates an obligation to that person. A just response, then, involves some attempt to make it right. It is the "right" thing to do, regardless of its other impacts.

Inherent in the effort to operate a program such as VOC in conjunction with the criminal justice system are serious challenges. How do we mesh a process that is reparative in focus with one that is more retributive? Can it be done, or will the larger system in the end overwhelm the smaller? Can VOC help transform the retributively oriented criminal justice system, or will the system transform VOC? Will VOC go the way of so many other "alternatives," perhaps even becoming a new instrument of control and punishment?

These are genuine questions, and researchers are sounding some warnings in this area. Some programs, for example, have come to reflect the system's offender orientation and have neglected victims. Criminal justice benchmarks such as restitution and recidivism can easily overshadow other more reparative or healing goals.

An early study of English programs warned of the dangers of tacking new experiments onto the existing criminal justice system.[9] This includes even (or especially!) reparative ones. At minimum, they remind us that we must keep value questions in the forefront. They call for a new understanding and language of justice and for research that will shape and test the viability of a reparative paradigm.

VOC AS A CATALYST

I have been a participant in the VOC movement since 1978. Initially, my participation was resistant and skeptical. Through previous work in criminal justice, I had developed a perspective I considered quite critical. And I suspected that

9 Gwynn Davis, Jacky Boucherat, and David Watson, *A Preliminary Study of Victim Offender Mediation and Reparation Schemes in England and Wales,* Research and Planning Unit Paper 42 (London: Home Office, 1987), 60–65.

VOC did not sufficiently challenge basic premises. As I experienced VOC firsthand, however, I came to realize that the parameters of my earlier "critical" framework were in fact quite conventional. It was VOC that had the potential to transform my ideas about justice.

In my earlier work with prisoners and defendants, I had not understood the perspectives of victims. Indeed, I did not want to, for they served primarily as interference in the process of finding "justice" for the offender. I did not fundamentally question the state's role in justice, nor did I ask whether the administration of pain was the proper focus. I was, however, well aware of the many and often systematic injustices in the way criminal justice selects and treats offenders.

VOC forced me to meet and listen to crime victims, and that caused me to begin rethinking what crime is and what ought to happen. The experience of seeing two hostile people—victim and offender—leave a meeting with new understandings of what happened could not help but make an impact. Often they left with new understandings of each other, sometimes with new or even friendly relationships. Eventually the implications of all this began to sink in. VOC has become, for me, the agent of a transformation of my understanding of justice and a demonstration that such justice is not just theoretical but can be practical. Yet the implementation and spread of VOC has also posed important questions and raised some warning flags.

When agriculturists want to solve certain problems in crops, they often experiment with new strains. To do that, they test by planting them in experimental plots. When such plots are successful, they may become demonstration plots to help persuade others to try. Since 1974, VOC has served as both an experimental and a demonstration plot.[10] VOC's demonstration role is important: VOC serves as a reminder that there

---

10 Credit for the plot analogy goes to Clarence Jordan and John H. Yoder.

are other ways to understand and respond to crime—that justice can repair. But the experimental role must not be abandoned. VOC itself must continue to experiment, to push out new boundaries. We need new experiments that go beyond VOC—experiments that will help develop and test new understandings of crime and justice. Increasingly, such experiments are taking place.

In planting and nursing such plots, the church's role is critical. Although the VOC movement is well established in the world at large by now, the church played a pivotal role in its development and spread and still remains deeply involved in many communities. That is as it should be. VOC embodies a vision of justice that is inherently biblical and thus provides an arena where the church can implement its vision.

The VOC movement desperately needs the church if it is to survive in a form that matters. Pressures to be sidetracked from the vision are many. The church can provide the kind of independent value base and independent institutional base that is necessary to carry the vision. Motivated by a biblical vision of justice as restoration, perhaps the church can continue to plant plots that will experiment and demonstrate another way. If VOC is to survive as a catalyst for change, the church must remain involved.[11]

FAMILY GROUP CONFERENCES AND CIRCLES

In the early days of victim-offender conferencing, Dutch law professor Herman Bianchi chided us that the approach was too individualized and private.[12] Many cultures are accustomed to addressing their conflicts and problems within larger family and

---

11 For a more thorough discussion of contemporary victim-offender conferencing, see Lorraine Stutzman Amstutz, *The Little Book of Victim Offender Conferencing* (Intercourse, PA: Good Books, 2009).

12 Adapted from the appendix of *Changing Lenses*, 3rd edition.

community contexts, he said. They would find the simple one-on-one dyads of a victim-offender encounter too isolated.

I filed this away as an idea that seemed sensible but hard to apply within our model. The theory of victim-offender reconciliation and restorative justice did recognize a role for the community; indeed, many of us saw it as a way to return conflicts to the community. We consoled ourselves with the assurance that the community was involved through volunteer mediators and the community-based organizations that hosted many of the programs.

In the case of juveniles, families have always been a factor to consider, although their role has been seen as somewhat problematic. Some programs see families of offenders as a potential nuisance; they must be informed but should be kept out of the actual encounter for fear that they will take responsibility away from the offender. Others encourage their attendance but try to ensure that the essential dialogue is between young offender and victim. In this situation the parents have a role, but it is supportive rather than central.

In other words, family and community have been recognized to have some role, but in practice the role has been ambiguous and often episodic or marginal rather than integral.

Two restorative approaches have forced us to reconsider these assumptions. They suggest ways to implement the role of community acknowledged in the concept of restorative justice. Interestingly, both represent ways of implementing principles from indigenous cultures within Western legal frameworks.

FAMILY GROUP CONFERENCES

Family group conferences emerged in New Zealand (and soon were adapted in Australia) in the late 1980s as a response, in part, to the concerns and traditions of the indigenous Maori population. The Western juvenile justice system was widely recognized to be working poorly, and many Maori argued that it was antithetical to their traditions. The system was oriented toward punishment rather than solutions, was imposed rather than negotiated, and left family and community out of the process.

In the new juvenile system adopted in 1989, all juvenile cases except a few very violent crimes are diverted from police or court into family group conferences (FGCs). As a result, judges reported substantial drops in caseloads as high as 80 percent. New Zealand judge Fred McElrea has called it the first truly restorative approach to be institutionalized in a Western legal framework.[13]

Instead of a court hearing, a youth justice coordinator (employed by the social service system, not the justice system) facilitates a meeting that is similar to VOC in that it provides a forum for feelings to be expressed, facts to be explored, and settlements to be negotiated. Offenders are held accountable and victims are provided opportunities to have some needs met. But there are significant differences from VOC in the makeup of the meeting and the scope of the discussions.

Compared to VOC, the meetings are large. Families of the offender are an essential ingredient. This may include both immediate and extended family members. In broken or dysfunctional families, more distant relatives or other significant people may be involved. Caregivers involved with the family may be invited, and a youth advocate—a special attorney—is

---

13 See, for example, McElrea's essays in Jonathan Burnside and Nicola Baker, eds., *Relational Justice: Repairing the Breach* (Winchester, UK: Waterside Press, 1994), 104–13, and B. J. Brown and F. W. M. McElrea, eds., *The Youth Court in New Zealand: A New Model of Justice* (Legal Research Foundation, Publication No. 34, 1993). Descriptions and evaluations of family group conferencing in New Zealand and Australia may be found in Christine Alder and Joy Wundersitz, eds., *Family Group Conferencing and Juvenile Justice: The Way Forward or Misplaced Optimism?* (Canberra, Australia: Institute of Criminology, 1994).

included to look out for the legal concerns of the offender. Victims, too, may bring family or supporters. Moreover, the police (the prosecutors in this legal system) take part in the meeting. So the meetings are not only large but include parties with divergent interests and perspectives.

That in itself may seem radical, but there is more: This group is expected to come up with a recommendation for the entire outcome of the case, not just restitution. And they must do this by consensus of the group! Even more startling is the fact that, in most cases, they manage to do so.

To be sure, the approach has needed fine-tuning. Restitution follow-up is sometimes inadequate, for example, and the initial legislation did not adequately recognize the central role of victims. In spite of such glitches, however, the evidence emerging from this experience is impressive. Similarly, efforts in Australia, such as the police-based approach in Wagga Wagga, appear to be working well and are being tried in some American locations.

The involvement of families in FGCs maximizes possibilities for what Australian criminologist John Braithwaite calls "reintegrative shame." In his pioneering book, Braithwaite notes that one of the most powerful forms of social control is shame, but there are two kinds of shame—*stigmatizing* shame and *reintegrative* shame.[14]

Our retributive justice approach embodies stigmatizing shame. It sends the message that not only are your behaviors bad, but you are bad. There is really nothing you can do that will make up for it. It becomes very difficult, therefore, to be reintegrated into society. So people who offend feel permanently labeled as offenders and seek out other deviant people. Delinquent subcultures, differential association theory,

---

14 *Crime, Shame, and Reintegration* (Cambridge, UK: Cambridge University Press, 1989).

labeling theory—many criminological perspectives begin to come together through the concept of stigmatizing shame.

Reintegrative shame, on the other hand, denounces the offense but not the offender and, in addition, offers a way back. Through steps such as acknowledgment of the wrong and actions to make things right, self-respect and acceptance into the community become possible. Such shame uses wrongdoing as an opportunity to build character and community.

FGCs provide a forum for this positive application of shame. The potential for denouncing the wrong is tremendous within the circle of the family. It is bad enough to be shamed in front of the victim, but imagine facing your grandmother or grandfather! Since the offender is part of the family, however, FGCs also provide encouragement for affirming the worth of the offender. Family members reportedly often articulate their dismay and anger at the behavior yet affirm the essential value and gifts of the young person who has offended. Working together, the family discusses collaborative strategies that allow offenders to take responsibility to make things right and to feel supported in the process.

Cautions have been raised about the deliberate elicitation of shame in conferences, however. Shame is a powerful and volatile emotion and is easily misused. Shame is likely to be present in conferences, on the part of offenders, their families, and victims as well. Research is suggesting that conferences should not try to impose more shame but rather focus on ways to remove and transform shame.[15]

In addition, family involvement in determining the outcome of the case gives a sense of ownership in its success. This makes it more likely that the family will provide encouragement and support as the agreement is carried out.

15 Nathan Harris and Shadd Maruna, "Shame, Sharing and Restorative Justice: A Critical Appraisal," in *Handbook of Restorative Justice*, ed. Dennis Sullivan and Larry Tift (New York: Routledge, 2008).

FGCs are not a panacea, of course, but the evidence so far is hopeful. In my visits to New Zealand, I have heard dramatic stories, often from players I would not expect to be easy converts, including judges, police officers, and lawyers.

CIRCLE PROCESSES

Another approach that has emerged is the sentencing circles being used in Canadian First Nations communities and other circle processes. Like FGCs, sentencing circles provide a way to incorporate some traditional problem-solving approaches in the overall context of a Western legal system. With sentencing circles, case outcomes—including court-based sentencing plans—are developed through discussion and consensus. Compared to FGCs, however, more emphasis is placed on community involvement. Meetings, or "circles," may be quite large, with many community members attending.

Judge Barry Stuart, in whose Yukon jurisdiction such circles emerged, emphasizes that the community-building and community problem-solving dimension of this may be one of the most important outcomes of sentencing circles.[16] When the community is left out, as it is in the traditional criminal justice process, important opportunities for growth and community building are missed. When conflicts are processed properly, however, they provide the means to build relationships between people and communities. Take this away, and you take away a fundamental building block of community and of crime prevention. Judge Stuart says it like this:

> The principal value of Community Sentencing Circles cannot be measured by what happens to offenders, but rather by what happens to communities. In reinforcing and building

---

16 "Alternative Dispute Resolutions in Action in Canada: Community Justice Circles" (unpublished paper, Yukon Territorial Court, Whitehouse, Yukon).

a sense of community, Circle Sentencing improve[s] the capacity of communities to heal individuals and families and ultimately to prevent crime. Sentencing Circles provide significant opportunities for people to enhance their self-image by participating in a meaningful way in helping others to heal.

He argues that this is not a radical idea but draws on the traditions of aboriginal cultures as well as Western societies "before becoming dependent upon professional 'healers' and 'conflict resolvers.'"

A variety of circle processes are being used today and in many situations. Healing circles are used to address individual and community needs, including victim-offender relationships. Sentencing circles provide forums for developing sentencing plans while at the same time addressing community-wide causes and problems. Sentencing circles bring together offenders, victims (or their representatives), support groups, and interested community people to discuss what happened, why it happened, and what should be done about it. Discussions are reportedly wide-ranging and encompass not only specific sentencing plans but causes, community responsibilities, and needs for healing. Stuart lists these objectives: (1) to address causes, not symptoms; (2) to involve the parties personally, providing an opportunity to air their emotions and work toward solutions; (3) to reduce dependency on experts; and (4) to build a sense of community. He argues that the approach is as workable in the inner city as in more rural aboriginal communities.

Sentencing circles, like FGCs, widen the scope of problem solving and provide ways to remove and transform shame. Judge Stuart reports,

The community will [often] tell the offender that they have done something "bad" yet also they are not a "bad" person, but have many good qualities that can be developed. . . . Bringing love, concern, support, and a willingness to forgive into the sentencing process, profoundly influences the attitude and actions of many offenders. As one offender stated, "I never heard that before—not that people cared for me. I didn't know that—for me it was always you know a bad guy doing bad stuff, so I became good at doing bad stuff. Why not, eh? I was angry about how they acted towards me, now I find out they really do care—want to help. I feel different—makes me want to be different."

Today, circle processes are being used in many situations outside the criminal justice system. They are often used in schools, for example, and to address community conflicts.[17] Because they resonate with many indigenous approaches to problem-solving and discussion, they provide a model with widespread applications.[18]

In some ways, the stories emerging from family group conferences and circle processes sound familiar to those of us involved in victim-offender reconciliation. However, the inclusion of family and community suggests important directions that we must take seriously as we move further to develop the theory and practice of a justice that heals and restores.

---

17 See Lorraine Stutzman Amstutz and Judy H. Mullet, *The Little Book of Restorative Discipline for Schools* (Intercourse, PA: Good Books, 2005); and Carolyn Boyes-Watson and Kay Pranis, *Circle Forward: Building a Restorative School Community* (St. Paul, MN: Living Justice Press, 2014). For higher education, see David R. Karp, *The Little Book of Restorative Justice for Colleges and Universities* (Intercourse, PA: Good Books, 2013).

18 For more information on family group conferences and sentencing circles, see: Kay Pranis, *The Little Book of Circle Processes* (Intercourse, PA: Good Books, 2005); and Allan MacRae and Howard Zehr, *The Little Book of Family Group Conferences, New Zealand Style* (Intercourse, PA: Good Books, 2004).

Part IV

A New Lens

10

A Restorative Lens

AS I AM THINKING about writing this chapter, I take time out to go to court. An eighteen-year-old boy, my neighbor, is scheduled to be sentenced. He has pleaded guilty to molesting the young girl next door. Her mother has asked for my help. She doesn't want him to go to prison, where he might become a victim himself, but she wants the behavior to stop. "If it were anyone else," she tells me, "I would want to string him up. But Ted just needs help."

"I'm going to continue this sentencing until a later date," says the judge. "Frankly, I don't know what to do. Howard, maybe you can help."

Where does one start in this sort of case? I begin by framing the issues in a conventional way. He has broken the law. What does the law require? What will the court accept? What should the court do with him? Then I remember what I've been writing, and my framework begins to shift.

The framework—it makes a difference. How do we interpret what has happened? What factors are relevant? What responses are possible and appropriate?

As I stated at the beginning of this book, the lens we look through determines how we frame both the problem and the "solution." We need to look not only at alternative punishments or even at alternatives to punishment. (Professor Kay Harris, a specialist in sentencing, has reminded us that it is a matter of alternate values, not of alternate technologies of punishment.[1]) We need to look to alternative ways of viewing both problem and solution.

A retributive lens has been the focus of this book. As we observed in the story at the beginning of the book and throughout other examples, the process that relies on that lens fails to meet many of the needs of both victims and offenders. Such failures are negative signposts that identify a need for change, but there are positive signposts that point a direction. The experiences and needs of victims and offenders indicate some of the concerns we must address. The biblical tradition offers some principles.

Our historical experience and more recent "experimental plots" suggest possible approaches. Perhaps these signposts can serve as elements for a new lens.

A new lens, perhaps, but a new paradigm as well? A paradigm is more than a vision or a proposal. It requires well-articulated theory, combined with a consistent grammar and a physics of application—and some degree of consensus. It need not solve all problems, but it must solve the most pressing ones and must point a direction. I doubt that we are there yet.

More realistic at this stage are alternative visions, rooted in both principle and experience, which can help to guide our search for solutions to the present crisis. We can adopt a different lens, even though it cannot yet be a full-fledged

---

1 See M. Kay Harris, "Strategies, Values and the Emerging Generation of Alternatives to Incarceration," *New York University Review of Law and Social Change* 12, no. 1 (1983–84): 141–90, and "Observations of a 'Friend of the Court' on the Future of Probation and Parole," *Federal Probation* 51, no. 4 (December 1987): 12–21.

paradigm. Such visions can help give direction to what must be a shared journey of experimentation and exploration.

In this search, we are seeking a vision of what the standard ought to be, what is normative, not what would be a realistic response in all situations. The current lens builds upon the unusual, the bizarre. It makes procedures for such cases normative for "ordinary" offenses. Some offenders are so inherently dangerous that they need to be restrained. Someone must make that decision, guided by rules and careful safeguards. Some offenses are so heinous that they require special handling. But these special cases should not set the norm. Our approach, then, should be to identify what crime means and what normally ought to happen when it does, while recognizing the need for certain exceptions. For now, then, we will not preoccupy ourselves with whether our vision can encompass all situations. Rather, we will try to envision what ought to be the norm.

One way to start this exploration is to take crime down from its high plane of abstraction. This means understanding it as the Bible understands it and as we experience it: as injury and as a violation of people and of relationships. Justice ought, then, to focus on repairing, on making things right.

In that case, the two contrasting lenses might be sketched like this:

Retributive Justice

Crime is a violation of the state, defined by lawbreaking and guilt. Justice determines blame and administers pain in a contest between the offender and the state directed by systematic rules.

Restorative Justice

Crime is a violation of people and relationships. It creates obligations to make things right. Justice involves the victim, the offender, and the community in a search for solutions which promote repair, reconciliation, and reassurance.

In chapter 12, I will note some cautions about the term *retributive justice* and the stark contrast drawn here between it and *restorative justice*. I also refine the way I articulate the concept of restorative justice. This critique will build upon rather than invalidate this chapter, however, as sometimes too-stark dichotomies give us initial language with which to make important distinctions.

CRIME: VIOLATION OF PEOPLE AND RELATIONSHIPS

I pointed out earlier that a person often experiences even minor property crimes as an attack on the self. Victims feel personally violated, even when the direct harm is only to property. The shalom vision reminds us that this material level is important to a sense of well-being.

But the shalom vision also reminds us that crime represents a violation of human relationships. Crime affects our sense of trust, resulting in feelings of suspicion, of estrangement, sometimes of racism. Frequently it creates walls between friends, loved ones, relatives, and neighbors. Crime affects our relationships with those around us.

Crime also represents a ruptured relationship between the victim and offender. Even if they had no previous relationship, the crime creates a relationship. And that relationship is usually hostile. Left unresolved, that hostile relationship in turn affects the well-being of victim and offender.

Crime represents an injury to the victim, but it may also involve injury to the offender. Much crime grows out of injury. Many offenders have experienced abuse as children. Many lack the skills and training that make meaningful jobs and lives possible. Many seek ways to feel validated and empowered. For many, crime is a way of crying for help and asserting their personhood. They do harm in part because of harm done to them. Often they are then further harmed in the "justice" process. This dimension grows in part out of larger distributive justice issues. It also is an integral part of the shalom vision.

Crime, then, is at its core a violation of a person by another person, a person who himself or herself may be wounded. It is a violation of the just relationship that should exist between individuals. There is also a larger social dimension to crime. Indeed, the effects of crime ripple out, touching many others. Society too has a stake in the outcome and a role to play. Still, these public dimensions should not be the starting point. Crime is not first an offense against society, much less against the state. Crime is first an offense against people, and it is here that we should start.

This interpersonal dimension of crime reminds us that crime involves conflict.[2] Indeed, several European scholars working toward a new lens for viewing crime have urged us to define *crime* as a form of conflict. After all, crime creates interpersonal conflict, and sometimes it grows out of conflict. Certainly crime is related to other harms and conflicts in society. Properly approached, many such conflictual situations can be opportunities for learning and growth whether or not one defines them as crimes.

Marie Marshall Fortune has warned that to label crime as *conflict* can be misleading and dangerous.[3] In situations of domestic violence, for example, we have too often defined violent acts with serious consequences as simply an outgrowth of conflict. This has tended to mute responsibility for behavior by blaming the victim. It also assumes that violence is simply an escalation of conflict. Violence is not, Fortune reminds us,

---

2 See, e.g., Louk Hulsman's work, cited above. See also John R. Blad, Hans van Mastrigt, and Niels A. Uldriks, eds., *The Criminal Justice System as a Social Problem: An Abolitionist Perpective* (Rotterdam, Netherlands: Erasmus Universiteit, 1987).

3 Fortune raised this concern in a consultation on restorative justice and "tough cases" held in Guelph, Ontario, in 1986.

simply an escalation of conflict. It is categorically different. It is one thing to have a difference of opinion and to argue. It is quite another to attack another physically.

Because of its interpersonal dimensions, crime obviously involves conflict. To equate it with conflict, however, may be misleading and may obscure some important dimensions.

What about the term *crime?* Some would have us avoid the term altogether. *Crime* is a result of a legal system that makes arbitrary distinctions between various harms and conflicts. It is an artificial construct that throws into one basket a variety of unrelated behaviors and experiences. It separates them from other harms and violations and thereby obscures the real meaning of the experience.

Because of this, Dutch criminologist and lawyer Louk Hulsman has suggested the term *problematic situations*.[4] That term helpfully reminds us of the connection between crimes and other types of harms and conflicts. It also suggests the learning possibilities that are inherent in such situations. But *problematic situations* feels vague and, for serious harms, may seem to minimize the dimensions of the hurt. Certainly it is difficult to imagine *problematic situations* taking the place of *crime* in ordinary discussion!

An alternate term would be helpful, but so far I have not found an acceptable replacement. So for now I'll stick to *crime,* keeping in mind its inadequacies.

Crime involves injuries that need healing. Those injuries represent four basic dimensions of harm:

1. To the victim

2. To interpersonal relationships

---

4 See also "Critical Criminology and the Concept of Crime," *Contemporary Crises: Law, Crime and Social Policy* 10 (1986): 63–80.

3. To the offender

4. To the community

The retributive lens focuses primarily on the latter: social dimensions. It does so in a way that makes *community* abstract and impersonal. Retributive justice defines the state as victim, defines wrongful behavior as violation of rules, and sees the relationship between victim and offender as irrelevant. *Crimes*, then, are categorically different from other types of wrongs.

A restorative lens identifies people as victims and recognizes the centrality of the interpersonal dimensions. *Offenses* are defined as personal harms and interpersonal relationships. *Crime* is a violation of people and of relationships.

UNDERSTANDINGS OF CRIME

Retributive Lens	Restorative Lens
Crime defined by violation of rules (i.e., broken rules)	Crime defined by harm to people and relationships (i.e., broken relationships)
Harms defined abstractly	Harms defined concretely
Crime seen as categorically different from other harms	Crime recognized as related to other harms and conflicts
State as victim	People and relationships as victims
State and offender seen as primary parties	Victim and offender seen as primary parties
Victims' needs and rights ignored	Victims' needs and rights central
Interpersonal dimensions irrelevant	Interpersonal dimensions central
Conflictual nature of crime obscured	Conflictual nature of crime recognized
Wounds of offender peripheral	Wounds of offender important
Offense defined in technical, legal terms	Offense understood in full context: moral, social, economic, political

So far we've limited most of our discussion to the harms and conflicts that we usually label as crimes. Such a narrow focus, however, is not biblical. The Bible holds out for us a vision of how people ought to live together—in a state of shalom, in a state of right relationship. Behaviors we call crime violate such relationships, but so do a variety of other harms, including acts of injustice and oppression by the powerful against the powerless. To be biblical in our understanding, we will have to see injustice holistically, without artificial lines between crimes and other injustices. We must see the whole continuum of harms. Crimes merge into other harms and conflicts between individuals that we normally term *civil*. But those injustices join with injustices of power and wealth. The Old Testament prophets remind us that structural injustice is sin and that such injustice in turn breeds more injustice.

RESTORATION: THE GOAL

If crime is injury, what is justice? Again, a biblical understanding points the way. If crime harms people, justice should be a search to make things right to and between people. When a wrong occurs, the central question ought not to be, "What should be done to the offender?" or "What does the offender deserve?" Instead, the primary question ought to be, "What can be done to make things right?"

Instead of defining justice as retribution, we will define justice as restoration. If crime is injury, justice will repair injuries and promote healing. Acts of restoration—not further harm—will counterbalance the harm of crime. We cannot guarantee full recovery, of course, but true justice would aim to provide a context in which the process can begin.

If the harm of crime has four dimensions, reparative energies ought to address these dimensions. The first goal of justice, then, ought to be restitution and healing for victims.

Healing for victims does not imply that one can or should forget or minimize the violation. Rather, it implies a sense of recovery, a degree of resolution or transcendence. The violated should again begin to feel like life makes some sense and that they are safe and in control. The violator should be encouraged to change. He or she should receive freedom to begin life anew. Healing encompasses a sense of recovery and a hope for the future.

Healing of the relationship between victim and offender should be a second major concern of justice. The victim-offender reconciliation movement has identified this goal as reconciliation.

Reconciliation implies full repentance and forgiveness. It involves establishing a positive relationship between the victim and offender. The VOC experience suggests that this is possible. Yet it would be unrealistic to expect reconciliation to occur in all cases. In many cases, nothing like reconciliation will be accomplished. In other cases, a satisfactory relationship may be worked out that does not imply intimacy or complete trust. In no way should participants feel coerced toward reconciliation. Ron Kraybill, former director of Mennonite Conciliation Service, has reminded us that reconciliation has a rhythm and dynamic of its own. Even if we consciously want reconciliation, our emotions may go a different direction.

To the brain's concern with what *ought* to be, the heart responds with what *is*. The head can set a direction for the heart, but the heart must arrive at its own pace. Heart reconciliation is a cycle with stages along the way.[5]

According to Ron Claassen, founder of the VORP in Fresno, California, we must see reconciliation as a continuum.[6] On the one end is outright hostility. On the other is the restoration or

5 Ron Kraybill, "From Head to Heart: The Cycle of Reconciliation," *Conciliation Quarterly* 7, no. 4 (Fall 1988), 2.

6 Ron Claassen and Howard Zehr, *VORP Organizing: A Foundation in the Church* (Elkhart, IN: Mennonite Central Committee, 1988), 5.

creation of a strong, positive relationship. When a crime occurs, the relationship is usually at the hostile end of the scale. Left unaddressed, the relationship usually remains there or even moves toward deeper hostility. The aim of justice, then, ought to be to move the relationship toward reconciliation. Such healing of relationships, even if only partial, is an important step toward healing for individuals. Justice cannot guarantee or force reconciliation, but it ought to provide opportunities for such reconciliation to occur.

I have been involved in cases where little progress toward a reconciled relationship seems to have occurred. Having met to discuss the offense and its resolution, victim and offender remained hostile. Yet the nature of their hostility had changed. No longer were they mad at an abstraction, at a stereotype of a victim or offender. They were now mad at a concrete person. Even that represents some improvement.

Offenders too need healing. They must be accountable for their behavior, of course. They cannot be "let off the hook." Yet this accountability can itself be a step toward change and healing. And their other needs must receive attention.

The community also needs healing. Crime undermines a community's sense of wholeness, and that injury needs to be addressed.

The experience of justice is a basic human need. Without such an experience, healing and reconciliation are difficult or even impossible. Justice is a precondition for resolution.

A full sense of justice may, of course, be rare. However, even "approximate justice" can help.[7] Even a partial experience can lay the groundwork necessary for a sense of recovery and

---

7 Marie Marshall Fortune suggested this terminology at the Guelph consultation. See also Fortune, "Making Justice: Sources of Healing for Incest Survivors," *Working Together* (Summer 1987), 5; and "Justice-Making in the Aftermath of Woman-Battering," in *Domestic Violence on Trial*, ed. Daniel Sonkin (New York: Springer Publishers, 1987), 237–48.

transcendence. For example, when an offender has not been identified or refuses to take responsibility, the community can play a role in providing an experience of justice. They can truly hear and value victims, agreeing that what happened was wrong and listening and attending to their needs. Approximate justice is better than no justice and aids the process of healing.

How should we envision justice? The blindfolded goddess with balance in hand symbolizes well the impersonal, process-oriented nature of the contemporary paradigm. What is our alternative?

One possibility is to imagine justice as healing a wound. My colleague Dave Worth has spelled out this image well:

> New tissue must grow to fill the space where the old was torn away. The proper conditions and nutrients must be present to allow the new to grow. There must be safety and cleanliness and time. Sometimes there is a scar, and sometimes there is impairment. But when it is healed we can move and function and grow. And through our experience of wounding and healing, we can have some understanding of the conditions which brought about that wound and the conditions which brought about that healing. [Then] we can work to change the former and to offer the latter to others who are wounded.[8]

Wilma Derksen, whose daughter was brutally murdered, has suggested still another metaphor that I find even more hopeful. Crime creates an emptiness, she says, so justice is filling a hole.[9]

The biblical approach to justice shows that restorative justice must often be "transformative justice."[10] To make things

---

8 Dave Worth, note to author.

9 Wilma Derksen, *Have You Seen Candace?* (Wheaton, IL: Tyndale, 1992).

10 I am indebted to Marie Marshall Fortune for this term.

right, it will likely be unadvisable and even impossible to return situations and people to their original condition; justice must go beyond a return to the status quo. In cases of wife abuse, for example, it is not enough to make amends for the damages. True justice cannot occur unless people and relationships are transformed into something that is healthy so the injury does not recur. Justice may mean moving in a new direction rather than returning to the situation of the past.

Justice may involve more than filling a hole and leveling it off. The hole may need to be heaped up until it overflows. Again Dave Worth summarized this image of justice better than I can.

> Second Corinthians 5:18ff. makes a link between reconciliation and new creation. That is perhaps the essence of reconciliation: something new has happened between two people. Not something based on the way it was in the past, but on the way it should be. Reconciliation is really a forward-looking approach to the problem.
>
> [Overflowing] is what justice is about. It is not the level-over-the-top kind of legalistic approach to justice that we are talking about. We are not talking about the scales of justice. We are talking about a situation where true justice has occurred which has made a new thing come to pass. A thing which leaves people not lower, not just equal, but full and overflowing so they can go out and spread justice to others around them. Perhaps the problem with the present legalistic approach to justice is that it doesn't heap people up so they have no justice left to give others.

JUSTICE BEGINS WITH NEEDS

Justice that aims to fill and overflow must begin by identifying and seeking to meet human needs. With crime, the starting point must be the needs of those violated. When a crime occurs (regardless of whether an "offender" is identified), the first questions ought to be, "Who has been harmed?"; "How have they been harmed?"; and "What are their needs?" Such an approach would, of course, be far from that of retributive justice, which first asks, "Who did it?" and "What should be done to them?"—and then rarely moves beyond that point.

Victims have a variety of needs that must be met if one is to experience even approximate justice. In many cases, the first and most pressing needs are for support and a sense of safety.

Soon after that, however, come a variety of other needs, some of which I noted in the first chapter. Victims need someone to listen to them. They must have opportunities to tell their story and to vent their feelings, perhaps over and over. They must tell their truth. And they need others to suffer with them, to lament with them the evil that has been done.

Somewhere in the process, victims need to feel vindicated. They need to know that what happened to them was wrong and undeserved and that others recognize this as wrong. They need to know that something has been done to correct the wrong and to reduce the chances of its recurrence. They want to hear others acknowledge their pain and validate their experience.

The language of truth-telling, lament, and vindication may sometimes be harsh and angry. We must accept that and truly hear it. Only then can people move beyond. Mort MacCallum-Paterson has concluded that crime victims' cries of anguish are much like the cries of anguish found so frequently in the Old Testament. Cries of pain and demands for vengeance are "prayer-cries," intended for God's ears, asking for God's sympathy and lament. Often they sound angry and vengeful, but they are not necessarily demands for community action. As one murder victim's father said to Paterson, "We may sound as if we're asking for the death penalty. We really aren't . . . but what else can we say?" Paterson observes,

What else can we say? That's the point. There are no words more ultimate than a blood-cry as a way of expressing the grief, the pain and the rage of the survivors of murder victims. Whether or not those words become active strategizing toward the goal of executing the murderer requires another move. It requires a further decision. Lament as such does not contain the decision, but . . . lament does contain the *language*. It takes the form of a curse. In effect, it is a prayer that God will damn that one who took the life of the victim.[11]

Retribution may be one form of vindication, but so also is restitution. In an important little book entitled *Mending Hurts,* John Lampen of Northern Ireland notes that restitution is at least as basic a human response as is retribution.[12]

Restitution represents recovery of losses, but its real importance is symbolic. Restitution implies an acknowledgment of the wrong and a statement of responsibility. Making right is itself a form of vindication, a form that may promote healing better than retribution.

Retribution often leaves a legacy of hatred. Perhaps it is more satisfying as an experience of justice than no justice at all, but it does little to address hostilities. Such hostilities can impede healing. That is the beauty of forgiveness. By addressing hostilities, it allows both the victim and the offender to take control of their own lives. Like reconciliation, however, forgiveness is not easy and cannot be forced. For many, an experience of justice is a necessary precondition for forgiveness to occur. For some, forgiveness will not seem possible.

Both retribution and restitution have to do with righting an imbalance. While both retribution and restoration have

---

11 Morton MacCallum-Paterson, "Blood Cries: Lament, Wrath and the Mercy of God," *Touchstone* (May 1987), 19.

12 John Lampen, *Mending Hurts* (London: Quaker Home Service, 1987), 57.

symbolic importance, however, restitution is a more concrete way to restore equity. Also, retribution seeks to right the balance by lowering the offender to the level to which the victim has been reduced. It tries to defeat the wrongdoer, annulling his or her claim to superiority and confirming the victim's sense of worth. Restitution, on the other hand, seeks to raise the victim to his or her previous level. It recognizes his or her moral worth and acknowledges the role of the offender and possibilities for repentance. It thereby acknowledges the moral worth of the offender as well.[13] Most of us assume that retribution is high on victims' agenda. Most surveys of victims, however, suggest a different picture. Victims are often open to nonincarcerative, reparative sentences—more frequently, in fact, than is the public.[14]

Moreover, they often rank rehabilitation for the offender as an important value. Help for the offender, after all, is one way of addressing the problem of safety and the prevention of future wrongs.

Victims also need to be empowered. Justice cannot simply be done to and for them. They must feel needed and listened to in the process. Since one dimension of the wrong was that they were robbed of power, one dimension of justice is to return power to them. At minimum, this means they must be a key in determining what their needs are, how they should be met, and when they should be addressed. But victims should have some role in the overall process.

Victims need reassurance, reparation, vindication, and empowerment, but they especially need to find meaning. Remember Ignatieff's insight: justice provides a framework

---

13 See also Jeffrie C. Murphy and Jean Hampton, *Forgiveness and Mercy* (Cambridge: Cambridge University Press, 1988).

14 See, for example, Russ Immarigeon, "Surveys Reveal Broad Support for Alternative Sentencing," *National Prison Project Journal,* no. 9 (Fall 1986): 1–4.

for meaning. Victims need to find answers to questions about what happened, why, and what is being done about it. They need to address the six questions that I suggested in chapter 2 that provide steps to recovery. Only the victims themselves can answer some of these questions, although it may be that we can help them in their search. However, some of these questions are questions of fact. Who did it, why, what kind of person are they, what is being done about it? At minimum, justice should provide such information.

Thus, victims often seek vindication. This vindication includes denunciation of the wrong, lament, truth-telling. Vindication also requires that the wrong be publicly acknowledged and not minimized. Victims seek equity, including reparation, reconciliation, and forgiveness. They sense a need for empowerment, including participation and safety. Another need is reassurance, including support, "suffering with," safety, clarification of responsibility, and prevention. And they have a need for meaning, including information, fairness, answers, and a sense of proportion.

Victims feel violated by crime, and these violations generate needs. Communities feel violated as well, however, and they have needs too. Since one cannot ignore the public dimensions of crime, the justice process in many cases cannot be fully private. The community, too, wants reassurance that what happened was wrong, that something is being done about it, and that steps are being taken to discourage its recurrence. Here too information can be important as it can help to reduce stereotypes and unfounded fears. Here too restitution can play an important role by providing a symbol of the restoration of wholeness. In fact, the role of symbolism is important. Crime undermines the sense of wholeness in a community. For a community, reparation often requires some sort of symbolic action that contains elements of denunciation of the offense, vindication, reassurance, and repair.

The public dimensions of crime are important, therefore, but they should not be the starting point. Also, the community needs to be challenged in some of its assumptions about crime. One of these assumptions is that full order and safety is possible, at least within the framework of a free society.

At a fundraising party for the organization that operates our local VORP, I sat across a picnic table from a well-to-do young man. A spectacular storm was approaching, and everyone else had abandoned us for the safety of the house. As we sat watching the storm, he asked about the organization to which he had just contributed, and that led to a discussion of justice. He told me with considerable candor of his own internal struggle with the question. He had known since childhood a man who was a perpetual thief. Part of him was concerned about that friend's rehabilitation and well-being. On the other hand, he saw himself as conservative and felt that the thief deserved harsh punishment. "Sometimes," he said, "I think we should do what Iran does—cut off an arm, punish severely. Then we'd be safe."

"Perhaps," I replied, "but would you want to live here then?"

Order and freedom are two opposites on a continuum. Complete freedom, at least in the sense of freedom to do whatever we wish without formal or informal controls, would likely be chaotic and unsafe, a Hobbesian world. Complete order, on the other hand, even if it were attainable, would come at the price of freedom. If harsh punishment were to deter crime, for instance, it would have to be swift and sure. The price? We would have to be willing to make mistakes and to give arbitrary power to central authorities—a power that would surely be misused. Most of us would not wish to live in such a world. So we find ourselves moving back and forth somewhere in the middle of that continuum, seeking to balance freedom and order. The conservatives among us find themselves closer to the order end, the liberals closer to the freedom end.

There is yet another error in usual assumptions about freedom and order. Most of the time we think of order as rules and penalties, formal controls. We forget, however, that throughout history order has been maintained by informal controls—by belief systems, by social pressures and obligations, by the rewards of conforming. This is true also in our own everyday lives. To assume that order derives simply from laws and punishment is to overlook what holds society together.

The point in all this is that we cannot live in complete safety and retain other values we hold dear. At the same time, our freedom is also at risk when we do not call people to account when their attempt to exercise their will infringes on the freedom of others.

CRIME CREATES OBLIGATIONS

A discussion of needs quickly leads to questions of responsibility and liability. Violations create obligations.

The primary obligation, of course, is on the part of the one who has caused the violation. When someone wrongs another, he or she has an obligation to make things right. This is what justice should be about. It means encouraging offenders to understand and acknowledge the harm they have done and then taking steps, even if incomplete or symbolic, to make that wrong right.

Making right is central to justice. Making right is not a marginal, optional activity. It is an obligation. Ideally, the justice process can help offenders to acknowledge and assume their responsibilities willingly. This can happen. It often does in the victim-offender conferencing process. More often, however, persons accept this responsibility reluctantly at first. Many offenders are reluctant to make themselves vulnerable by trying to understand the consequences of their action. After all, they have built up edifices of stereotypes and rationalizations to protect themselves against exactly this kind of information. Many are reluctant to take on the responsibility to make right. In many ways taking one's punishment is easier. While it may hurt for a time, it involves no responsibility and no threat to rationalizations and stereotypes. Offenders often need strong encouragement or even coercion to accept their obligations.

The VOC movement in North America and elsewhere has discussed this often. Obviously this acceptance of responsibility is better when voluntary. Obviously too, coercion can be abused. Still, in principle I do not object to the requirement that offenders must assume their responsibilities. After all, if someone harms someone else, he or she has created a debt, an obligation. The offender should recognize that and willingly accept responsibilities. The justice process should encourage that.

However, persons often will not willingly assume their responsibilities. One of the reasons many offenders get into trouble is a lack of certain kinds of responsibility. One cannot overcome such irresponsibility quickly. What society *can* say to offenders, then, is simple: "You have done wrong by violating someone. You have an obligation to make that wrong right. You may choose to do so willingly, and we will allow you to be involved in figuring out how that should be done. If you do not choose to accept this responsibility, however, we will have to decide for you what needs to be done and will require you to do it."

One can require offenders to accept the obligation to make right. One can strongly encourage them to take fuller responsibility by facing their victims. However, one cannot and must not force them to do so. And one certainly should not coerce victims to participate! Forced encounters are unlikely to be good for either offender or victim and may well backfire.

We can require offenders to make right, but they cannot be fully responsible without some degree of voluntarism.

One purpose of both punishment and reparation is to send messages. The utilitarian aim of punishment is to say to offenders, "Do not commit offenses because they are against the law." "Those who do wrong deserve to get hurt." Reparation or restitution seeks to send a different message. "Don't commit offenses because it harms someone. Those who harm others will have to make it right." The message of our actions does not always sink in, as British author Martin Wright has noted. But when it does, we need to make sure it is the right message.[15]

Regarding the need to send a message that crime is wrong, Wright also observes: "We can denounce crime more constructively by doing things *for* the victim (and requiring the offenders to do so), rather than against the offender."[16]

Crime creates a debt to make right, and that debt remains regardless of whether forgiveness happens. When we offend, we cannot assume that because we have experienced forgiveness from God or even from the one wronged no other obligation remains. Nevertheless, it is also true that victims may choose to forgive even the concrete obligation that is owed. Rarely is an offender able to make up completely for what both the victim and the offender have lost. Herman Bianchi has noted that crime creates a liability and that forgiveness is about removing the liability for that which cannot be restored.

Insofar as it is possible, offenders should make amends. However, in many cases there are considerable delays before offenders are identified. Often offenders are never identified at all. Also, many of the needs that the victim and the

---

15 Martin Wright, "Mediation," *Mediation UK* 5, no. 2 (March 1989): 7.

16 Martin Wright, "From Retribution to Restoration: A New Model for Criminal Justice," *New Life: The Prison Service Chaplaincy Review* 5 (1988): 49.

community have as a result of crime are beyond the means of offenders to set right. And offenders have needs as well. This is society's responsibility: to attend to the needs to which individuals alone cannot attend. Certain obligations on the part of the community are thus also generated by crime.

OFFENDERS HAVE NEEDS, TOO

Biblically, justice is done not because it is deserved but because it is needed. Although in a retributive or just deserts model offenders may not "deserve" to have their own needs given priority, society's self-interest dictates that these needs be part of a just response. Identifying and addressing offenders' needs is a key element of restorative justice.

In the story with which I opened this chapter, Ted needs to receive treatment. The legal system interprets his behavior as sexual molestation. This behavior is part of a larger pattern of inadequacy and dysfunction. Left unattended, it will only get worse. Part of the treatment needed involves helping Ted recognize the impact of his actions on his young victim.

Offenders have many needs, of course. They need to have their stereotypes and rationalizations—their mis-attributions—about the victim and the event challenged. They may need to learn to be more responsible. They may need to develop employment and interpersonal skills. They often need emotional support. They may need to learn to channel anger and frustration in more appropriate ways. They may need help to develop a positive and healthy self-image. And they often need help in dealing with guilt. Like with victims, unless such needs are met, closure is impossible.

In the aftermath of crime, victims' needs form the starting point for restorative justice. But one must not neglect offender and community needs.

A MATTER OF ACCOUNTABILITY

Needs and responsibilities—these are matters of accountability. When harm is done, offenders need to be accountable and in ways that represent natural consequences of their actions. This accountability means understanding and acknowledging the harm and taking steps to make things right.

There is a third, intermediate dimension of accountability by offenders: to share in the responsibility for deciding what needs to be done. Judge Challeen speaks of responsible sentencing.[17]

Since offenders' behavior often reflects irresponsibility, simply telling them what is going to happen lets them off the hook, encouraging further irresponsibility. In his court, therefore, he tells offenders the dimensions they must address. Then he tells them to come back with a proposal on how they expect to meet these requirements and how the sentence will be monitored and enforced. VOC works at this by having offenders negotiate and agree to restitution.

In a juvenile reparations experiment operated by the Center for Community Justice in Indiana some years ago, young offenders came to our program before the "sentence" was decided. There they were encouraged to understand that their behavior does harm (1) to the victim, (2) to the community, and (3) to themselves. The staff worked with them to help them propose a sentence that addressed all three. Through a victim-offender encounter, for example, they could learn of victims' needs and make restitution. Through community service they could seek to repay the community. Through tutoring, art therapy, or other activities they had an opportunity to address some of their own needs. The point is this: accountability should empower and encourage responsibility. And it should take seriously all three levels of obligation: victim, community, and offender.

17 Dennis A. Challeen, *Making It Right: A Common Sense Approach to Crime* (Aberdeen, SD: Mielius and Peterson Publishing, 1986).

Offenders must be held accountable, but so too must society. Society must be accountable to victims, helping to identify and meet their needs. Likewise, the larger community must attend to the needs of offenders, seeking not simply to restore but to transform. Accountability is multidimensional and transformational.

UNDERSTANDINGS OF ACCOUNTABILITY

Retributive Lens	Restorative Lens
Wrongs create guilt	Wrongs create liabilities and obligations
Guilt is absolute, either/or	Degrees of responsibility
Guilt is indelible	Guilt is removable through repentance and reparation
Debt is abstract	Debt is concrete
Debt is paid by taking punishment	Debt is paid by making right
Debt is owed to society in the abstract	Debt is owed to victim first
Accountability as taking one's "medicine"	Accountability as taking responsibility
Assumes behavior chosen freely	Recognizes difference between potential and actual realization of human freedom
Free will or social determinism	Recognizes role of social context as choices without denying personal responsibility

THE PROCESS MUST EMPOWER AND INFORM

Judges and lawyers often assume that what people want most is to win their cases. But recent studies show that the process matters a great deal and that the criminal justice process often does not feel much like justice. Not only *what happens* but also *how it is decided* is important.[18]

18 See Wright, "Mediation"; and Martin Wright, *Making Good: Prisons, Punishment and Beyond* (London: Burnett Books, 1982), 246ff.

Justice has to be lived, not simply done by others and re-ported to us. When someone simply informs us that justice has been done and that we should now go home (as victims) or to jail (as offenders), we do not experience that as justice. Justice that is actually lived, experienced, may not always be pleasant. But we will know that it has happened because we have lived it rather than having it done for us. Not simply justice, but the *experience* of justice must occur.

The first step in restorative justice is to meet immediate needs, particularly those of the victim. Following that, restor-ative justice should seek to identify larger needs and obliga-tions. In identifying these needs and obligations, the process should, insofar as possible, put power and responsibility in the hands of those directly involved: the victim and offender. It should also leave room for community involvement. Second, it should address the victim-offender relationship by facilitating interaction and the exchange of information about the events, about each other, and about each other's needs. Third, it should focus on problem solving, addressing not only present needs but future intentions.

I have already spoken of the importance of participation for both victim and offender. For victims, disempowerment is a core element of the violation. Empowerment is crucial to recovery and justice. For offenders, irresponsibility and a sense of disempowerment may have been some of the bricks on the road to the offense. Only by participating in the solution can they move toward responsibility and closure.

The community has a role to play here too. Part of the tragedy of modern society is our tendency to turn over our problems to experts. That is our tendency with regard to health, education, and childraising. And it certainly applies to the harms and conflicts we call crime. In doing that, we lose the power and ability to solve our own problems. Even worse, we give up opportunities to learn and grow from these situations. Restorative responses must recognize that the community has a role to play in the search for justice.

An important part of justice is the exchange of information—about each other, about the facts of the offense, about needs. Victims want answers to their questions about what happened, why it happened, and who did this thing. Offenders need to understand what they have done and to whom. Faces should take the place of stereotypes. Misattributions need to be challenged. The exchange of such information is crucial, and ideally it can occur through direct interaction. In that context, the question of what to do about what has happened in the past and what is to happen in the future can be addressed. Such outcomes need to be registered in the form of agreements and settlements that are measurable and monitored.

Mediation or dialogue between victim and offender is one approach to justice that meets these criteria.[19] Victim-offender mediation empowers participants, challenges misattributions, provides for an exchange of information, and encourages actions aimed at making right. Through the use of community mediators, it provides for community participation. Mediation is fully compatible with a restorative approach to justice.

Mediation assumes certain preconditions, however. Safety must be assured. Participants must receive the emotional support they need and must be willing to participate. Trained mediators are essential. The timing must be right.

When such preconditions are met, mediation must be conducted appropriately and must address key issues. Mark Umbreit has pointed to the importance of an empowering style of mediation rather than one in which the mediator

---

19 Although practitioners in the field still use the term *mediation* sometimes, I am no longer comfortable with it, especially when applied to serious harm. See Zehr, *The Little Book of Restorative Justice*, 2nd ed. (New York: Good Books, 2015). I prefer terms such as *dialogue* and *conferencing*.

imposes his or her agenda and personality, either directly or through manipulation.[20]

One must not bypass the exchange of information and expression of feelings on the road to agreements. Ron Claassen teaches his VORP mediators that, for mediation to be complete, three types of questions must be satisfactorily answered:

First, has the injustice been recognized and acknowledged? Has the offender owned up to and accepted responsibility for his acts? Have victims' questions been answered? Has the offender had a chance to explain what has been going on in his life?

Second, has there been agreement on what needs to be done to restore equity as far as possible?

Third, have future intentions been addressed? Does the offender plan to do it again? Is the victim feeling safe? Is there provision for follow-up and for the monitoring of agreements?

In biblical language, Claassen summarizes the three categories as confession, restitution, and repentance.[21]

But mediation is not always appropriate. The fear may be too great, even with support and assurances of safety. Power imbalances between parties may be too pronounced and impossible to overcome. The victim or the offender may be unwilling. The offense may be too heinous or the suffering too severe. One of the parties may be emotionally unstable. Direct contact between victim and offender can be extremely helpful, but justice cannot depend only on such direct interaction.

There are, in such cases, other ways to keep interaction and exchange of information in focus. The use of surrogate victims, pioneered by programs in Canada and England, is one example. Here offenders meet with victims other than their

---

20 Mark Umbreit, *Victim Understanding of Fairness: Burglary Victims in Victim Offender Mediation* (Minneapolis: Minnesota Citizens Council on Crime and Justice, 1988), 25ff.

21 Classen and Zehr, *VORP Organizing,* 24–25.

own as a step toward assuming responsibility and sharing information. This can be particularly helpful in emotionally charged situations such as sexual offenses or where cases remain unsolved.[22]

Most sexual abuse therapy treats victims and offenders separately. It provides little recognition or ways to work at the abuse of trust involved in the offense. It offers few avenues for closure. Little attention is given to how events of the offense are perceived or to misattributions about the event or the individuals.

Victim-sensitive sex offender therapy, developed by therapist Walter Berea, is different.[23] This therapeutic approach has three stages. The first is the communication switchboard stage. Here the therapist makes contact with the probation officer, previous therapists, and, perhaps most unusually, with the victim. Contact with the victim provides more complete information about the events, lets the victim know that the offender is in therapy, and allows the therapist to inquire whether the victim's needs are being met.

In the second stage of therapy, misattributions about the victim are challenged. The offender is helped to acknowledge responsibility and to understand the consequences of his behavior. During this time, he writes a letter of apology to the victim. For the victim, this stage provides a time to make sure that he does not take fault or blame on himself.

---

22 See, for example, Russ Immarigeon, "Reconciliation between Victims and Imprisoned Offenders: Program Models and Issues" (Akron, PA; Mennonite Central Committee, 1994). Another example of a pioneering program, this one addressing serious violence, is run by Community Justice Initiatives Association in British Columbia; see www.cjibc.org.

23 Walter H. Berea, "The Systematic/Attributional Model: Victim-Sensitive Offender Therapy," in James M. Yokley, ed., *The Use of Victim-Offender Communication in the Treatment of Sexual Abuse: Three Intervention Models* (Orwell, VT: Safer Society Press, 1990).

The third and final stage of this therapy has a reconciliation focus. Options include actually receiving the letter of apology that the offender has written, a face-to-face meeting, or a "no-contact" contract with the offender for the future. The choice is the victim's. Such an approach takes seriously the harm and the interpersonal dimensions of the offense as well as the needs of both victim and offender.

"Genesee justice—crafted with pride in New York State." So reads the logo of a program operated by the sheriff's department in Batavia, New York. Concerned about overuse of the jail and about victims' needs, this program was designed specifically for cases of serious violence: manslaughter, assault, and homicide. When such an offense occurs, immediate and intensive aid is offered to victims and survivors. The support offered is holistic. It concentrates not simply on their legal needs but on emotional and spiritual needs.[24]

Staff persons walk through the victimization experience with victims. In the process they help them in providing full information to the "system" about their experience. During that process, victims are allowed some involvement in decisions such as bail and even sentencing—for example, through a victim-offender encounter. Given all that support and participation, victims' wishes often turn out to be surprisingly creative and redemptive. At minimum, their needs are addressed and the various dimensions of the harm are recognized.

The ideals of direct victim-offender interaction and empowerment cannot always be fully attained. Some third-party decisions are inescapable. Cases with important implications for the community cannot simply be left up to victim and offender. There must also be some sort of community oversight. But these cases need not set the norm for how we view and

---

24 This describes the program as it was when the earlier edition was written. The program still exists at this time, but these comments may not describe its current status.

respond to crime. Even in such cases, we need to keep before us a vision of what crime really is and what really should happen.

JUSTICE INVOLVES RITUALS

Our legal system makes much of ritual. Indeed, trials are to a large extent ritual, drama, theater. But we usually ignore the most important needs for ritual.

One of these points of need is when an offense has occurred. This is where the ritual of lament, stated so eloquently in the Psalms, is appropriate. Genesee justice has recognized this need by facilitating religious services of lament and healing for those who are interested.

But as justice is done—whether complete or approximate—we also need rituals of closure. Louk Hulsman has called these "rituals of reordering." They may be important for both victim and offender.

Such rituals provide an arena in which the church could play a particularly important role.

IS THERE A PLACE FOR PUNISHMENT?

I have argued that punishment should not be the focus of justice. But is there room in a restorative concept for some forms of punishment? Certainly options such as restitution will be understood by some as punishment, albeit a more deserved and logical punishment. In one major study of VOC, for example, offenders described their outcomes as punishment but viewed them more positively than traditional punishment. Perhaps punitive language arose due to a lack of alternate terminology (although some did use the language of "making right" to describe justice). However, accepting responsibility is painful and will of necessity be understood in part as punishment. Similarly, isolation of those who are dangerous, even under the best of conditions, is painful.

The real question, then, is not whether persons will experience some elements of restorative justice as punishment, but whether punishment *intended as punishment* has a place. Christie has argued that if pain—intended as pain—is used, it should at least be used without an ulterior purpose.[25]

Pain should be applied simply as punishment, not as a way of reaching some other goal such as rehabilitation or social control. To apply pain with other utilitarian purposes is to be dishonest and to use people as commodities. Christie makes the analogy with sorrow. When we mourn a death, we mourn for the sake of mourning, not for some other purpose. Christie also urges that we inflict pain only under conditions that will reduce the level of pain infliction.

Perhaps punishment cannot be eliminated entirely from a restorative approach, but it should not be normative, and its uses and purposes should be carefully prescribed. The biblical example suggests that the goal, nature, and context of punishment are critical. In the biblical context, for example, punishment usually is not the end. It aims at liberating and creating shalom. Biblical justice is administered in a context of love. Possibilities for forgiveness and reconciliation are the light at the end of the tunnel. Punishment is limited, while love is unlimited. Redeeming love, not punishment, is the primary human responsibility.

When we as a society punish, we must do so in a context that is just and deserving. Punishment must be viewed as fair and legitimate, Ignatieff notes, because we cannot experience justice unless it provides a framework of meanings that make sense of experience. For punishment to seem fair, outcome and process need to relate to the original wrong. However, the societal context must also be viewed as fair, and this raises larger questions of social, economic, and political justice.

---

25 See works previously cited.

If there is room for punishment in a restorative approach, its place would not be central. It would need to be applied under conditions that controlled and reduced the level of pain and in a context where restoration and healing are the goals. Perhaps there are possibilities for restorative punishment. Having said that, however, I hasten to add that possibilities for destructive punishment are much more plentiful.

TWO LENSES

Earlier I summarized briefly the retributive and restorative lenses. These two perspectives can be formulated in somewhat longer form. According to retributive justice, (1) crime violates the state and its laws; (2) justice focuses on establishing guilt (3) so that doses of pain can be measured out; (4) justice is sought through a conflict between adversaries (5) in which offender is pitted against state; (6) rules and intentions outweigh outcomes. One side wins and the other loses.

According to restorative justice, (1) crime violates people and relationships; (2) justice aims to identify needs and obligations (3) so that things can be made right; (4) justice encourages dialogue and mutual agreement, (5) gives victims and offenders central roles, and (6) is judged by the extent to which responsibilities are assumed, needs are met, and healing (of individuals and relationships) is encouraged.

Justice that seeks first to meet needs and to make right looks quite different from justice that has blame and pain at its core. The following chart attempts to contrast some characteristics and implications of the two concepts of justice.

UNDERSTANDINGS OF JUSTICE

Retributive Lens	Restorative Lens
Blame-fixing central	Problem-solving central
Focus on past	Focus on future
Needs secondary	Needs primary
Battle model; adversarial	Dialogue normative
Emphasizes differences	Searches for commonalities
Imposition of pain considered normative	Restoration and reparation considered normative
One social injury added to another	Emphasis on repair of social injuries
Harm by offender balanced by harm to offender	Harm by offender balanced by making right
Focus on offender; victim ignored	Victims' needs central
State and offender are key elements	Victim and offender are key elements
Victims lack information	Information provided to victims
Restitution rare	Restitution normal
Victims' truth secondary	Victims given chance to tell their truth
Victims' suffering ignored	Victims' suffering lamented and acknowledged
Action from state to offender; offender passive	Offender given role in solution
State monopoly on response to wrongdoing	Victim, offender, and community roles recognized
Offender has no responsibility for resolution	Offender has responsibility in resolution

Outcomes encourage offender irresponsibility	Responsible behavior encouraged
Rituals of personal denunciation and exclusion	Rituals of lament and reordering
Offender denounced	Harmful act denounced
Offender's ties to community weakened	Offender's integration into community increased
Offender seen in fragments, offense being definitional	Offender viewed holistically
Sense of balance through retribution	Sense of balance through restitution
Balance righted by lowering offender	Balance righted by raising both victim and offender
Justice tested by intent and process	Justice tested by its fruits
Justice as right rules	Justice as right relationships
Victim-offender relationships ignored	Victim-offender relationships central
Process alienates	Process aims at reconciliation
Response based on offender's past behavior	Response based on consequences of offender's behavior
Repentance and forgiveness discouraged	Repentance and forgiveness encouraged
Proxy professionals are the key actors	Victim and offender central; professional help available
Competitive, individualistic values encouraged	Mutuality and cooperation encouraged
Ignores social, economic, and moral context of behavior	Total context relevant
Assumes win-lose outcomes	Makes possible win-win outcomes

Retributive justice, restorative justice. The world looks quite differently through these two lenses. Retributive justice, we have. It may not do what needs to be done, or even what its practitioners claim it does, but it "works" in the sense that we know how to carry it out. What about the more elusive perspective that I've called restorative justice? Where do we go from here?

11

Implementing a Restorative System

HOW **WILL WE** go about fully implementing a restorative system? It is fun to speculate.[26]

SYSTEM POSSIBILITIES

Some have urged that we "civilize" the law.[27]

Unlike criminal law, civil law defines wrongs in terms of injuries and liabilities rather than guilt. Outcomes, therefore, focus on settlement and restitution rather than punishment. Civil law allows for degrees of responsibility without defining them in win/lose terms. Since the state is not the victim, the actual participants remain center stage, retaining significant power and responsibility in the process. Because outcomes are not primarily punitive, procedural safeguards are of less concern, and the relevant facts are less circumscribed. What if we were to modify civil procedures to ensure certain safeguards? What if we made sure that victims had advocates in

26 This chapter is included with only minor changes from the earlier editions.

27 See also Martin Wright, *Making Good* (London: Burnett Books, 1982), 249–50.

the process, allowing for third-party decisions when we could not reach agreements or when questions of danger were involved? What if we removed cases from criminal procedures and processed them through a modified civil procedure?

The application of criminal law is what triggers the retributive paradigm. Yet criminal law is a relatively new addition to Western society and operates under assumptions that are in many ways at variance with the rest of life. The existing structure of civil law might provide an alternative framework for a concept of justice that avoided some of these assumptions.

Perhaps we should not dream of dismantling the retributive system but develop a parallel system with choices about which to use. Herman Bianchi has argued that the existence of two parallel tracks—state justice and church justice—in the medieval period was in some ways a good thing. The existence of two tracks provided choices for participants in certain cases. Moreover, each track served as a conscience and check on the other.

Development of a separate justice track has been the strategy of the Community Boards in San Francisco. These programs have been developing neighborhood-based structures for resolving disputes outside the system. The programs train people from the community to serve as case workers and as mediators and place a high value on community education and empowerment. Their mediation processes serve as an alternative to civil or criminal courts. Indeed, they refuse to take on a case while it is in the legal process. The programs are a means of educating and empowering the community to solve its own problems.

The Community Boards and other dispute resolution programs have shown much promise.[28] They represent one way

---

28 Founded in 1976, the Community Boards are considered the oldest public mediation center in the U.S.

of actually implementing a problem-solving, community-oriented vision of justice. Yet such forms of informal justice have come under increasing attack in recent years.[29]

Various warnings are sounded. Outcomes may have no uniformity and thus contradict a basic sense of fairness. Informal justice may be reserved primarily for the poor and the powerless, denying them access to other forms of justice. Victims may be given too much power. In the end, the state and the formal justice system may actually receive more, not less, power and legitimation. The dispute resolution movement is being encouraged to consider its assumptions and goals carefully.

The Japanese model is particularly interesting in this context. John O. Haley, a specialist in Japanese law, reports that a unique two-track judicial system operates there.[30] Separate formal and informal tracks operate parallel to one another, but with considerable dependence upon and interaction between them. A common pattern is for serious cases to begin in one but be transferred to the other.

One track is a Western-style, formal criminal system with many familiar characteristics. The process focuses on guilt and punishment. It is governed by formal rules and is operated by professionals such as public prosecutors. This track is used for many crimes. Yet few cases proceed all the way through the system, ending in long imprisonment or other serious legal penalties. Cases are constantly shunted aside. To an outsider, the overall system seems remarkably lenient.

---

29 See Roger Matthews, ed., *Informal Justice?* (London: Sage Publications, 1988).

30 I have drawn upon John O. Haley, "Mediation and Criminal Justice: The Japanese Model—Confession, Repentance, and Absolution" (unpublished paper, CLE Seminar "Creative Justice Through Mediation," Seattle, Washington, on October 29, 1988). See also John O. Haley, "Victim-Offender Mediation: Lessons from the Japanese Experience," *Mediation Quarterly* 12, no. 3 (Spring 1995): 233–48.

This apparent leniency and the lack of long-term involvement by the formal legal system is the result of a second, less formal track for which there is no Western parallel. Haley summarizes it like this:

> A pattern of confession, repentance, and absolution dominates each stage of law enforcement in Japan. The players in the process include not only the authorities in new roles but also the offender and the victim. From the initial police interrogation through the final judicial hearing on sentencing, the vast majority of those accused of criminal offenses confess, display repentance, negotiate for their victims' pardon and submit to the mercy of the authorities. In return, they are treated with extraordinary leniency; they gain at least the prospect of institution[al] absolution by being dropped from the formal process altogether.

Cases are moved out of the formal legal system at each stage of the process. Only a fraction enter prosecution, and an even smaller fraction are fully prosecuted. A smaller minority is incarcerated and few serve more than one year. This does not mean, however, that Japanese offenders are not convicted. In fact, conviction rates in Japan stand at about 99.5 percent!

A variety of factors influence decisions to shunt cases from the formal process or to impose nonpunitive sentences. Some of these considerations are familiar to Westerners, such as the seriousness of the offense and the nature of the offender. Added to this, however, are some unique variables: the willingness of the offender to acknowledge guilt and to express remorse and make compensation to the victim, and the victim's willingness to receive compensation and to pardon.

Conviction rates are high in Japan largely because offenders are willing to confess and take responsibility. The roots of this willingness are in part cultural, of course. In part, however, it is due to the understanding that, if they do, the outcome is likely to focus on compensation and correction more than punishment. Where the complex, punitive legal system in Western society discourages confession, the Japanese system appears to make it normative.

Victims have an important role to play in this process. Restitution for losses is expected. And they have a voice in the authorities' decisions to report, prosecute, or sentence the offender. Yet they do not control the process, nor do they assume the role of adversary or prosecutor.

Westerners are surprised at authorities' willingness to divert cases from the formal legal system. This is only because of our assumption that the formal process is primary and that its main focus is to establish guilt and apply punishment. The basic aim of the criminal process in Japan is to correct, and this governs authorities' decisions. Haley writes, "Thus [the authorities'] roles are not confined to the formal tasks of apprehending, prosecuting and adjudicating. Rather, once personally convinced that a suspect is an offender, their concern for evidentiary proof of guilt shifts to a concern over the suspect's attitude and prospects for rehabilitation and reintegration into society, including acceptance of authority. Leniency is considered an appropriate response if the correctional process has begun."

Haley says that typical of the Japanese pattern of responding to crime are "acknowledgment of guilt, expression of remorse including direct negotiation with the victim for restitution and pardon as preconditions for lenient treatment, and sparing resort to long-term imprisonment."

Westerners assume that such a "lenient" response would fail to deter crime. Haley, however, concludes that this pattern of response is in fact partly responsible for low crime rates in Japan.

Haley marvels that the Japanese have institutionalized the concepts of repentance and forgiveness while the West has not. The imperative to repent and forgive is at least as strong in the Judeo-Christian tradition as it is in the Japanese. Yet the West has, he says, "failed to develop institutional props for implementing such moral commands. Instead, the legal institutions and processes of Western law both reflect and re-inforce societal demands for retribution and revenge."

While the Japanese pattern is obviously tied to Japanese culture, Haley believes that we have much to learn from that example. It suggests intriguing possibilities for linking formal and informal, adversarial and nonadversarial, systems. The Japanese model suggests a place for the formal machinery of justice and for the state while leaving space for restoration and giving victim and offender an enlarged role. While the West cannot simply imitate this model, it suggests that justice might be both personal and formal. Jerome Auerbach has worried about the dangers of law without justice but especially of injustice without law. The Japanese pattern gives hope that these are not the only two possibilities.

The possibilities are intriguing. However, I must admit to considerable skepticism about blueprints for system-wide implementation, certainly at this stage. I was relieved when I heard Kay Harris, at a workshop on restorative justice, urge us to continue to develop the vision and to resist pressures for "premature practicality."[31]

Much conceptual work remains to be done. In the previous chapter I noted that restorative justice is not yet a paradigm. Many issues remain undeveloped or unanswered. *Community* is an elusive, oft-abused term. What does it mean, and how

---

31 See M. Kay Harris, "Alternative Visions in the Context of Con-temporary Realities," in *Justice: The Restorative Vision*, Issue No. 7 of *New Perspectives on Crime and Justice: Occasional Papers* (Akron, PA: Mennonite Central Committee, 1989): 31–40.

could it be given reality in a restorative approach? What is the proper role of the state?

I have emphasized the responsibilities *of* offenders, but what about responsibilities *to* offenders? What do we do with the dangerous few? Do we incarcerate? If so, how do we make these decisions? Is there a place for punishment? How does the idea of restorative justice in the area of crime mesh with larger questions of social, economic, and political justice? The biblical material assumes a close connection, but what does this mean in practical terms today?

Furthermore, to what extent does my formulation reflect a white, middle-class, male, North American perspective? Kay Harris's work on a feminist concept of justice points in some of the same directions but not entirely.[32] The idea of restorative justice needs to be tested against the perspectives of a variety of cultures, traditions, and experiences.

Even if one could present restorative justice as a full-fledged paradigm, however, I must admit that I would remain wary about system-wide implementation.

One of the deficiencies of Kuhn's theory of paradigm change is that it treats paradigm change as an intellectual activity, neglecting the politics and institutional dynamics of paradigm shifts. Political and institutional interests and processes certainly affect whether shifts occur and what form they finally take. The retributive paradigm is closely tied to the interests and functions of the modern state. That will have considerable impact on whether the paradigm changes and, if it does, what shape it takes.

The history of change in the area of law and justice is not a hopeful one. Efforts at change have often been co-opted and diverted from their original visions, sometimes in perverse

---

32 See "Moving into the New Millennium: Toward a Feminist Vision of Justice," in *Criminology as Peacemaking*, ed. Harold Pepinsky and Richard Quinney (Bloomington: Indiana University Press, 1991).

and harmful ways. The origin of prisons is a case at point and must stand as a constant reminder and warning to those of us who think about change. Perhaps such "improvements" have gone wrong because they did not question fundamental assumptions, as I suggested earlier. But the issues are more complex than that.

Sometimes so-called alternatives have used new language to clothe ideas that were not new.[33] Often ideas have hidden implications that take time to emerge. And a variety of pressures—internal and external—tend to sidetrack such efforts from their original directions. Sometimes they end up reshaping them so they serve interests and goals quite different from those projected.

Before we dream too grandly, then, we have an obligation to think through implications carefully. We must be as literate as possible about the dynamics of change, and we must project how our dreams can go wrong.

IN THE MEANTIME

While we contemplate larger possibilities, we must also pursue interim goals and activities. There are things that we can and must do here and now, in the meantime.

We must continue to dialogue, to *palaver* with those who are sympathetic and those who are not.[34] We must test, explore, and develop our vision.

---

33 Matthews, *Informal Justice?*, 102.

34 We are using this term (from the Portuguese *palavra*, to talk) for our discussions at the suggestion of Herman Bianchi. Russ Immarigeon of the Maine Council of Churches has pointed out that, according to *The American Heritage Dictionary*, it is defined as "idle chatter," or "talk intended to charm or beguile," or "a parley between European explorers and representatives of the local populations, especially in Africa." Are we up to "idle chatter?" he asks. And why "especially in Africa"? The dictionary shows another, more neutral level of meaning having to do with discussion and debate, but perhaps these other connotations need to be kept in mind!

We must also become justice farmers, planting our experimental and demonstration plots. We must plant more VOCs, for example, and test new forms and applications of VOC. We should offer new services to victims that operate from a restorative framework. These include all-important rituals that will show that we as a community stand with them in their suffering, in denouncing the wrong, and in seeking healing. Likewise, we need to offer new services to offenders and their families. Through it all, we need to explore alternatives to punishment that offer possibilities for accountability, repair, and empowerment.

Through VOC, we know something about restorative approaches to property crime. Now it is time to further apply the tough case test. What about murder? What about spouse and child abuse? Rape?[35] What are the possibilities and what are the limits? What procedures work and which do not? What safeguards do we need?

Discussion and testing of such issues has begun, but much work remains. This will require creativity, risk-taking, and dreaming as well as realism, hard work, and caution. It will require cooperation between theoreticians and practitioners, between "experts" and laypersons. The involvement of former victims and offenders will be essential.

As we pursue our alternatives, we will have to test constantly whether they really are alternatives. Do they in fact reflect alternative values? Or are they simply alternative technologies? Are they consistent with a restorative focus? Do they move us in that direction?

We must develop interim strategies and approaches, but we must be thoughtful about where they can take us. At

---

35 Much encouraging work has been done in these areas since *Changing Lenses* was written. Domestic violence remains a controversial area of application fraught with challenges and dangers, though some promising approaches have emerged.

minimum, we should ask the following of our efforts: Do they encourage or discourage punishment values? Can they be used to construct new modes of control or punishment? Will they provide a reservoir of experience, serving as experimental or demonstration plots? Do they incorporate key elements of a restorative vision?

What are those key elements of a restorative vision? Perhaps we could begin to develop a restorative yardstick against which to measure our efforts. I have attempted a fuller listing in the resources section, but primary would be questions such as these: Does the program or outcome seek to make right the harm to the victim? Does it address the needs of the offender? Does it take into account community needs and responsibilities? Does it address the victim-offender relationship? Does it encourage offender responsibility? Are victim and offender encouraged to participate in both process and outcome?

NEW WITHIN THE OLD

Meanwhile, the church has a key role to play. Old Testament scholar Millard Lind has reminded us that biblical justice stood, then as now, in marked contrast to state justice. He poses an important question: "How do Christians relate this new, transformed model of justice to the justice systems of this world?" What is the Christian community's responsibility?

Lind looks at four of the church's responses over the centuries. The first is a strategy of withdrawal. At points the church has tried to insulate itself from the world. The withdrawal strategy is a strategy of unfaithfulness, however, because it ignores the aggressive character of God's justice, which is to be shared with others. A second response is the Constantinian one, a strategy of capitulation. This has been the predominant response of the church, which has largely adopted the assumptions of the secular world. A third strategy was that adopted by the Enlightenment, a strategy that denies the tension between models of justice.

Christ's strategy, however, presented a fourth option: to create the new in the midst of the old. In *Easy Essays*, Peter Maurin captured this spirit nicely in his words about the Catholic Worker: "The Catholic Worker believes in creating a new society within the shell of the old with the philosophy of the new, which is not a new philosophy but a very old philosophy, a philosophy so old that it looks like new."

Christ's strategy was to create a new society (the church) with new operating principles and assumptions that would operate in the midst of—and serve as an example and challenge to—the old.[36]

Part of the answer to Lind's question, then, is to get our own act together. Too often within the church, we have ignored the victims and have responded to wrongdoing with a retributive lens borrowed from the larger society. The apostle Paul warned that Christians should avoid taking their disputes to state courts, which operate under inappropriate assumptions. His point was not merely negative, however. He assumed that the church should develop its own alternative structures to implement covenant justice. Surely we must reexamine the lenses we use for dealing with harm and conflict within the church and create new structures that incorporate a restorative understanding. In this way, the church can provide a model to others.

When we operate outside the church's framework, we need to take our restorative lens with us, allowing it to shape and inform what we do. The church must also lead the way in setting up alternative structures within the old framework. We must take the lead in planting plots that can serve as tests and models.

---

36 See John H. Yoder, *The Original Revolution* (Scottdale, PA: Herald Press, 1971).

If we are ever to develop an alternative to retributive justice that is in fact a genuine paradigm, we will have to move beyond theory to a new grammar and a new physics. That is, we need a new language but also a set of principles and procedures for implementation that can make sense of the paradigm. The church has a special responsibility in this process.

IF NOTHING ELSE

Retributive justice is deeply embedded in our political institutions and our psyche. Perhaps it is too much to hope for that to change in fundamental ways. Yet we must recognize the importance of the paradigms we use and free ourselves to question these paradigms. We can also begin to use a new lens to inform and shape what we decide is worth doing. And we can begin to use another lens in the areas of our lives where we do have some control: within our families, our churches, our daily lives.

If restorative justice is not a paradigm, perhaps it nevertheless can serve as what one writer has called a "sensitizing theory."[37] Perhaps it can at least cause us to think carefully before we impose pain.

Observers have sought to understand why Holland has had such low incarceration rates since World War II. One study has concluded that the reluctance to impose prison there is less the result of a particular philosophy of sentencing than the result of a "bad conscience" about prison.[38]

The experience of imprisonment at the hands of the Nazis and a law-school curriculum that questioned imprisonment shaped a whole generation of jurists. The result has been a hesitation to impose pain in the form of imprisonment. If

---

37 Sebastian Scheerer, "Towards Abolitionism," *Contemporary Crises: Law, Crime and Social Policy* 10, no. 1 (1986): 9.

38 Willem de Haan, "Abolitionism and the Politics of 'Bad Conscience,'" *The Howard Journal of Criminal Justice* 26, no. 1 (February 1987): 15–32.

nothing else, discussions about our lenses can contribute to a milieu in which the infliction of pain is a last resort, a statement of failure, rather than the hub of justice.

THE IMPORTANCE OF VISIONS

What I have written in this book may sound impossibly visionary and unrealistic.[39] So the abolition of slavery once sounded. In fact, much of what we today assume as common sense was once considered utopian. Lenses do change.

Still, I must confess that for me personally, in my own life, it sometimes does feel utopian. Confronted with my own anger, my own tendencies to blame, my own reluctance to dialogue, my own distaste for conflict, I have at times been afraid to write this book.

Yet I believe in ideals. Much of the time we fall short of them, but they remain a beacon, something toward which to aim, something against which to test our actions. They point a direction. Only with a sense of direction can we know when we are off the path. The place to begin experiencing restoration is not from the top but from the bottom, in our own homes and communities. I continue to have faith that the community of God's people can lead in this direction. Certainly we will often fail, as those in the biblical record did. But just as certainly, God will forgive and restore us.

I have confessed that restorative justice is in part an ideal, but that raises another concern. I worry that because of this confession, the reader will not take this vision seriously. I recall the preface to Copernicus's book—not to imply that my own is in the same class, but for the lesson that we can learn from it.

Copernicus's book revolutionized the way we think about the cosmos itself. It was a key element in the paradigm shift

---

39 This section appeared as the afterword to the first edition.

known as the scientific revolution. Yet a century passed before people took it seriously.

People did not take Copernicus's book seriously at first—in part because it went counter to the common sense of the era. However, its preface may have encouraged its neglect. In that preface, the writer Oreander said, in effect, "Look, reader, what an interesting book. It deserves to be read. But remember, it's just an idea, a model, a vision. It is not necessarily reality." That comment may have made this radical book more palatable to its enemies, but it let the reader off the hook by suggesting that the Copernican paradigm was just an imaginary model. I fear that I may do so as well.

My hope is that you will understand this as a vision—a vision that is less an elusive mirage than it is an indistinct destination on a necessarily long and circuitous road.

12

Reflections Twenty-Five Years Later

WHEN I WAS writing *Changing Lenses* in the mid-1980s, I sometimes wondered whether it would be the object of laughter and derision. To be sure, victim-offender conferencing was being practiced in several countries by that time, but it was not widely known, and the conceptual framework of restorative justice was new and seemed a little crazy.

Twenty-five years later, restorative justice *is* well established internationally as a movement and as a field of study and practice. To be sure, restorative justice does remain marginal in many communities and unknown in others, but awareness of it is widespread and growing throughout the world. Academics now study and debate it at conferences and in a rapidly growing literature in various languages; governments sometimes finance and even advocate it; a growing number of communities and countries throughout the world are implementing it; and increasing numbers of people are seeking to make careers of the field.

Those of us who were involved in the 1980s never would have dreamed it possible that restorative justice would be a topic of debate and even practice in countries like Russia, South Africa, Brazil, South Korea, Pakistan, and Iran . . . and the list could go on. Nor could we have imagined that a restoratively oriented process might become the default justice process, with the courts serving as backup, as is the design of New Zealand's youth justice system.[1]

The field of restorative justice began with relatively "minor" criminal offenses but is now being applied to cases involving severe violence and even in death penalty cases. Moreover, the approach has moved far beyond the criminal justice arena to schools, the workplace, and even postconflict at a societal level. In fact, educational settings are probably the fastest growing arenas of application today.

In a relatively short time, the trickle has become a river.

Much has been learned through all this experimentation and interaction. One thing that we have learned is that although restorative justice is essentially a very simple concept, its implications are profound, complex, and even problematic. Indeed, along with the good news of restorative justice's positive impact is the bad news that the inevitable forces of co-optation and diversion outlined in the resources section are well under way.

In what follows, I note some topics deserving more attention than we can give them here. The bibliographic essay for this edition suggests sources, including some of my own more recent writing, for further exploration of these issues.

In my graduate restorative justice classes, I often require participants to write an essay about how *Changing Lenses* might be strengthened in light of later experience and writing. In this context, Gary Shapiro articulated a fundamental characteristic of this book that is important to keep in mind:

---

1 For more information, see MacRae and Zehr, *The Little Book of Family Group Conferences, New Zealand Style.*

"The context is basically modern, western, rationalist, Christian, liberal democracy, and individualistic. What is missing is a deeper and broader perspective that integrates non-western collectivist political and social culture with a non-hierarchical non-theistic spirituality."

The validity of this description has become increasingly clear as this Western articulation of restorative justice interacts with other cultures and faith traditions. In my own classes, which have included practitioners from many countries and traditions, participants often find that restorative justice has deep connections with their own cultural and religious traditions, but that the theory, practice, and underlying assumptions cannot simply be transported to their own contexts.

On the other hand, restorative justice does provide an important catalyst for discussion in diverse contexts—as long as it is taken as that and not as a simple blueprint for implementation. Restorative justice at its best is a compass, pointing a direction, but not a detailed map describing how to get there. Ultimately, what is most important about restorative justice may not be its specific theory or practice but the way it opens a dialogue, an exploration, in our communities and societies about our assumptions and about our needs. What do we mean by justice? Do our established systems deliver justice? What needs to change? What are our values? What matters to us? When I lead workshops on restorative justice, I inevitably find that we begin to talk not only about our formal justice systems but also about our schools, our communities, about how we live as individuals within society. These discussions often open windows of hope that we might try to do some things differently.

Here, then, are some themes that I might address were I writing *Changing Lenses* today.

STAKEHOLDER ISSUES

Restorative justice developed in part out of an analysis of the needs and roles of those who have a *stake* in justice.[2] *Changing Lenses* identifies those stakeholders primarily as victims, offenders, and communities. It says relatively little about the role of governments as stakeholders. Although this does reflect a personal bias toward grassroots approaches and skepticism of government (derived, in part, from my Anabaptist religious tradition), government does have an important stake and a role in restorative processes. At minimum, government has an important role in undergirding these processes, safeguarding human rights, and providing backup processes when fully restorative approaches are not possible. However, the appropriate role of government is a complex and much debated issue in the field.

In the intervening years, the topic of community has become much more integral to restorative justice but also more complex and even contentious. Many restorative justice advocates believe that restorative justice is incomplete unless the community is fully represented in restorative processes. Some argue that restorative justice approaches such as circle processes have the potential to encourage a more participatory form of democracy at the community level. They suggest that one measure of restorative justice ought to be the extent to which it actually strengthens communities. At any rate, communities have a stake because they are, to varying extents, victims but also because they have obligations and because they represent important resources.

While the importance of community in restorative justice has been increasingly emphasized, definitions of *community* have been much debated. How do we define *community*?

---

2 My former student Jarem Sawatsky has warned that *stakeholder* may be an unfortunate term, since it may derive from the historical experience of white settlers driving a stake to claim land from indigenous peoples.

What does it mean in practice? What is the proper role of government in relation to community initiatives? Some argue that communities should own and operate restorative processes while others wonder whether communities are not too traumatized and unhealthy to trust with the process. Those who live in contexts such as Western Europe, where most governments have played an important and positive role in social welfare, argue that governments do, in their experience, legitimately represent community interests.

I have much more experience with crime victims than I did in the 1980s and thus could say more about their perspectives. Were I starting over, I would be more specific about what they seem to need from a justice process but also about the challenges of making restorative justice truly victim-oriented. Similarly, there is much more that could be said about the needs of offenders. I have become particularly interested in the role of shame and trauma in the lives of offenders and victims and the importance that creating new life narratives— "re-storying" lives—plays in overcoming the past.

Since the release of John Braithwaite's groundbreaking book *Crime, Shame and Reintegration*, shame has become an important topic of debate within restorative justice.[3] Braithwaite argues that if not appropriately managed, shame becomes stigmatizing and that stigmatizing shame encourages offending behavior; he also argues that most justice as we know it in the West is stigmatizing, helping to perpetuate the cycle of offending. However, he argues that shame may be positive and reintegrative if properly applied and managed, for example in restorative conferences.

Some question, however, whether shame can ever be a positive force. Others are concerned that some practitioners

---

3 John Braithwaite, *Crime, Shame and Reintegration* (Cambridge, UK: Cambridge University Press, 1989).

are taking the wrong message from Braithwaite and others. Instead of focusing on how to remove and transform shame so that it might be reintegrative, practitioners and participants sometimes put their energy into making sure offenders feel shame, a strategy that is likely to backfire.

I am convinced that issues of shame and humiliation (and their opposites: respect, dignity, honor) are indeed important in understanding the experiences and needs of offenders as well as victims. Shame and respect, humiliation and honor all have tremendous analytic power to help us understand the experiences, motivations, and perspectives of offenders as well as victims. Experiences of shame and disrespect also help explain why justice so often backfires. However, I do not believe we should deliberately impose shame on offenders. In the restorative justice process, the experience of confronting victims and family members and of developing understanding and empathy often results naturally in shame on the part of offenders. Our focus ought to be, rather, on providing ways for shame to be released and, as much as is possible, transformed into a sense of self-respect.

HISTORY AND ORIGINS

Although I wrote about my own European "indigenous" tradition, I did not adequately realize in those early days what a tremendous debt restorative justice owes to many indigenous traditions. Two peoples have made very specific and profound contributions to practices in the field: the First Nations people of Canada and the U.S., and the Maori of New Zealand. In many ways, however, restorative justice represents a validation of values and practices that were characteristic of many indigenous groups. While some have tried to dismiss this claim as a "myth of origin," I have found restorative justice to resonate widely with people from various indigenous traditions whom I have encountered in my own classes and travels. Braithwaite has written that he has yet to find an indigenous tradition that does not have elements of both restorative and retributive justice, and that is true of my own experience as well.

I have come to view restorative justice as a way to legitimate and reclaim the restorative elements in our traditions—traditions that were often discounted and repressed by Western colonial powers. However, modern restorative justice does not represent a simple recreation of the past but rather an adaptation of some basic values, principles, and approaches of these traditions combined with modern human rights sensibilities and realities. To put it another way, a Maori youth court judge in New Zealand once commented to me that my approach to restorative justice was a way to articulate key elements of his own tradition in a way that Westerners could understand and accept.

In chapter 7, I briefly describe the "legal revolution" that brought a more retributively focused legal system to the fore. Were I to integrate more recent historical work, it would be possible to draw a more complete picture of how developing legal theory and developing theology mutually distorted and reinforced each other, embedding punitive values deeply into Western culture.

THE CONCEPT OF RESTORATIVE JUSTICE

Although my basic concept of restorative justice has not changed fundamentally, through hundreds of lectures and discussions my articulation of it has become clearer.[4] Here is one way I sometimes formulate restorative justice:

Restorative justice:

1. Focuses on *harms* and consequent *needs* (of victims, but also communities and offenders);

---

4 See Zehr, *The Little Book of Restorative Justice*, 2nd ed. (New York: Good Books, 2015).

2. Addresses *obligations* resulting from those harms (offenders' but also communities' and society's);

3. Uses *inclusive, collaborative* processes;

4. Involves those with a *stake* in the situation (victims, offenders, community members, society); and

5. Seeks to repair harms and *put right* the wrongs to the extent possible.

I sometimes describe restorative justice as a wheel. At the center of this wheel is a hub: the effort to put right, to the extent possible, the wrong (number 5, above). However, my understanding of *putting right* has expanded. After listening to victims and also observing participants in New Zealand family group conferences—and especially Maori participants—I have realized that *putting right* means that we have to address the harms and needs of victims but also the causes of offending. Thus the plan that emerges from youth justice conferences in New Zealand is supposed to have two crucial parts: a plan to address the harms and needs of victims and a plan to address whatever is happening in the young offenders' lives that is contributing to their offending. This represents an effort to put right in a holistic way.

Around the hub of the wheel—the effort to put right—are four spokes (numbers 1–4 above): restorative justice addresses harms and needs as well as obligations, and involves those who are affected or otherwise have a stake in the situation using, to the extent possible, collaborative inclusive processes.

A wheel cannot work with only a hub and spokes: it requires a rim, and I increasingly see the rim as the values that surround and undergird our work. One important criticism of restorative justice as articulated in *Changing Lenses* is that it focuses on principles but not enough on the values underlying those principles. Indeed, it is likely that we could follow the principles of restorative justice and yet do some very unrestorative things—unless we clearly articulate and are guided by the underlying values. I will discuss three of these values a bit later.

At its core, changing lenses requires us to change our questions. Instead of our preoccupation with the three questions that dominate the Western legal system—What rule or law was broken? Who "done" it? What do they deserve?—I propose that we be guided by what I'd call the "Guiding Questions of Restorative Justice":

1. Who has been hurt?
2. What are their needs?
3. Whose obligations are these?
4. What are the causes?
5. Who has a stake in this situation?
6. What is the appropriate process to involve stakeholders in an effort to address causes and put things right?

In the preceding pages I have described retributive justice in stark contrast to restorative justice. Although it does capture a key characteristic of our justice system's approach, I rarely use the term *retributive justice* for the Western legal system, as it oversimplifies and also ignores positive attributes of the system. Also, while I still believe that these comparisons can be helpful tools, I no longer speak in such clear dichotomies. Indeed, some critics have charged that these dichotomies reflect the very adversarial approach that I am seeking to critique here.

Let me note three dimensions of this.

1. Conrad Brunk's essay in *The Spiritual Roots of Restorative Justice* helped me realize that at the theoretical level, retribution and restoration actually have

much in common.[5] A primary goal of both retributive theory and restorative theory is to achieve reciprocity by evening the score. Where they differ is in what effectively will right the balance. Both acknowledge a basic moral intuition that a balance has been thrown off by the wrongdoing. Consequently, the victim deserves something and the offender owes something. Both approaches argue that there must be a proportional relationship between the act and the response. They differ, however, on the currency that will fulfill the obligations and right the balance.

Retributive theory believes that pain will vindicate, but in practice that is often counterproductive for both victim and offender. Restorative justice theory, on the other hand, argues that what truly vindicates is acknowledgment of victims' harms and needs combined with an active effort to encourage offenders to take responsibility, make right the wrongs, and address the causes of their behavior. By addressing this need for vindication in a positive way, restorative justice has the potential to affirm both victim and offender and help them transform their lives.

Painting retribution and restoration as mutually exclusive, then, cuts off possibilities for exploration of commonalities and mutual interests between those who hold these positions. Posing them as total opposites also obscures the retributive elements that may be part of a restorative approach.

---

5 Conrad Brunk, "Restorative Justice and the Philosophical Theories of Criminal Punishment," in *The Spiritual Roots of Restorative Justice*, ed. Michael L. Hadley (Albany: State University of New York Press, 2001), 31–56.

2. Rather than opposites, then, the two approaches to justice—the legal approach and the restorative approach—might be viewed as points on each end of the scale on a gauge or meter. Sometimes the gauge will be more toward the legalistic side and sometimes more toward the restorative. As I noted earlier, my work in parts of the world without well-functioning legal systems and clear human rights traditions has helped me to realize that we need well-grounded legal systems to safeguard these rights and to establish some sort of truth when it is being denied. These cannot be taken for granted. However, we also need to be clear about the failures of the Western legal approach and work in our systems and our individual cases to have processes and outcomes that are as restorative as possible. Sometimes we may go a long way toward the restorative pole, while at other times we may only move a short way. The goal ought to be to make the processes as restorative as possible within the realities of the situation, perhaps with restorative options as the default, as is the design of New Zealand's youth justice system.

The ideal, perhaps, would be a system that is restorative at its base and core, with less restorative options available when more restorative ones fail or are clearly inappropriate. In *Restorative Justice and Responsive Regulation*, Braithwaite argues that, used as a last resort, less restorative options such as deterrence and incapacitation are actually more effective in a restorative context than in a punitive one.[6]

3. Within restorative justice, I envision a continuum that ranges from fully restorative at one end to nonrestorative

6 John Braithwaite, *Restorative Justice and Response Regulation* (Oxford: Oxford University Press, 2002).

at the other. Between these two poles are a variety of options with restorative qualities. Some, for example, are partially restorative and some are potentially restorative. Some approaches—such as victim services—are absolutely essential in a restorative system but cannot alone meet all criteria of a restorative system as they cannot address offender issues completely. Other approaches, such as community service restitution programs, might be restorative if properly conceived and implemented, although most existing programs probably are not. This precision in analysis or terminology has become more important as the term *restorative justice* has become a catchword applied to a wide variety of approaches, some of which are not restorative at all.

Debate is ongoing about the adequacy—or inadequacy—of the term *restorative justice*, with criticism on at least two levels. First, as *Changing Lenses* acknowledges, *re-* words are problematic because many stakeholders and others interested in this field are not seeking to go back to a previous state of being but forward to new or better conditions. In fact, what is necessary in most cases is to find a new reality. Some have suggested that *transformative justice* might be more accurate as a term.

Those who advocate *transformative justice* also point out, with justification, that if *restorative justice* replicates the legal system's emphasis on individuals and does not address the larger, often structural, causes of offending and victimization, it will continue to perpetuate crime. They argue, then, for a transformative approach to justice that not only addresses individual wrongdoing but addresses the harms and obligations inherent in social, economic, and political systems.

In recent years, Michelle Alexander's important book, *The New Jim Crow: Mass Incarceration in the Age of Color Blindness*, has brought widespread awareness of the reality of racial disparities in the American justice system and its implication for our communities.[7] Is the restorative justice field ignoring or even replicating these patterns? Are we adequately monitoring and addressing these issues? Are we exploring ways that restorative justice might help to address this issue? Are we who are practitioners and advocates adequately aware of our own biases and complicity in all this? These are the kind of questions that will have to be addressed if restorative justice is to be truly transformative.

My own vision is that restorative justice should lead to transformative justice, but to do this, we will have to confront such questions. I acknowledge the formulation of restorative justice in *Changing Lenses* probably does not adequately address these larger structural issues.

In *Changing Lenses* I tried to explore the basic assumptions—spoken and unspoken—that underlie our understandings of crime and justice. To use a more recent term, I invited us to *reframe* our understandings. What I did not then understand, however, was the extent to which our frames or assumptions are embedded in, and shaped by, language and metaphor. Were I to start over, I would want to explore this dimension.

Changing lenses, in short, involves changing questions and changing metaphors.

IN PRACTICE

As I noted earlier, the practice of restorative justice has gone far beyond the use of victim-offender encounters in cases such as burglary. Nevertheless, although victim-offender dialogue or conferencing remains the predominant form of restorative justice practice in the U.S., two new forms of conferencing have emerged—both with roots in indigenous communities—that greatly widen the circle of involvement and

---

7 Michelle Alexander, *The New Jim Crow: Mass Incarceration in the Age of Colorblindness* (New York: New Press, 2010).

impact. Family group conferences and circles are described in chapter 9. Increasingly, however, these various forms are being blended so that the distinctions between them are less clear. What is clear is the value of expanding the number of stake-holders involved in many situations as well as the agenda of issues addressed in these settings.

One relatively new form of practice in the criminal jus-tice arena, and one that I never anticipated, is its application in death penalty cases in the U.S. Defense victim outreach (DVO)—pioneered by Tammy Krause, a former student of mine, and Mickell Branham—works in death penalty cases to provide a link between the families of murder victims and de-fense attorneys in order to help meet victim needs and reduce the trauma of the legal process. Operating from the restorative justice principles of victim needs and offender obligations, a victim liaison works with victims to identify what they need and want from the justice process that the offender and his or her attorneys can provide. Often this includes the need for gen-uine information about what happened in the crime or what is going to occur in the legal process. Surviving family members often also want offenders to acknowledge their responsibility. Sometimes work with victims actually results in plea agree-ments that address their needs, including the need for the of-fender to acknowledge responsibility. Other times the work of victim outreach specialists is limited to addressing those needs of victims that can be done within the confines of the usual legal process. Although these cases sometimes result in actual encounters between survivors and offenders, more often this is partial restorative justice, with an emphasis on providing ways for victims to be empowered, have some of their needs ad-dressed, and reduce the trauma created by the trial process. In the space of only a few years, defense victim outreach is mov-ing toward becoming the norm in federal capital cases. As de-fense attorneys learn more about the importance of victims' needs in criminal cases, its use is growing in state capital and noncapital cases as well.

In a number of California communities, restorative justice conferences are being used to keep young people out of the system entirely. Adapted from the New Zealand model, the conferences include the young person who caused the harm and family members, the person harmed and their supporters, community members, and occasionally law enforcement. By agreement with the prosecutor, facilitators are able to offer a "reverse Miranda"—that is, the process is confidential and information revealed will not be used against them in later proceedings. Consensus-based plans have four parts: to do right by one's victim, family, community, and self.[8] Recidivism rates have been remarkably low, especially for African American young men.

Restorative justice has moved far beyond criminal justice applications. As I noted earlier, schools and universities represent the fastest growing arena of application with, of course, appropriate modification of language and processes for these contexts.

My former student Barb Toews, now a professor at the University of Washington Tacoma, and architect Deanna Van Buren are collaborating to explore the relationship between restorative values and the architecture and design of space in which justice occurs.[9] Using collaborative, dialogical processes, they work within prisons and communities to identify what is needed to create safe, life-giving spaces. I would never have imagined that restorative justice would be relevant to spatial and architectural design.

---

8 Training and support is provided by the Restorative Justice Project at Impact Justice in Oakland, Calif.; sujatha baliga is currently overseeing this project.

9 Their organization is called Designing Justice+Designing Spaces. See: http://www.designingjustice.com/.

WHERE TO FROM HERE?

In chapter 11, I outline some options for incorporating restorative justice more widely. New Zealand's youth justice system suggests another option. What if the courts were not the norm, but the backup and safeguard? What if a variety of restorative options were the default, with cases going to court when defendants denied their responsibility or there were aspects of the case too complicated or difficult for, say, a restorative conference?[10] We have essentially designed a process for the worst and most difficult kinds of cases, then made that the norm. What if we realized courts were a scarce resource and also that there is real value in encouraging community engagement in addressing harms and responsibilities? A number of legal scholars are arguing that justice is best served through a collaboration of professionals and laypeople.[11]

A functioning legal system is essential. Human rights and due process must be protected. There must be a system to identify those who do wrong. Wrongful actions do need to be named and denounced. The rule of law, and the orderly progression of law, is critical. But surely we can be more restorative in its focus and function.

My dream is of a justice system that consists of collaboration between laypeople—the community—and justice professionals. In this dream, all of those involved in the justice process would be guided by restorative justice values and principles. Police, prosecutors, judges, and lawyers would ask restorative justice questions of each situation they encounter: Who has been hurt? What are their needs? How can things be made right? Who is responsible to meet these needs and obligations? Who has a stake, and how can they be involved in the resolution?

10 Braithwaite explores this further in *Responsive Regulation*.

11 See, for example, Albert W. Dzur, *Punishment, Participatory Democracy, and the Jury* (New York: Oxford University Press, 2012).

In this world, those harmed would be assisted in defining their needs and have them addressed, regardless of whether the one who caused the harm was available or able. The lawyers involved would view themselves not as gladiators but as healers and peacemakers. As Braithwaite has suggested in *Responsive Regulation,* there would be a place for incapacitation and pure deterrence, but they would be used as a last resort, after more restorative, respectful, and less coercive options were tried—and they would be carried out as restoratively as possible.[12]

A WAY OF LIFE?

Over the years I have heard many people argue that restorative justice is a way of life. Initially, I found this very puzzling: How can a conceptual framework—a very simple concept, actually, designed to respond to crime—be seen as life-changing or even as a way of life?

Eventually I concluded that restorative justice as a way of life has to do with the ethical system that restorative justice embodies. Some argue that restorative justice reflects, and taps into, some universal values, and that is why it connects with so many indigenous and religious traditions. Whether this is accurate or not (and I think it probably is), restorative justice does embody a coherent, internally consistent value system in a way that criminal justice does not.

The Western criminal justice system is intended to promote some important positive values: the rights inherent in each person, the boundaries of acceptable behavior, the importance of fairness and consistency. However, it does so in a way that is largely negative, saying, "Do this, or else." We will do to you what you have done to others; suffering requires suffering; the

---

12 For thoughts on restorative justice as a third way, see Howard Zehr, "Three Justice Orientations," *Zehr Institute for Restorative Justice* (blog), September 7, 2009, http://emu.edu/now/restorative-justice/2009/09/07/three-justice-orientations/.

penalty is a mirror image of the offense. One reason for the vast literature rationalizing the principle of punishment is that the state is empowered to inflict pain, and inflicting pain in most circumstances is seen as morally questionable.

To keep the system humane and to mitigate the suffering we cause, we are, therefore, forced to bring to bear important values from outside the ethical system of justice. We have to instruct practitioners to treat offenders humanely, for example, because a punitive and just deserts–based understanding of justice does not emphasize this value. Imported values are never as effective as values derived from within. Moreover, in itself, the punitive approach to justice does not offer us a vision of the good or of how we want to live together.

Restorative justice, on the other hand, offers an inherently positive and relatively coherent value system. It implies a vision of the good and of how we should live together. Like many indigenous and religious traditions, restorative justice is premised on the assumption that we as individuals are interconnected and that what we do matters to others and vice versa. Thus the basic principles of restorative justice, however they are articulated, suggest guidelines by which most of us want to live in everyday life. Restorative justice reminds us of the importance of relationships. It calls us to consider the impact of our behavior on others and the obligations that our actions entail. It emphasizes the dignity that we and others deserve. Perhaps, then, restorative justice does indeed suggest a way of life.

VALUES

As I noted earlier, the justice "wheel" must be surrounded by a rim of values. Three have come to be especially important to me.

RESPECT

The first is *respect*. I am convinced that issues of respect are fundamental to much offending and to the negative ways in which offenders so often experience justice. Likewise, issues of respect and disrespect play important roles in victims' trauma and recovery as well as the negative way they so often experience justice.

Restorative justice, in a word, is about respect. If we take that value seriously, seeking to profoundly respect the perspectives, needs, and worth of all involved, we will inevitably do justice restoratively.

HUMILITY

The second key value is *humility*. Within the meaning of *humility* I include its common usage, the idea of not taking undue credit. Indeed, this is an important value for restorative justice practitioners. When justice is practiced well, participants often overlook the role of the facilitator, and it is important for practitioners to be able to live with that lack of recognition.

But by *humility* I primarily mean something more basic and more difficult: a profound recognition of the limits of what we "know." A core principle of restorative justice is that it must be contextual, shaped from the ground up in a particular context. As a result, humility requires a real caution about generalizing and applying what we think we know to others' situations. Humility also requires a deep awareness of how our biographies shape our knowledge and biases. Our gender, culture, ethnicity, and personal and collective histories all profoundly shape how we know and what we know, and in ways that are often difficult to bring to consciousness. Humility calls us, then, to a deep appreciation for and openness to others' realities. Such openness is imperative in an increasingly polarized world.

Only if we are humble can we guard against a justice that, while it may seem liberating to us, becomes a burden on others—or, as has happened in so many previous "reforms," becomes a weapon that is used against people. A lesson from the birth of the modern prison haunts me. It was introduced as a reform, and incarceration had been a positive experience for some of its advocates. Yet it very soon became so brutalizing that the movement to reform prison is almost as old as the modern prison itself. Humility requires that those of us who champion restorative justice undertake an obligation to listen to our detractors, to measure our visions against realities, and to be both advocate and critic.

WONDER

The third value is *wonder*, or awe. The Western way of knowing has been deeply influenced by the philosopher Descartes. Descartes's primary epistemological approach was doubt. Doubt everything, he said, until you can find something that *is* certain; for him, the one thing that couldn't be doubted was the axiom "I think, therefore I am." This stance of doubt has strengths—indeed, I argued above that humility requires us to maintain some skepticism about what we know and do—but an overall attitude of skepticism can lead to a great deal of cynicism.

Professor Delbert Wiens began one of my college philosophy courses by acknowledging this stance in Western thought and then suggesting a corrective: The proper approach to the world, he said, is wonder. This perspective is increasingly important to me and, I believe, to the field. Wonder involves an appreciation of mystery, of ambiguity, of paradox, even of contradictions. An ability to live with the unknown, with surprises, and with the seemingly irreconcilable is essential to good restorative justice practice.

David James Duncan, in his book *My Story as Told by Water*, defines wonder like this: "wondering is unknowing, experienced as pleasure."[13] Given that, the field of restorative justice promises a great deal of pleasure! Even though the contemporary field now has more than a quarter century of experience, even though it has deep roots in our histories, we are still very early on the learning curve. There is still very much we do not know.

At the end of chapter 11, I describe restorative justice as "an indistinct destination on a necessarily long and circuitous journey." Now, several decades later, I can confidently say that, although it is still a journey with many curves, many detours, and wrong turns, the road and its destination are not as indistinct as they once were.

I believe that if we embark on this journey with respect and humility, and with an attitude of wonder, restorative justice can lead us toward the kind of world we want our children and grandchildren to inhabit.

---

13 David James Duncan, *My Story as Told by Water* (San Francisco: Sierra Club Books, 2001).

RESOURCES

Essays

Safeguarding the Restorative Justice Vision

As REFORMING VISIONS are made operational, they tend to be diverted or subverted from their original intents. Sometimes they end up serving purposes quite opposed to their original intent. This tendency is obvious in many areas, including—and some would argue, especially—in criminal justice. Restorative justice too could become something quite different than what was envisioned. Indeed, some have argued that the process is well under way.

Over the years that I have been involved in some way with restorative justice, I have struggled to understand the forces that tend to distort our visions. Such distortion may be inevitable, but it can be minimized if we understand the dynamics of the process. The following is an attempt to catalog some of the sources of this diversion or subversion as I understand them. I've organized them under three categories.

CRIMINAL JUSTICE INTERESTS

In restorative justice circles, a frequently discussed source of diversion has to do with the conflict between retributive and restorative goals. The criminal justice system is essentially retributive, seeking primarily to punish. Restorative justice, however, claims to be concerned with restoration. Can those two goals coexist, or will the larger system pressure us to share its goals? If we speak language the system understands, the language of punishment, the punitive may come to overshadow the restorative. If we refuse to speak the language of punishment, chances are that we will remain marginal, nonessential for "minor" cases.

The criminal justice process creates diversionary pressures in other ways. Criminal justice is inherently offender-oriented. The event, the case, and the principal actors are all defined in terms of the offender. The victim has little legal standing. If we work alongside and get referrals from an offender-oriented system, can we retain equal and genuine justice for victims?

A third source of pressure from the criminal justice process has to do with its own self-interests. As I have noted before, the various parts of the "system" have their own interests, and they tend to find ways to co-opt and control new concepts to fit these interests. In *Justice without Law?*, Jerome Auerbach has provided an anatomy of this process for conflict resolution processes in American history.

THE DYNAMICS OF INSTITUTIONALIZATION

For ideas to become reality, institutions need to be created. The dynamics of those institutions themselves create diversionary pressures.

Administrative considerations become important. Administration requires measurements that are easily collected, tabulated, and processed. One can, in turn, use these measurements to justify the organization's existence. With victim-offender conferences or dialogues, for instance, it is tempting to measure our value by the number of cases handled and by successful outcomes.

Outcomes such as satisfaction or reduced hostility or fear are not usual criminal justice goals and are harder to measure than more easily quantifiable ones. Consequently, we may come to emphasize restitution, which is much easier to measure. We may put pressures on mediators to finish cases quickly to maintain volume, without regard to the quality of outcome. We could turn to professional mediators. Administrative goals and measurements can easily reshape the vision.

As this implies, subsistence questions are involved. This quickly takes us to the issue of funding and funding sources. To do our good things, we have to have money. As someone has said, programs tend to end up looking like their funding sources.

Another dimension to the dynamics of institutionalization has to do with the development of staff identities and career goals. As institutions develop, people begin to look to careers within them. And they begin to make decisions about themselves and about the program with career goals in mind. The effects of this are subtle but important.

All of us look to others around us for support, for peers. Where do those of us involved in restorative justice look for our peers? As we establish ourselves, we probably begin to look for peers within criminal justice circles. That has its strengths, but it also creates pressures to conform to the values and assumptions that operate within that system.

The hired staff and the values they hold are critical. Most analyses of the subversion of reform have focused on a gradual co-optation process. The process, however, is more fundamental and begins sooner. While leaders articulate a grand vision, the staff may come from traditional criminal justice jobs and hold traditional criminal justice values. Guided by a traditional perspective instead of an alternative paradigm, they tend to do things the traditional way. If not all share alternate values, it is hard to make a real difference.

As they develop, organizations move through various stages. These stages call forth certain types of leadership, each with its own strengths and weakness. This too affects the shape of a program.

The early stages of an organization require entrepreneurs. Usually a handful of people provide leadership. Among them are visionaries, risk-takers. Creativity must be high. Ideas have to be shaped and made workable. Resources have to be found and fit together in creative ways.

People with these entrepreneurial qualities bring considerable energy, enthusiasm, and creativity to their work. Often, however, they are not managers. At some point, therefore, it is important for leadership to become more managerial to cope with the realities of maintaining an organization and program. Managers, however, often are not visionaries. They may be preoccupied with the necessities of day-to-day operations and less concerned about long-term implications, program evaluation, and dreaming. They may not like to take risks. If programs move into the managerial stage without building in prophetic and visioning functions, another potential source of diversion is created.

PROGRAM DESIGN AND OPERATION

Programs often seek to meet a variety of goals. But good operation often requires only one primary goal. Moreover, goals may be contradictory.

We found that true early on for the VOC program in Elkhart, Indiana, and recent research in England suggested the same there. The goal of diverting people from jail sometimes conflicts with the goal of reconciliation, for example. Programs begun primarily to divert from jail may come to deemphasize reconciliation and victim concerns.

As this suggests, it is easy to implement policies without examining their long-term implications, both practical and philosophical. A series of small, concrete steps, unexamined, may take us far off our path. And we may unknowingly lose our way.

Group activity: **Force field analysis.**

Make a chart with two columns. One column is headed something like "Forces encouraging a truly restorative approach." The other column is labeled "Forces resisting or encouraging co-optation and subversion of RJ." Either as a whole group or in small groups, identify the cultural, political, and social forces that belong on each side. If time, discuss strategies to counter or discourage the "subverting" forces and encourage the restorative ones.

A Restorative Justice Yardstick

1. Do victims experience justice?
   - Are there sufficient opportunities for them to tell their truth to relevant listeners?
   - Are they receiving needed compensation or restitution?
   - Is the injustice adequately acknowledged?
   - Are they sufficiently protected against further violation?
   - Does the outcome adequately reflect the severity of the offense?
   - Are they receiving adequate information about the event, the offender, and the process?

- Do they have a voice in the process?
- Is the experience of justice adequately public?
- Do they have adequate support from others?
- Are their families receiving adequate assistance and support?
- Are other needs—material, psychological, spiritual— being addressed?

2. Do offenders experience justice?
- Are they encouraged to understand and take responsibility for what they have done?
- Are misattributions challenged?
- Are they provided encouragement and opportunity to make things right?
- Are they given the opportunity to participate in the process?
- Is there encouragement toward changed behavior (repentance)?
- Is there a mechanism for monitoring or verifying changes?
- Are their own needs being addressed?
- Are their families receiving support and assistance?

3. Is the victim-offender relationship addressed?
- Is there opportunity for a meeting, if appropriate— either direct or therapeutic?
- Is there opportunity and encouragement for an exchange of information—about the event, about one another?
- Are misattributions being challenged?

4. Are community concerns being taken into account?
- Is the process and outcome sufficiently public?

- Is community protection being addressed?
- Is there need for some restitution or symbolic action for the community?
- Is the community represented in some way in the process?

5. Is the future being addressed?
   - Is there provision for solving the problems that led up to this event?
   - Is there provision for solving problems caused by this event?
   - Have future intentions been addressed?
   - Is there provision for monitoring, verifying, and troubleshooting outcomes?

Group activity: **Case study.**

Choose a case or program from your context or from the Internet and discuss to what extent it measures up to this yardstick. What could be done to make this situation or program more restorative?

Ten Ways to Live Restoratively

1. Take relationships seriously, envisioning yourself in an interconnected web of people, institutions, and the environment.

2. Try to be aware of the impact—potential as well as actual—of your actions on others and the environment.

3. When your actions negatively impact others, take responsibility by acknowledging and seeking to repair the

harm—even when you could probably get away with avoiding or denying it.

4. Treat everyone respectfully, even those you don't expect to encounter again, even those you feel don't deserve it, even those who have harmed or offended you or others.

5. Involve those affected by a decision, as much as possible, in the decision-making process.

6. View the conflicts and harms in your life as opportunities.

7. Listen, deeply and compassionately, to others, seeking to understand even if you don't agree with them. (Think about who you want to be in the latter situation rather than just being right.)

8. Engage in dialogue with others, even when what is being said is difficult, remaining open to learning from them and the encounter.

9. Be cautious about imposing your "truths" and views on other people and situations.

10. Sensitively confront everyday injustices including sexism, racism, and classism.

Group activity: **Discussion.**

Discuss ways that taking these seriously would affect our personal and social lives. Are there suggestions for revisions or additions?

Group Study and Teaching Suggestions

THE FOLLOWING STUDY QUESTIONS and activity ideas are intended to provide help for those who wish to use this book in a group study setting. More activity ideas are provided in the next section.[1]

CHAPTER 1 A VIGNETTE
Questions

1. Think about an issue or event on which your perspective has changed. What initiated your change of perspective? How does changing lenses on a particular issue begin?

2. "The [criminal justice] process neglects victims while failing to meet its expressed goals of holding offenders accountable and deterring crime." What do you think of this claim?

---

1 For additional discussion and activity ideas, see also https://good books.com/assets/media/pdf/1356125331.9781561483761.pdf.

3. Reread "The Story" in chapter 1. Talk about what headlines might appear on news articles about this event. Then talk about ways that the media transforms events.

CHAPTER 2 **THE VICTIM**
Questions

1. Suppose you came home to find that your home had been broken into and vandalized. Valuable property, including several family heirlooms, are gone, and an ax was obviously used to get in. How would you feel? How would it affect you? What questions would you have? What would you need?

2. Have you known crime victims personally? Have you been victimized yourself? How did you react? How did you feel?

3. What do you believe should have happened in the case outlined in part 1, from the victim's perspective?

4. Do you agree that anger is a natural part of healing and that its expression should be encouraged? How do you personally respond to someone who is hurt and angry?

5. Charlotte Hullinger lists four types of helpers (see footnote 2). What are the strengths and weaknesses of each? Which are you? What can you do to be a positive helper?

6. Some argue that retribution is an inherent human need. They say if it is not fulfilled by government action, it will be taken on by individuals. Others argue that it is learned. Some argue that it represents a need that is better filled through other processes such as restitution and forgiveness. What do you think?

7. What are some of the ways we tend to blame victims? Why do we do so?

8. Discuss the six questions for healing (see "The Recovery Process"). What will it take to answer each? Who can do it?

9. In the preface, the author notes concerns about terminology. In what ways might the term *victim* be problematic?

Activities

1. On a board or flip chart, list a series of victim-related words such as these:

   - victim
   - burglary
   - court
   - justice
   - prosecutor
   - revenge
   - restitution

   Go through the list, having people call out whatever associations or ideas come to mind for each word. Write these down. After the list is complete, analyze these associations together.

2. Invite a victim or victim-assistance worker to talk about his or her experience. Invite a lawyer, prosecutor, or judge to talk. What are the victim's rights? What is the victim's usual role? How is he or she usually treated? You might also invite a crime victim to share in this session.

CHAPTER 3 **THE OFFENDER**
Questions

1. What do you think of the outcome for the offender in this case? If you were asked to develop an alternate proposal, what would you propose?

2. What does the author suggest about concepts of self-worth and personal power and their relationships to offending? Do you agree? (See also chapter 4.)

3. What are the various nonprison sentences typically used in today's society? (Examples may include community service, probation, treatment, halfway houses, and restitution.) What are the advantages and disadvantages of each? What does each attempt to accomplish? To what extent does each seek to punish?

4. What, if any, is the appropriate purpose and place of prison in our legal system?

5. How does the author define the term *accountability*? How does this square with your own concept? Should accountability be a central goal of justice, and if so, how should it be obtained?

6. Is it helpful to view offenders as people who have themselves been violated? To what extent does their behavior grow out of abuse at home or restricted educational and employment opportunities? How should this affect their responsibility? How does it affect society's responsibility?

7. In the preface, the author notes concerns about terminology. In what ways might the term *offender* be problematic?

Activities

1. As in the suggestions for chapter 2, list a series of words on the board. Have the group call out their associations. After they have run out of ideas, analyze their responses.

   Suggested words: revenge, offender, criminal, prison, judge, punishment, court

2. Invite a judge or probation officer to talk about how sentencing recommendations and decisions are made.

3. Invite a counselor who works with offenders to discuss common *misattributions* and *exculpatory strategies*—stereotypes and rationalizations used to justify and rationalize wrongful behavior.

CHAPTER 4 SOME COMMON THEMES

Questions

1. What do repentance and forgiveness mean to you?

2. What does the author mean by "forgiveness is a gift; it should not be made into a burden"? Does this fit your understanding of forgiveness?

3. What is the role of repentance and forgiveness in the process of moving from victim to survivor? Can this recovery happen without forgiveness? How?

4. The author argues that certain preconditions facilitate forgiveness. What are they? Do you agree? Is this biblical?

5. Discuss ways the church could use rituals of lament and rituals of reordering (e.g., rituals of forgiveness and reconciliation) with victims and offenders.

6. What are the requirements for punishment to be just? To be effective?

7. The author suggests that wrongful behavior is often rooted in self-hate more fundamentally than in self-love. Is this true? If so, how does that affect our approaches to healing and rehabilitation?

8. What can we do as individuals, society, and the church to demystify crime?

Activities

1. Examine news clippings of crime coverage from a local paper. List and discuss ways news coverage of crime encourages fear as well as stereotypes and misconceptions about crime, victims, offenders, officials, and the justice process.

2. Invite a reporter who covers crime to talk to your group about how this news is obtained and reported.

CHAPTER 5 **RETRIBUTIVE JUSTICE**
Questions

1. In what ways does our legal system encourage a *them* and *us* mentality? (And who are *them* and *us*?) What are the consequences?

2. Define *punishment*. Is the implied definition of *punishment* as "pain, intended as pain," adequate?

3. Does punishment satisfy victims? Offenders? What is your own experience with punishment?

4. How do the following terms relate to one another: punishment, retribution, vengeance, revenge?

5. Examine your own tendencies and experiences with your friends, your spouse, or your children. When you feel wronged, is yours basically a tit-for-tat perspective, a problem-solving perspective, or do you take some other approach?

6. Examine your own assumptions about wrongdoing. Do you tend to define it in terms of breaking rules or in terms of consequences and harm? What are the consequences of those two perspectives?

7. Did you realize before reading this chapter that the state, not the individual, is the legal victim of a crime? What are some of the implications for you if you were (or have been) a victim?

Activities

1. Make up a case. Ask a variety of criminal justice officials (judges, probation officers, lawyers, prosecutors) to say what they think should be the sentence or outcome. Report back and compare the results.

2. Continuum activity: Ask the group to take their places along a line in the room according to their position on contrasting statements such as those listed below. Participants may place themselves at the far end of the continuum, or they may place themselves anywhere on the continuum between the two poles. While they are there, ask them to explain why they placed themselves where they did.

   Sample statements (make your own):

   a. Punishment is natural and inherent vs. punishment is learned.

   b. Punishment is a necessary part of justice vs. punishment should be avoided.

 c. I find myself most closely aware of, or concerned about, victims vs. I find myself most closely aware of, or concerned about, offenders.

CHAPTER 6 **JUSTICE AS PARADIGM**

Questions

1. What does the author mean by *paradigm*?

2. What is it about crime that makes us view and treat it differently from other wrongs and harms? Should we view and treat it differently? If so, where would we draw the line between them?

3. What are some of the ways civil law differs from criminal law? What decides whether a situation will be treated as civil or criminal?

4. What nonlegal means of resolving harms and conflicts do we use in our everyday lives and in society as a whole? Give examples from your own experience.

5. What signs, if any, are there that we may be on the verge of a shift in justice paradigms? (In other words, what are some of the signs of dysfunction or crisis?)

6. Evaluate current criminal justice reforms (e.g., victim assistance, intensive probation, private prisons, electronic monitoring, community service). To what extent do they point in new directions? To what extent are they simply patches in the paradigm?

Activity

 Suppose two children get into a fight at school and one knocks a tooth from the other. This could be treated as a problem requiring punishment, a conflict needing resolution, or a damage requiring restitution. It could be seen as something to settle within the school, as a criminal case, or it could be taken to civil court. All these and other responses can and do occur in such situations.

Discuss what governs the response to such a situation. What are the likely consequences of each? Which is likely to be most satisfactory and why? How does the response chosen affect the eventual understanding of the original fight?

CHAPTER 7 **COMMUNITY JUSTICE: THE HISTORICAL ALTERNATIVE**
Questions

1. The author notes the importance of *moral vindication* when wrong has been committed. What does this mean? Is it important? What are some of the ways this has happened in the past? How does it happen today? How could it happen in an improved system?

2. In what ways might Christian theology have served to underpin the emerging retributive understanding of crime?

3. In what ways does modern punishment try to reach the soul, as Michael Foucault puts it, and not just the body?

4. What has been positive and what has been negative about the legal revolution?

5. In what ways does punishment serve a symbolic role today?

CHAPTER 8 **COVENANT JUSTICE: THE BIBLICAL ALTERNATIVE**
Questions

1. The author argues that the law in the Old Testament had a different meaning and function than law today. What are some of the differences? What are the implications?

2. Test the basic tenets of your faith against the concept of shalom. Does it change anything if you try to base your thinking in a vision of shalom?

3. What has been your assumption in the past about the role and meaning of "eye for an eye"? Has your understanding changed? If so, how?

4. Our understandings of biblical justice may ultimately rest on our images of God. For some, the image of God as a loving parent is predominant. Others see God first of all as a stern judge. What other possibilities are there? What is your predominant image?

5. What is the relationship between shalom justice and tit-for-tat justice in the Old Testament? How does our concept of tit for tat or reciprocity change if it is rooted in shalom?

6. How does the biblical concept of justice square with your own understandings? Are the comparisons with modern justice valid?

7. What would happen if we measured justice by its fruits (i.e., by the outcome rather than by the process)? What are the possible benefits and dangers?

8. What happens to our understandings of the Ten Commandments and the Sermon on the Mount if we treat them as invitations and promises more than prohibitions and prescriptions? Does this seem an appropriate way to understand them?

9. If we take shalom seriously as a goal and vision, can we continue to treat criminal justice without addressing other justice issues? If not, what are the implications?

10. Modern justice is usually imaged as a blindfolded goddess holding a scales. What are the meanings of this

image? In what ways is this a healthy image? In what ways might it be a dangerous image? What might be an appropriate image for restorative justice?

Activities

1. Read and discuss Psalm 103. What vision of justice emerges here? How does it relate to other, more retributive, themes in the Old Testament? (You may also wish to examine Leviticus 26 and Deuteronomy 4.)

2. Outline a particular case taken from the newspaper. Examine what was done with it against the biblical conception of justice. Now discuss what might have been done with such a situation.

CHAPTER 9 **VORP AND BEYOND: EMERGING PRACTICES**

Questions

1. What are some potential benefits of the VORP/VOC approach? What are some potential problems?

2. If you were a victim (or offender) contemplating participation in VOC or one of the other practices mentioned here, what potential benefits might you see for yourself? What would be your worries? What would be the factors that might make you decide to participate or not?

3. What should be the one primary goal for VOC? What other goals might be appropriate? Which would not?

4. Should reconciliation be a goal of VOC, and what would that mean in practice? How would it be measured?

5. Can you think of other ways this approach might be used in our society (e.g., outside criminal justice)?

6. How can and should the church be involved in VOC? What are the possibilities and responsibilities of the church here? What form should this involvement take?

Activity

If you are in a community that has a restorative justice program, invite a staff member, volunteer mediator, victim, or offender from the program to talk with your group.

CHAPTER 10 **A RESTORATIVE LENS**
Questions

1. Where do traditional goals of criminal justice—such as incapacitation, deterrence, and rehabilitation—fit in a restorative model? Do they fit in a restorative framework?

2. What about so-called victimless crimes? Do such offenses exist? How should they be dealt with in a restorative way?

3. What should the role of the community be? How can this role be made concrete? Who is the community anyway?

4. What do you make of the author's contention that the victim's needs should be the starting point but that offender's needs are of equal concern? Is this appropriate? Can it work?

5. The author argues that retributive justice begins with guilt and rights, but that a restorative model begins with needs and obligations. What are the implications of these two starting points?

6. A justice model that takes victim and offender needs seriously and gives them more participation would result in outcomes that were quite varied. Traditional

expectations of uniformity of outcome might be violated. What are the implications of this? How do you see this?

7. Discuss the term *vindication*. What is its biblical meaning? (See, e.g., Psalm 103:6.) What does it mean to you? What might it mean for victims?

8. Given the needs that have been identified here, in what ways can the church assist in the healing of victims and offenders?

9. The author argues that the present system exaggerates the public dimensions and minimizes the private dimensions of crime. What are the public dimensions of crime, and how should they be addressed within a restorative framework?

10. What should be the role of coercion in a restorative model? Should victims be coerced to participate? Should offenders? What are the implications?

11. Think of justice as a communication system designed to send various messages. What messages does the present system seek to send, and to whom? What messages does it actually send? What messages would a restorative system need to send, and how might it do this?

12. What are some of the necessary rituals in the healing and justice process? When and where should they occur? How could the church be helpful in this?

13. Is there a legitimate role for punishment? If so, in what circumstances and to what end? How can its misuse be minimized?

Activity

Take a case example. Design a restorative process and outcome for the case. Keep in mind the four dimensions of harm as well as key elements of the restorative model. When done, test your outcome against the "Restorative Justice Yardstick" (pp. 255–56) or develop a yardstick of your own.

Think carefully about where to start. What are the primary needs that must be met? Who can best decide what they are and how they should be met? What are the primary goals and concerns that need to be addressed in your response?

Now look at what normally happens in such a case. (Or, if using an actual case, examine what the actual outcome was.)

CHAPTER 11 IMPLEMENTING A RESTORATIVE SYSTEM
Questions

1. What is the proper role of the state in the justice process? How would it change in a restorative model?

2. What are some of the political and institutional dynamics that might affect possibilities for a shift in our justice paradigm? What are the possibilities for an actual paradigm shift?

3. To what extent does the church practice restorative justice internally? How could it be more restorative?

4. Will you respond differently to crime and other harms or conflicts now that you have read this book? In what ways?

CHAPTER 12 REFLECTIONS TWENTY-FIVE YEARS LATER
Questions

1. Does the concept of restorative justice resonate with your own family, cultural, or religious traditions? In what ways? And in what ways is it not in tune with your experience and traditions?

2. Does the discussion of shame ring true? How do shame, humiliation, honor, and respect play out in our personal and social lives?

3. Who is your community, and how do you imagine them being involved in difficult situations? How do you define community?

4. Discuss the differences and similarities between restoration and retribution.

5. Can restorative justice lead to transformative justice? Why or why not?

6. Think of some approaches to wrongdoing in your community. Where do they fit on a restorative justice continuum?

7. The author lists a number of values that underlie restorative justice. What other values are important?

8. What would it look like if we tried to make restorative justice a way of life? (See "Ten Ways to Live Restoratively" on p. 257).

Activity

Apply the "Guiding Questions of Restorative Justice" (p. 237) to a real or imagined situation. How does the process and outcome differ when one applies conventional justice questions: What rules or laws were broken? Who did it? What do they deserve? (Option: divide into two groups, one applying restorative justice questions, the other applying the other, more common, set of questions.)

Additional Group Exercises

Defining Justice

Eric Gilman, with Matthew Hartman

Objective: To provide an opportunity for participants to reflect upon and voice the values that they believe define justice for victims, offenders, and the community.[1]

Number of Participants: 2+

Materials:
- Flip chart and markers
- Tape to hang flip chart pages

Time: 1–1½ hours

---

1 Many of my former graduate students at the Center for Justice and Peacebuilding, Eastern Mennonite University, are gifted trainers and educators. I invited a few of them to submit some favorite activities for this edition. Unfortunately, due to space considerations, it was not possible to include all that were offered.

Introduction: This exercise is best done as the starting point in the process of studying restorative justice concepts, as it elicits learners' own intuitive responses to some of the basic questions restorative justice aims to address.

Description:

1. Share a story of crime from a neutral perspective. Choose a scenario that is neither highly violent nor too minor to elicit serious reflection. Provide some context details regarding the offender (for example, if using a burglary scenario, you might explain that the offender's intent for the burglary was to sell the goods for money to use toward a drug addiction).

2. Tell learners: "As you are listening to the following story, I want you to hear it as if it is something that happened in your community. Most likely you know, or know of, the people you'll be hearing about. You can define your community in any number of ways, but make sure it represents the people, groups, or organizations with whom you find a sense of belonging."

3. After finishing the story, give participants a few minutes to think about how they would feel, how different members of their community might react, how the justice system might respond, and who all might be impacted in some way.

4. Present the following questions as different ways of articulating the same question, allowing the participants time to reflect and write down their answers. Elicit participants' responses and write answers on a sheet of flip chart paper labeled "Victim."

When the justice system's response to this crime is complete, what outcome would you want for the victim? What should have happened? What are you looking for? What do you want for the victim to have experienced?

5. Use the same questions to elicit participants' thoughts about the offender, then the community. Write answers on separate sheets of flip chart paper labeled by stakeholder ("Offender"; "Community").

6. Facilitate a closing discussion by explaining to the group that the questions they have just been asking are the same basic questions restorative justice asks. At its heart, restorative justice asks: As a community, how do we want to respond to crime, and what are the goals or hoped for results of those responses? Additional questions you can ask as you debrief:

   a. What are you noticing about these lists?
   b. Is what you have articulated here what we get from our current criminal justice system? If not, why do you think that might be?
   c. Do you believe your lists look different than the lists others in your community might make? What leads you to that belief?

Note: When discussing these questions with participants, it's important to note that this exercise has been done hundreds of times, with very diverse groups—conservative, liberal, young, old, ethnically diverse, and so forth—with the lists almost identically reflecting each other. Hence the question: If this is what we (meaning, our communities) want, why aren't we getting it?

Graffiti-Be-Gone

Catherine Bargen[2]

Objective: To provide an experiential example of a punishment approach and a restorative approach in a school discipline context. This exercise also touches on how each approach can affect trust and potential for relationship-building.

Number of Participants: 4–100+

Materials: None required. However, the facilitator can copy or create printable forms describing the scenario for those role-playing "student" and those role-playing "principal," as some learners prefer to read a scenario and have responses prepared, rather than hear instructions verbally. (See "Information to Distribute to Participants" at the end of this exercise.)

Time: Approximately 20–30 minutes including time for debriefing.

Introduction: This exercise is effective at helping people feel the experiences of punitive and restorative approaches to wrongdoing. Accordingly, this exercise can be particularly fun and informative in mixed groups of adults and youth, with the youth playing the role of disciplinarian and the adults in the role of the student. That said, the exercise can work well and be enlightening for any type of group. It is most effective early on in a course of study, before philosophical concepts of punitive and restorative justice have been identified, so that learners have a felt experience to reference.

---

2 *In partnership with Fraser Region Community Justice Initiatives Association and Langley (B.C.) School District.*

278 ··· CHANGING LENSES

Description:

1. Divide learners into two groups. You may decide in advance how you want to divide them (e.g., all adults in one group, all youth in another), or randomly divide the groups in two. Group one is the "students"; group two is the "school principals."

2. Ask the "students" group to leave the room and wait out in the hallway or another suitable place apart from the main room. Tell them you will be with them in a moment.

3. Explain to the remaining "school principals" group that there will be three rounds in the following role play.

   a. Round 1, Punitive Approach: In the first round they will use a punitive approach with the students.

   b. Round 2, Restorative Approach: In the second round, they each will be matched with a new student and use a restorative approach.

   c. Round 3, Restorative Approach: In the third round, each principal will be back with the original student, but this time taking a restorative approach.

   Both student and principal groups will work with the same scenario: A student has committed graffiti on the school wall. (Ideas for questions and statements to use in each round are included on the following pages. If possible, make copies of these questions and statements for principals to refer to during the role play. Otherwise, give them some sample questions for each round that they can jot down.)

4. Have each principal arrange an empty chair so a student can sit facing him/her.

5. Now attend to the awaiting student group. Simply explain to them that in the role play each of them is a student who has been caught for committing graffiti on a school wall. They feel their graffiti was artistic and therefore not harming anyone. However, after some reflection they do think that it was probably a poor choice to graffiti on the school and that there could have been other ways and other places to express themselves. The role play will involve the students meeting with the principal to determine next steps.

6. Let the students enter the room and sit across from the principals. If there is an odd number, assign two students to one of the principals, or vice versa.

7. Tell the groups to proceed with Round 1 (principals taking the lead). Allow 5 minutes.

8. Tell the students to rotate one principal to the left. Proceed with Round 2 (again, principals taking the lead). Allow 5 minutes.

9. Tell the students to return to their original principal. Proceed with Round 3 with principals taking the lead. Allow 5 minutes.

10. Call time and have everyone return to their seats to debrief with any of the following questions:

    a. For "students": How did Round 1 feel? Round 2? Round 3? What impact did each approach have on your ability to take responsibility for your actions? How was the problem solved, if at all? What did you learn from being in the student role?

    b. For "principals": How did Round 1 feel? Round 2? Round 3? What impact did you notice on how the students were able to take responsibility for their

actions? How was the problem solved, if at all?
What did you learn from being in the principal
role?

c. Why did we have a Round 3? How does that con-
nect to real life and building trust?

d. How does this exercise get at power dynamics?

e. Did this exercise help you understand the importance of relationship-building? How?

f. How does this exercise help you understand punitive and restorative approaches?

g. Is this exercise realistic or unrealistic? Why or why
not?

h. What are the benefits and challenges of each
approach?

i. Are *punitive* and *restorative* the correct names for
these approaches?

INFORMATION TO DISTRIBUTE TO PARTICIPANTS:

For learners in the role of "student"

Scenario: A student has been caught for doing graffiti on an
outside wall of a school. The graffiti was not offensive in nature; however, it is an obvious location and will need to be
removed.

Student: You have been caught for doing graffiti on the wall.
You feel your graffiti was artistic and therefore not harming
anyone. However, after some careful consideration you do recognize that it was a poor choice to graffiti on the school wall
and that there could have been other ways and other places to
express yourself.

For learners in the role of "principal"

Scenario: A student has been caught for doing graffiti on an outside wall of a school. The graffiti was not offensive in nature; however, it is in an obvious location and will need to be removed.

Round 1:

Using a *punitive approach*, have a meeting with a student who has been caught for doing graffiti on an outside wall of your school. There was no offensive writing and the graffiti was apparently "artistic." However, you want to send a strong message through punishment.

Types of things to say:

a. Why did you do this?! (Don't wait for the answer ... cut them off!)

b. Don't you know that it's wrong to write on property that is not yours?

c. Do you really think graffiti is art?

d. You realize I have to suspend you, don't you?

e. What do you think your fellow students will think of you now? This is bringing shame to their school!

f. We may involve the police, you know.

g. Parents are asking questions regarding who could have done such a thing. What am I supposed to tell them?

h. You are going to have to pay to get this wall cleaned! Graffiti costs the school district $300,000 per year!

i. We are all very disappointed in you. We expect more from our students.

Round 2:

Using a *restorative approach*, ask questions that will help the student reflect on what they have done without judging them. Be open and willing to listen to their side. Be clear about the impact of uninvited graffiti on the school. Encourage them to think about how they will be accountable for their actions.

Types of questions to consider:

    a. So tell me what happened?

    b. What did you draw on the school wall?

    c. What was going on in your mind while you were doing it?

    d. What do you think about it now?

    e. How do you think this will affect your friends or other schoolmates?

    f. As you know, our school is not prepared to keep uninvited graffiti on the wall. So, what should we do about this wall? How will you help make things right?

    g. Where else could we have you express your feelings and artistic ability at school?

Round 3:

You are back with your original student, but this time you apologize for the first time you met and ask the student if he or she is willing to start over and work things out together. You will now use the *restorative approach* with this student to see if you can come to a solution about this graffiti problem.

Types of questions to consider: See Round 2.

Mantles of Restorative Justice and Criminal Justice

Jef From

Objective: To explore the strengths and challenges of the restorative justice and criminal justice systems.[3]

Number of Participants: 2–22

Time: 45 minutes

Materials:
- Flip chart paper and markers
- Lengths of fabric (one for each small group; see below, step 4)
- Optional: Prewritten interview questions (see below, step 5)

Introduction: This exercise requires some prior knowledge of the restorative justice and criminal justice systems. (Some people will have more knowledge of one or the other, and that should provide balance in the groups.) See chapters 10 and 12 for a related discussion of retributive versus restorative justice, but note this caveat: though such comparison is useful for exploring concepts, setting up too stark of a dichotomy can be unhelpful. As this exercise points out, the criminal and restorative justice approaches each have strengths and weaknesses, and any pursuit of justice likely involves aspects of both systems and approaches.

---

3 Adapted from "Mantles of Restorative Justice and Criminal Justice," *Training Activities Used in Defense Initiated Victim Outreach Training* (Council for Restorative Justice, 2009), 37–38.

Description:

1. Break the participants into an even number of small groups; then, make sure each group is paired with another. One group in each pair is to discuss and list the strengths of restorative justice (RJ); the other group in each pair is to do the same for the criminal justice system (CJS). Be sure that the participants understand that the lists of strengths should reflect how RJ or the CJS meet the needs of victims, offenders/defendants, and the community.

2. Ask each group to identify one member to be a scribe (to write the group's list of strengths on flip chart paper) and a spokesperson (to present the list to the whole group). The rest of the group should come up with ways they will support the spokesperson when she or he is presenting (e.g., act as a cheerleading squad, hold up signs that say "We Love RJ," stand next to the presenter). Try to create an atmosphere of playful competition.

3. Allow 25 minutes for each group to make their lists.

4. Bring the groups back together for presenting. As facilitator, ask the spokesperson from each group to step forward and, very ceremoniously (with farcical undertones), drape each spokesperson with a piece of fabric. These pieces of fabric are the "mantles" of RJ and the CJS.

5. Ask one spokesperson to present first. Encourage this spokesperson's group to show support. When this person has finished presenting, facilitate an interview of the spokesperson. The interview questions you choose should point out some of the weaknesses in the spokesperson's presentation. Another participant can be asked

to represent and interview the spokesperson from the perspective of a victim. Group members should continue to show support for their spokesperson throughout the interview. This portion of the activity should take twenty minutes for each pair of groups: five minutes for each group to present and five minutes interviews with each spokesperson.

6. Optional: To debrief, post the flip chart lists from each group on a wall in the room. Ask participants to compare the various lists and discuss outcomes.

Image Theater

Adapted by Jef From

Objectives:
*   To use body sculpture to express thoughts and feelings.[4]
*   To help participants focus and center upon an issue or theme.

Number of Participants: 1–22

Time: 10–15 minutes (or 20–30 minutes if using Part I below)

---

4 Adapted from "Complete the Image," and "Image," in *Training Activities Used in Defense Initiated Victim Outreach Training* (Council for Restorative Justice, 2009), 32–33. Originally from Augusto Boal, *Theatre of the Oppressed.* C. McBride and M. McBride, trans. (New York: Urizen Books, 1979), 174–80.

Introduction: This activity invites participants to use their bodies to sculpt images around a theme or issue. The images elicited allow participants to experience and embody restorative justice concepts or more deeply explore the use of metaphors in harm and conflict. By drawing out emotions, image theater also signals restorative justice's aim to help people work through or with their emotions and holistically put things right in the context of interconnected relationships. This contrasts with the modus operandi of the criminal justice system, which tends to break harm and restitution into tangible units.

Description:

Part I: Complete the Image

If the majority of participants have never done image theater, or if you sense some resistance to participation—or if you simply want to get the creative juices flowing before delving into deeper concepts—warm up with this sequence before continuing to Part II.

1. Ask the participants to pair up. Have them shake hands with each other, then freeze. Direct them to identify one member of the pair as Actor A and one as Actor B.

2. Direct Actor B to stay frozen with her/his hand extended in a handshake, while A releases from the handshake and interacts with B's frozen position in a new way (e.g., A could put her/his head in B's hand).

3. Next, direct A to stay frozen in that new position while B steps away and interacts with A in a new way. Ask them to continue freezing and unfreezing.

4. You can then direct the pairs to form groups of four, with A, B, C, and D taking turns freezing and moving to interact in new ways.

5. Eventually you can bring the participants into groups of eight, or into one large group, with one person at a time moving and interacting.

6. Debrief with questions such as:

    a. What did you notice?

    b. What changed as you moved from being a pair, to a group of four, to a group of eight?

    c. What were the themes and/or story lines you observed?

Part II: Image Theater

1. Ask the participants to stand in a circle.

2. As the facilitator, step into the middle of the circle and form an "image" (e.g., sit on the floor, pull your knees to your chest, and look down toward the ground). Then ask the question, "What do you see?"

3. Allow participants time to offer and explore their perspectives. (Answers usually include feelings, thoughts, and the basic observation, "a person on the floor with their knees pulled to their chest.")

4. After a minute or two, tell the participants you are going to change the image slightly. (Model the same image as before, but now, instead of looking at the floor, look up.) Again, ask participants, "What do you see?"

5. Next, select a theme that refers to what you are discussing in the class session (e.g., the victim/offender experience, a vision of shalom, harm, punishment, restoration, needs and obligations).

6. If the group is small, ask the participants to work as a full group to form an image around that theme. If the

group is larger, ask them to split up into smaller groups to develop an image to present to the larger group.

7. When images are formed, ask participants to reflect on the following questions:
   a. What do you see?
   b. If this person were talking, what might he or she say?
   c. What are some of the sounds you think might be coming from this image?
   d. What would you like to change about this image?
   e. What would you like to add to this image?
   f. What would you like to take away from this image?

8. As facilitator, you may ask different people in the image to give a monologue. Or, if applicable, ask members of the audience to interact with the image and build upon it.

Restorative Justice: Rebuilding the Web of Relationships

Barb Toews, with Melissa Crabbe and Danny Malec

Objectives:
- To explore the impact of crime on offenders, victims, their communities of care, and the wider community.
- To consider the ways in which the dominant approach to justice affects interpersonal and community relationships.
- To visually and experientially define restorative justice.

Number of Participants: 10–24

Materials:
- Flip chart and markers
- Nametags: Nametags without a border are ideal for the way they increase the space in which participants can write.
- Markers: One for each participant. Thin-tipped are best.
- Yarn: One skein each of red, blue, and purple (or three other different colors) and one skein of variegated yarn with red, blue, and purple hues in it (or skein with the single colors that have been chosen). This yarn should be thin enough to rip apart by hand. If it isn't, scissors will be needed for the group exercise. Depending on skein size, more than one skein of each color may be needed.
- A community crime scenario with unique roles for each participant to play
- A community crime newsflash
- Supporting documents for the scenario

Time: 1½ hours minimum (2–2½ is ideal; depends on size of the group)

Introduction:
To prepare the yarn: From each of the single color skeins, cut strands of yarn that are 12–18 inches in length. Cut eight to ten strands of each color for each participant. Bundle the strands so each bundle has eight to ten strands of each color. Create a ball of yarn from the variegated skein, leaving one end free and easy to find.

To prepare role plays: Consider a crime(s) that has occurred in your community and all the people who were affected by it. Create a scenario in which each participant can take on a role within the community. Describe these roles in one or two paragraphs. Include these roles: offender, specific offender family members and friends, victim(s), victim family members and friends, neighbors, faith leaders, business leaders, educators, specific community members, law enforcement, justice professionals (e.g., attorneys), and government leaders. Each role should include the following: a description of the person; their relationship to the crime and other people impacted; their feelings related to what happened; and their ideas for how to do justice. Across all the roles, there should be diverse responses and perspectives, just as there are in any real-life community. Feel free to use the real-life crime as just the starting point for the scenario, and to deepen the scenario by adding additional crimes and events to raise questions or tensions. Ensure that each role is given a label to identify who the person is (e.g., offender, victim). You can assign each role a gender-neutral name or let the participants chose their own names. Print out two lists of the roles—one list for you, and one list that you can cut into slips of paper (one role per slip of paper) so participants can select their roles.

Preparing the community crime newsflash: The activity begins with all participants hearing a newsflash that summarizes the crime and events happening in the community. It also identifies who the players are in the community and what they have done or said. It may be helpful to imagine that a news reporter is giving a report. Write this newsflash in advance of the training.

Preparing the supporting documents to organize the scenario:
If the group is large, it can quickly become difficult to keep
all the roles and perspectives organized in your head. Create
a key that includes the role label (e.g., offender, mayor) and
the corresponding role name, if appropriate (e.g., Jerry, Sam).
It is worthwhile to plan in advance which roles will not be
used if the number of participants changes at the last minute.
Depending on how complex the connections are, you may also
want to create a diagram of the relationships among the roles.

Prior to starting:
- To each single color of yarn, assign a *strength of relationship*. For instance, red represents a strong relationship, purple represents a weak relationship, and blue
  represents a moderate relationship that is neither
  strong nor weak. Write a key on the flip chart so that
  strong is written in red, *moderate* is written in blue, and
  weak is written in purple. Display so every participant
  can see the list.
- On the flip chart, write out a list of the roles using the
  role labels (e.g., offender, victim) and name, if assigned
  in advance. Display so every participant can see the list.
- Set up the room so that there is some space for people
  to mingle and move around. Also, create a space in
  which participants can stand in a circle.
- Give each participant a nametag, thin-tipped marker,
  and bundle of yarn. These can be put at each person's
  seat prior to starting.

Description:
1. Introduce participants to the idea that they are now part
   of a community in which a crime(s) has occurred and
   that they will be taking on roles of various people within

that community. Introduce participants to the types of roles by reviewing the list written on the flip chart.

2. Hand out the descriptions of individual roles by either letting each participant select blindly from the stack of roles or by handing each participant a role from the top of the stack. Give participants a few minutes to read their roles and, if necessary, to give themselves a name and write it on the top of the nametag. Note: the name cannot take up the whole nametag, as participants will be writing more on it later.

3. Read each role that is written on the flip chart and have participants raise their hands to identify which role they are and give their role name, if appropriate. This is a preliminary way to see who is who in the community.

4. Read the newsflash to the group. Ask that each time you say their role label or name, individuals raise their hands to identify themselves to the group. This is another way for them to become familiar with who is who in the community.

5. Ask participants (in role) to think about the following questions and write brief responses on their nametags:

   a. What is a word that describes how you feel about what is going on the community?

   b. What is a value that you hold dear when it comes to justice?

6. Using a circle process (see pp. 301–4 for detailed instructions), invite participants to introduce themselves, their perspectives and feelings about what has been happening, and the value they hold dear to the rest of the group. After one full circle, open it up for people to respond to and ask questions of each other. This open discussion should not last longer than five or ten minutes. If you

are short on time, the open discussion is not a necessity for the activity.

7. Give the instructions listed below for the activity that will follow, which consists of mingling and exchanging strands of yarn:

   a. Introduce participants to the yarn bundles and the meaning of each color, using the key on the newsprint. Ask participants to determine for themselves what *strong*, *weak*, and *moderate* mean to them, individually. Later, they will discuss their definitions with the group.

   b. Explain that participants, in role, are going to mingle with each other and exchange strands of yarn based on how they feel about that relationship. When exchanging strands, each person will tell the other person why that particular strand is being given. For instance, the faith leader may give the offender a purple/weak strand because she is disappointed in the offender. The offender may give the faith leader a red/strong strand because he has always appreciated how the faith leader greets him on the street. Note: When exchanging strands, people do not need to agree on the strength of the relationship. As in the example here, people can give each other differently colored strands.

   c. Participants will need to keep the strands that they have to give away separate from the ones they get from others. They can put the strands they get from others in a pocket or over their shoulders while keeping the other ones in their hands.

   d. They will have approximately eight to ten minutes to mingle. After this time, you will all gather as a group to discuss what they learned.

8. Invite participants to mingle and exchange strands. Keep time.

9. After eight to ten minutes, ask the participants to return to their seats and take out all the strands that they received. Facilitate a large group discussion about their experiences exchanging strands. Be sure to inquire specifically about the experiences of the victim and offender in the scenario. Sample questions include:

   a. How did you define *strong*, *weak*, and *moderate* relationships?
   b. What are your reactions to the strands you have and the people who gave them to you?
   c. What interactions and strands surprised you?

10. After some discussion, invite participants to stand in a circle for the purpose of continuing to explore the community relationships in the context of restorative justice. As the facilitator, stand in the circle along with participants, holding the ball of variegated yarn.

11. Give participants instructions for the next phase:

   a. Participants will reflect on what they heard during the mingling and the debriefing discussion and consider three questions, in role:
      i. How are you feeling now, after this mingling and conversation?
      ii. What value do you consider important for this community?
      iii. Which person in the circle is most important to you for working through the crime(s) and community relationships?
   b. Participants will share their responses, one by one. As they do this, they will toss the yarn ball to the person who they have decided is most important.

Prior to tossing the ball, however, each person will hold onto the end of the yarn tail so as to remain attached to the ball. The new person who holds the yarn ball will give his or her answers and then repeat, also holding the end of the yarn tail so as to remain attached to the ball. For instance, Person A answers the three questions and identifies Person B as the most important person. Person A throws the yarn ball to Person B, holding the end. Person B answers the three questions and throws the yarn ball to Person C, holding the end. This will continue until everyone has answered the questions and is holding onto yarn.

c. The yarn ball may be thrown to one person multiple times. For example, Person F throws the ball to Person A, who has already answered. Person A holds the end of tail and throws the ball to Person G, because G has not spoken yet. Person A does not answer the questions again. It is ok for one or more people to have multiple strands coming to and from them.

d. The last person to speak tosses the yarn ball back to the facilitator, holding onto the end of the yarn tail so as to remain attached to the ball.

12. After giving the instructions, start by tossing the ball to one of the participants, holding onto the end of the tail. As facilitator, watch and prompt, as needed, as the ball makes its way to all the participants. As participants are sharing, a web will emerge that connects them together.

13. Ask the last person who speaks to toss the yarn ball back to you, the facilitator. Rip the ball off from the tail so you are just holding onto the end of the yarn and you are part of the web.

14. Begin a discussion by asking participants to reflect on their reactions to the web that now binds them. Participants may vacillate between speaking in role or as him/herself, personally; this is okay. Be sure to ask those who hold many strands (and thus are important to several others) how they feel about being so important. You may point out that:

    a. Relationships bind us together regardless of whether they are strong, moderate, or weak, as represented in the different colors in the variegated yarn.

    b. Each strand represents the complexity of relationships, as represented by the variegated yarn.

    c. Each strand represents different needs we have from different relationships.

15. After some initial reactions, ask participants to consider the following question: What happens to this web when crime occurs?

16. Participants will likely start suggesting that the web is destroyed. As the discussion starts, hand off the yarn that you, the facilitator, are holding to the person beside you, and enter the web from below. With each comment about what happens to the web, tear a strand apart (or cut with scissors), thus separating two people from each other. Let the ends of the yarn just fall to the ground. Continue this ripping process with each comment, until one-quarter to one-half of the web is torn apart. Be sure to invite specifics for vague or general comments and ensure that comments about both victims and offenders surface.

17. Shift the discussion and ask people to consider typical approaches to justice and how they affect the web.

18. Participants will likely start suggesting that justice approaches often further damage the web. As such, continue to break the web with each comment. Be sure to invite specifics for vague or general comments and ensure that comments about both victims and offenders surface. Continue this ripping process with each comment, until one-half to three-quarters of the web is torn apart.

19. Again, shift the discussion and ask: If we wanted to do justice in such a way that rebuilds the web, rather than destroys it, what would we do?

20. Participants will likely start to suggest ideas such as restitution, dialogue, support, education, employment, and so forth. With each restorative idea, pick up two strands of yarn and tie them together in a knot. Continue to tie the web with each comment. Be sure to invite specifics for vague or general comments and ensure that comments about both victims and offenders surface. Continue this tying process with each comment until the web is rebuilt, albeit with very visible knots.

21. Step out of the middle of the web and invite participants to reflect and comment on the newly built web. Engage with the participants' comments and summarize the exercise to make the following points:

    a. Crime breaks the web of relationships.
    b. Experiences within the dominant criminal justice system often break the web of relationships.
    c. Restorative justice aims to repair the web.
    d. The knots in the rebuilt web represent the needs of individuals that are met through a restorative justice process.

22. The session can end with this final discussion, or participants can return to their seats to continue the discussion
about restorative justice in a more concrete, nonmeta-
phorical way.

Drawing/Diagramming RJ Values

Barb Toews

Objectives:
- To explore the meaning of restorative justice values.
- To examine the tensions among restorative justice
  values.
- To explore how values in tension with each other can
  coexist, if not complement each other.
- To explore the way in which competing interests can
  come together.
- To visually explore the relationship between values.

Number of Participants: 6–24

Materials:
- Flip chart paper (one sheet for each group; see step 1
  below)
- Markers (thick, one for each group)

Time: 1½ hours

Introduction:
This activity is based on an exercise created by John Paul
Lederach (see *Reconcile: Conflict Transformation for Ordinary*

Christians [Herald Press, 2014]). You may supplement this activity with additional readings or videos related to truth and reconciliation commissions, such as *No Future without Forgiveness* by Desmond Tutu or the *Greensboro Truth and Reconciliation Commission Report: Executive Summary*. Prior to the activity, decide which values you would like participants to explore and grapple with in the exercise.

Description:

1. Divide participants into small groups of approximately three to five people.

2. Assign each small group one value related to restorative justice: truth, justice, peace, and mercy.

3. Give groups the following instructions for Part A: Imagine your concept is a person.

    a. What is most important to your concept/person?
    b. What is your relationship to the other concepts/people? (e.g., Must you exist before another can be present?)
    c. Which of the other concepts/people do you fear and why?
    d. Which of the other concepts/people do you consider an ally and why?
    e. What comments or questions do you have for the other concepts/people?

    Give groups approximately twenty minutes to discuss these questions.

4. Give groups instructions for Part B: Draw a picture/diagram/map that illustrates how you see all the concepts related to each other. Give groups approximately 20–30 minutes to create these diagrams.

5. Give groups instructions for Part C: Pick an individual(s) who will represent your concept/diagram alongside the other concepts. This individual(s) will present your concept according to the above questions, ask questions of the others, and respond to what the other people say and their questions.

6. Ask the representative from each concept group to give a five-minute presentation of his/her concept and diagram. After each representative has presented, ask all representatives to ask questions of each other and respond. Other members from their groups can also join the conversation.

7. Debrief by transitioning the conversation to the learnings of the exercise. To discuss conceptual/philosophical learnings you might ask:

    a. Where do you agree or disagree with what other concepts/people have said?

    b. What does it take for all the concepts to work together?

    c. What do you call that space where all four concepts work together?

    Note: John Paul Lederach has proposed that reconciliation emerges from the space where truth, mercy, justice, and peace work together.

    To discuss practical learnings you might ask:

    a. Which of these concepts might a victim say is most important? An offender? The community?

    b. Do you believe it is realistic and possible to meet the needs of victim, offender, and community?

    c. What have you learned about building strong and healthy communities through this activity?

    d. How can you use the models you have created to work through the situations of community violence or conflict that you encounter every day?

The Circle Process

Jef From

Objectives:
- To provide a tool for practicing listening skills.[5]
- To provide participants the opportunity to share in a safe and egalitarian space.

Number of Participants: 2–25

Time: 15 minutes to indeterminate

Materials:
- Enough chairs in a circle for each participant to sit.
- A talking piece: A small, hand-held item that can be passed from person to person. Ideally, this item should symbolize something about the group, the activity, or the topic at hand. If nothing symbolic is available, any hand-held item can be used.
- Optional centerpiece: A visual symbol related to the topic at hand (a picture, an object, etc.) that can be placed in the center of the circle to focus attention.

---

5 Adapted from "Circle and Circle Process," *Training Activities Used in Defense Initiated Victim Outreach Training* (Council for Restorative Justice, 2009), 9–10. This explanation of the circle processes draws upon the work of Kay Pranis.

Introduction: Circles are sometimes implemented as a method for responding restoratively to harm, wrongdoing, or crime (see chapter 9 for a discussion about sentencing circles). Their structure allows participants to practice deep listening, authentically express feelings, and show respect for all perspectives represented. In cases of harm or crime, preparation for facilitating or participating in a circle can be quite extensive, and training in "circle keeping" is highly recommended for facilitators. In a classroom setting, however, circles can be used to debrief activities in a respectful, egalitarian way without much prior preparation on the part of facilitator or participants. Familiarize yourself with the basics of the circle process, as described below, before trying the next exercise, which simulates a sentencing circle (see "Circles in Response to Drug Offenses," pp. 304–9). For a much deeper exploration of the circle process, see Kay Pranis, *The Little Book of Circle Processes*.

Description:
Preparing for the Circle

1. Set up chairs in a circle, with no tables. It is important that there are exactly as many chairs as there are people in the circle, no more and no less. As the number of participants changes, be prepared to add or remove chairs from the circle.

2. Prepare a reflection question relevant to the activity or classroom experience, and prepare to set a peaceful and open tone for the circle.

Convening the Circle

1. Invite participants into the circle.

2. If a centerpiece is used as a focal point, begin by describing its significance.

3. Explain the significance of the talking piece, if applicable.

4. Explain the guidelines of the circle. (In applications related to harm, these guidelines are very important; in classroom activity settings, where the stakes may be lower, they may seem less necessary. However, abiding by them creates a space for all participants to speak and receive the attention and respect of others.) Common guidelines are:

   a. The person who has the talking piece is the only one who should speak. If you want to comment on what someone else has said, please wait your turn. This also means no side conversations or comments.

   b. Ask that no one leave the circle after the circle process has begun. It works well to schedule breaks between other classroom activities and the circle space to minimize any potential interruptions.

   c. Ask that electronic devices be silenced.

   d. Explain that if a participant feels unready to speak, they may "pass" when the talking piece comes to them.

   e. If there is time for open sharing, the talking piece can be placed in the middle of the circle, keeping in mind that as one person is speaking there should be no side conversations or comments.

5. As facilitator, open the circle by picking up the talking piece and posing the prepared reflection question. Then pass the talking piece to your left or right.

6. Pass the talking piece around the circle as many times as needed. If some participants "pass" during the first round, make sure to pass the talking piece an additional time to make sure those participants have a second chance to speak.

7. End the circle with a summary of what was spoken, being careful not to misrepresent others' words, and/or end with words of thanks to participants.

Circles in Response to Drug Offenses: Race, Economics, and Social Injustice

Barb Toews

Objectives:
- To explore the impact of crime on offenders, victims, their communities of care, and the wider community.
- To experience a restorative justice circle.
- To consider the use of circles to create sentences.
- To experience and consider the tensions in doing restorative justice in crimes influenced by social injustice and that involve the wider community

Number of Participants: 12–20

Time: 2–3 hours

Materials:
- Flip chart and markers
- Nametags and thin-tipped markers
- Process description
- Talking piece (see p. 301 for a more detailed description of the talking piece)

- A community crime scenario that explores the intersection of race, economics, and politics (e.g., drug crimes) with unique roles for participants to play
- Handouts for observers (see the end of "Introduction")

Introduction:
This circle simulation serves to explore the complexities of doing restorative justice when individual crime is connected to racial, economic, and social injustices and in seemingly "victimless" crimes. At the same time, it allows participants to explore these complexities by playing roles in the crime and justice process and to experience a circle process.

Role plays: Consider a crime(s) that has occurred in your community; that represents a situation in which race, economics, and politics intersect in the context of crime; and that has community impact. Drug-related crimes are just one example of such a crime. Write a one- to two-paragraph background scenario that introduces:

a. The crime and the community in which it occurred, including the racial, economic, and political realities.

b. The reasoning about why and how this crime has been referred to a circle so that a wider number of people can be involved in figuring out the offender's sentence or general justice response.

Next, create approximately twelve to fifteen roles based on this scenario. Role descriptions can be just one to two paragraphs long—enough to give participants an idea of what their role and perspectives are. Possible roles to include are: offender; grandparent of offender; offender's neighbor; arresting officer; partner/spouse of offender; community resident;

district attorney; defense attorney; community activist; neighborhood store owner; leader of neighborhood faith community; various neighborhood members.

Each role should include the following: a description of the person; their relationship to the crime and other people impacted (if relevant); their reaction to the crime (and others like it, if relevant); their reactions to coming to a circle; and their ideas for how to do justice. Across all the roles, there should be diverse responses and perspectives, just as there is in any real-life community. Ensure that each role has a label identifying who the person is (e.g., offender, victim). You can assign each role a gender-neutral name or let the participants chose a name at the training. At the top of each role, include the one- to two-paragraph background scenario. Print out two lists of the roles—one list for you, and one list you can cut into slips of paper (one role per slip of paper) so participants can select an individual role.

Observer roles: Participants without specific roles in the role play will serve as observers of the process and will facilitate a discussion after the simulation is complete. They will want to observe for such things as:

a. How participants are reacting to each other and what might be causing those reactions

b. Words people are using and to what effect

c. Nonverbal communication and its impact

d. Transformative moments in the process and their impact

e. Things the facilitator does and does not do

f. How restorative justice concepts are being practiced

You may also wish to give observers additional, more focused questions so they can home in on particular topics after the circle simulation. For example:

a. What does restorative justice mean when there is only an offender and no single or direct victim?

b. Who participates in the process of attending to offender needs and obligations?

c. What is the role of restorative justice in changing crime and justice policy and structural inequities?

d. What is the role and impact of community judgment of the offender?

e. To what degree does restorative justice include treatment and punitive goals and practices?

f. What does offender redemption and reintegration mean, and how is it experienced?

g. Is restorative justice an alternative to punishment or an alternate form of punishment?

h. What comes first: fulfillment of offender needs/obligations or community needs/obligations?

Create a handout for each observer that includes questions to guide their observations, the background to the scenario, and the list of circle participants.

Description:
Prior to starting

- The activity facilitator serves as the circle keeper. In advance of the session, write a description of the process you will use to keep the circle and decide what will serve as the talking piece. You will want to plan to facilitate a circle from beginning to the end, when an agreement has been made. Depending on the amount of time you have, you may need to wrap things up in the middle of the process.

- On the flip chart, write out a list of the roles using the role labels (e.g., offender, neighbor) and name, if assigned in advance. Display so every participant can see the list.

- Set up the room so that there is a circle of chairs, enough for each circle participant and the keeper(s). Create a second circle of chairs on the outside of the participant circle for the observers.

- Give each circle participant a nametag and thin-tipped marker.

Implementing the circle process

1. Introduce participants to the idea that they are now part of a community in which a crime(s) has occurred and that they will be taking on roles of various people within that community. As a community, they will be participating in a circle process to determine how to respond to the crime. Introduce participants to the types of roles by reviewing the list written on the flip chart.

2. Hand out the roles to each participant by either letting each select blindly from the stack of roles or by handing each participant a role from the top of the stack. Give participants a few minutes to read their roles and, if necessary, to give themselves a name and write it on the top of the nametag.

3. Read each role that is written on the flip chart and have participants raise their hands to identify which role they will play and to give their role name, if appropriate. This is a preliminary way to see who is who.

4. Ask those who selected the observer roles to raise their hands. Review their instructions and ask for questions.

5. Read the background to the scenario aloud so everyone is on the same page. Remind those who have roles that they can assume that they have been prepared to participate in the circle and have chosen to voluntarily attend.

6. Take on the role of the circle keeper and facilitate the circle in the way you have outlined in advanced.

7. When an agreement has been reached (or when you have to end, due to time), close the circle. To transition participants out of the roles, facilitate another circle in which participants remove their role nametags and identify one way in which they are different from the role they played.

8. Facilitate a circle in which each participant says one thing that surprised them about participating in the circle.

9. Open the discussion to include the observers by inviting them to discuss their observations, ask questions of the circle participants, and generally initiate a dialogue about the circle process, using the observation question identified above.

Facing Victims (and/or Offenders)

Barb Toews

Objectives:
- To put a face on victims/offenders.
- Learn about the offender/victim experience and needs for justice from real life experiences.
- Challenge people to face stereotypes they may have about victims and offenders.

Number of Participants: up to 24

Materials:
- Quotations from men and women featured in Howard Zehr's books *Doing Life: Reflections of Men and Women Serving Life Sentences* and/or *Transcending: Reflections of Crime Victims*. These quotes will reflect themes that you want participants to consider and discuss—e.g., accountability, reintegration, community, and forgiveness. They can be typed up or copied out of the book and trimmed or highlighted to focus the reader on the sentence(s) of interest.
- Portraits of men and women who are being quoted. Ideally, portraits are cut out of the book itself and laminated to allow for handling multiple times. Alternately, you can photocopy the portraits out of the book. The downside of using photocopies is the reduced quality of the photo.
- Tape

Time: 45 minutes

Introduction:

Using the narrative text and portraits in these two books serves as a way to bring in the victim and offender voice and presence, albeit symbolically, when educating people about restorative justice.

Description:

1. Prior to class, tape each person's quotation to the back of his/her respective photo.

2. During the class session, spread the photos on a table, face up. If you are using both victim and offender photos, be sure to mix them up so all the victims and all the offenders are not together.

3. Introduce participants to the activity (based on steps below).

4. Draw participants' attention to the photos and invite them to approach the table, look at the photos, and pick one that catches their eye. Do not tell them which photos are of victims and which ones are of offenders.

5. Invite each person to select a photo and pair up with another participant. Ask them to tell each other why they selected that particular photo. Then, ask them to read the quotations on the back of the photos to each other.

6. Invite them to discuss such questions as:

   a. What does this person say is important to them for justice?
   b. What is challenging or surprising about what this person says?
   c. How do you respond to what this person is saying?
   d. What question might you want to ask this person?

    e. How do you share or differ in your perspectives?

    f. What can you learn about justice from this person?

    g. What about what this person says may move them toward or away from considering a restorative justice response to the crime they experienced (or committed)?

    h. What can you learn about restorative justice and/or restorative justice practice from this person?

7. Ask participants to return to the large group circle, sitting in their dyads. Going around the circle, invite each pair to:

    a. Introduce the people in their photo by name.

    b. Say whether the people in the photos are victims or offenders.

    c. Say a bit about why they chose that photo.

    d. Briefly discuss what participants learned from the person in the photo and his/her quotation.

8. As facilitator, lead a large group discussion, picking up on themes, questions, and learnings that emerge as participants share.

Variations:

1. Place a label on the back of each photo that identities each individual as a victim or offender. For instance, a red label might indicate a "victim" and a blue label might indicate an "offender." Invite participants to select a photo and return to the large group. Going around the circle, invite each participant to introduce each person on the photo by name and say why she or he selected that person. After everyone has shared, ask them to flip

the photo over and explain what each color label means. Invite responses to questions such as:

a. What is your reaction to learning about this person's experience?
b. What is contributing to that reaction?
c. What is surprising or challenging about learning about this person's experience?

Participants can then pair up to read and discuss the quote.

2. Provide participants with a copy of a full interview (a short one) and portrait. In pairs or triads, ask them to read the interview and reflect on the portrait. Together, they can discuss similar questions as above. After this, they can return to the large group and do similar sharing as above.

Designing Restorative Justice Space

Barb Toews and Deanna Van Buren

Objectives:
- To explore the characteristics of spaces that facilitate restorative justice values and outcomes.
- To consider the relationship between restorative justice theory and the architecture and design of spaces in which restorative justice occurs.
- To visualize concepts, ideas, or personal experiences.

Number of Participants: 1–24

Materials:
- Magazines (that can be cut up) and/or precut images or photographs (ideally printed on paper). The magazines should be related to topics such as architecture, art and photography, lifestyle, travel, culture, and nature. Ensure that the magazines and images represent a variety of socioeconomic, gender, racial, and cultural demographics, especially those of the people with whom you are working.
- Papers (e.g., construction, patterned, and tissue paper) and found objects (e.g., leaves, gum wrappers)
- Pens, markers, pencils, and/or paint.
- Glue sticks
- Scissors
- 14 x 17-inch to 18 x 24-inch chip board, poster board, or multiuse paper base on which to create the collages (one for each participant). This size allows for a range of large-scale images coming from a standard magazine. If you choose a smaller size, you will be limited by the number and size of images that you can use.

Time: 1–1½ hours

Introduction:
Collage—pulling together a collection of images and organizing them in a single composition—is an easy way to explore concrete design ideas for a space or explore feelings such as love and forgiveness and how they relate to the design of justice spaces. Images seen in relationship to one another can take on new associations and more complex meanings than they do just on their own. Collage is useful when participants

may not feel comfortable drawing or sketching, and the use of photographic imagery can be helpful in conveying more complex emotions, intentions, systems, and ideas. In the case of restorative justice, collage is also a helpful tool for representing spaces that may draw on our past experiences and our visions for new spaces.

More information on the relationship between restorative justice and architecture/design, as well as tools with which to facilitate dialogue about that relationship, can be found in the *Designing Justice+Designing Spaces* toolkit, available at http:// www.designingjustice.com.

Description:

1. Prior to the start of the session, put out all the supplies on tables.

2. Explain the activity to participants, explaining what a collage is and introducing them to the supplies. Give each participant a base on which to create their collage.

3. Give participants the following prompt: *Imagine you have to do one of the following:*

    a. Face someone with whom you have had a great deal of conflict.

    b. Deal with the worst thing you have ever done in your life.

    c. Deal with the worst thing that you have ever experienced in your life.

    What kind of space would you need to do that?

4. Allow students approximately 30–45 minutes to create their collages.

5. When everyone has completed their collages, ask them to gather in a circle and present their collages, highlighting the meaning of the images they have chosen.

6. After everyone has shared, facilitate a large group discussion about what can be gleaned from the collages. Sample questions include:

   a. In what ways does your collage represent restorative justice values? Which ones?
   b. What similarities do you notice across the collages?
   c. What differences stand out?
   d. How are collages different across culture? Gender? Age?
   e. What have you learned about restorative justice in this process?
   f. What have you learned about the design of the spaces in which justice occurs?
   g. How, if at all, would your collages look different if you had selected images that represent the current justice system?

Bibliographic Essay

Howard Zehr and Gerry Johnstone

IN THE TWENTY-FIVE YEARS since *Changing Lenses* was first released, the literature on restorative justice and related topics has grown exponentially.[1] This bibliography does not attempt to be comprehensive. Rather, it is a selection of books that may be of interest to readers who are relatively new to restorative justice and to those who wish to explore particular aspects and topics in more depth. Although it contains many works that are quite scholarly, the aim is to also suggest works that are accessible to general readers as well as to academics and researchers. Specific sources that were especially helpful in developing the concept and writing *Changing Lenses* are listed in footnotes in the text.

Academic readers and researchers should note that the bibliographic essay does not include journal articles. For readers who are keen to keep abreast of research and scholarly writing

---

1 This bibliographic essay was prepared by Gerry Johnstone, building on the bibliographic essay I wrote for the third edition. It is not an attempt to be comprehensive. Rather, it suggests some of the reading that Gerry and I have found helpful and believe the reader may as well. Gerry Johnstone is professor of law, University of Hull in the United Kingdom.

on restorative justice, there is now a peer-reviewed journal, launched in 2013, that presents the fruits of academic research as well as practice- and policy-related information on restorative justice worldwide: *Restorative Justice: An International Journal* (details at http://www.hartjournals.co.uk/rj/index .html).

For further references, Prison Fellowship International's excellent website Restorative Justice Online (www.restorative justice.org) has a large annotated restorative justice bibliography and contains useful links to other websites.

CHAPTER 2: **THE VICTIM**

Judith Lewis Herman's groundbreaking book *Trauma and Recovery* (New York: Basic Books, 1997) is essential reading in the areas of victimization and trauma. Sandra Bloom's *Creating Sanctuary: Toward the Evolution of Sane Societies* (New York: Routledge, 1997) provides important insights into trauma and the relationship between trauma and social structure.

Howard Zehr's synopsis of the victim experience, combined with the voices of victims, may be found in his *Transcending: Reflections of Crime Victims* (Intercourse, PA: Good Books, 2001).

Although published a decade ago, James Dignan's book *Understanding Victims and Restorative Justice* (New York: Open University Press, 2005) remains one of the best introductions available on what restorative justice might mean for victims of crime. Written clearly, Dignan's book provides a highly accessible introduction to the literature on victimization and its effects and explains how policies toward crime victims have emerged and evolved, before looking closely at restorative justice approaches to meeting the needs of victims. There is a good chapter on evaluating restorative justice from the perspective of victims. Heather Strang's book *Repair or Revenge: Victims and Restorative Justice* (Oxford: Oxford

University Press, 2002) remains one of the leading works on the subject. Based on detailed empirical research, Strang provides an in-depth account of victims' needs and how these might be met by restorative justice, with a particularly good account of "emotional restoration." For a shorter introduction, chapter 4 of Gerry Johnstone's *Restorative Justice: Ideas, Values, Debates*, 2nd ed. (London: Routledge, 2011) examines the restorative approach to bringing justice and healing to victims, placing this in the context of wider changes in societal attitudes and policies toward victims of crime. An important book on the issue of providing justice for victims, which to some extent complements the analysis provided in *Changing Lenses*, is Susan Herman's *Parallel Justice for Victims of Crime* (Washington, DC: National Center for Victims of Crime, 2010).

For readers interested in what restorative justice might offer to victims of particular types of offense and to particular types of victims, a number of specialized works now exist (and more are likely to appear in the future as this is a growing area of inquiry). Existing texts include *Restorative Justice for Domestic Violence Victims* by Marilyn Fernandez (Lanham, MD: Lexington Books, 2010); *Child Victims and Restorative Justice* by Tali Gal (New York: Oxford University Press, 2011); and *Victims of Violence and Restorative Practices* by Tinneke van Camp (London: Routledge, 2014).

CHAPTER 3: **THE OFFENDER**

Many writings by and about prisoners continue to be published. Anthologies include Bell Gale Chevigny, ed., *Doing Time: 25 Years of Prison Writing* (New York: Arcade Publishing, 2011); Robert Johnson and Hans Toch, eds., *Crime and Punishment: Inside Views* (Los Angeles: Roxbury Publishing Co., 1999); Lori B. Girshick, *No Safe Haven: Stories of Women in Prison* (Boston: Northeastern University

Press, 2000); and Judith Scheffler, ed., *Wall Tappings: An International Anthology of Women's Prison Writings 200 to the Present* (New York: Feminist Press CUNY, 2003). Jane Evelyn Atwood's *Too Much Time* (London: Phaidon Press, 2000) includes photos and writing about women in prison. Howard Zehr's *Doing Life: Reflections of Men and Women Serving Life Sentences* (Intercourse, PA: Good Books, 1996) features portraits and words of both men and women who are serving life sentences.

The prison industry is examined in a number of books. For the general reader, a useful short introduction is chapter 4 of Nils Christie, *A Suitable Amount of Crime* (New York: Routledge, 2004). Christie explored the topic in more detail in an earlier work: *Crime Control as Industry* (New York: Routledge, 1993). Other useful works include Joel Dyer, *The Perpetual Prisoner Machine: How America Profits from Crime* (Boulder, CO: Westview Press, 2000); and Daniel Burton-Rose, Dan Pens, and Paul Wright, *The Ceiling of America: An Inside Look at the U.S. Prison Industry* (Monroe, ME: Common Courage Press, 2002). Jerome Miller's *Search and Destroy: African-American Males in the Criminal Justice System* (Cambridge: Cambridge University Press, 1996) explores the role of race in the criminal justice system. The effects of this are examined in Michelle Alexander's *The New Jim Crow: Mass Incarceration in the Age of Colorblindness* (New York: New Press, 2012). An essential book for understanding the social forces that have produced mass incarceration and more broadly transformed the politics of law and order is David Garland's *The Culture of Control* (New York: Oxford University Press, 2001).

Indispensable books for understanding offender needs and perspectives are Shadd Maruna, *Making Good: How Ex-Convicts Reform and Rebuild Their Lives* (Washington, DC: American Psychological Association Books, 2001); and James

Gilligan, *Violence: Reflections of a National Epidemic* (New York: Vintage Books, 1996). The process of desistance from crime is further explored in Stephen Farrell and Adam Caverley, *Understanding Desistance from Crime: Emerging Theoretical Directions in Resettlement and Rehabilitation* (Maidenhead: Open University Press, 2006). A recent study of the process of prisoner "reentry" to society is Daniel Mears and Joshua Cochran, *Prisoner Reentry in the Era of Mass Incarceration* (Thousand Oaks, CA: Sage, 2015).

David Cayley's book *The Expanding Prison: The Crisis in Crime and Punishment and the Search for Alternatives* (Toronto: House of Anansi Press, 1998) began as a series of radio interviews on the Canadian Broadcast Corporation. It is important reading on the issue of punishment in theory and practice as well as for many of the following topics.

CHAPTER 4: **SOME COMMON THEMES**

The topic of forgiveness has become a popular one in recent years, resulting in a substantial literature. Cynthia Ransley and Terri Spy, *Forgiveness and the Healing Process: A Central Therapeutic Concern* (Hove, UK: Brunner-Routledge, 2004) provides a rich collection of perspectives. Wilma L. Derksen, the mother of a murdered daughter, has thought deeply about forgiveness; her books include *Confronting the Horror: The Aftermath of Violence* (Winnipeg, MB: Amity Publishers, 2002) and *This Mortal Coil* (Winnipeg, MB: Amity, 2014). Elliot Cose's very readable *Bone to Pick: Of Forgiveness, Reconciliation, Reparation, and Revenge* (New York: Atria Books, 2004) examines the phenomenon of forgiveness and restoration in a variety of settings internationally. Donald W. Shriver Jr., *An Ethic for Enemies: Forgiveness in Politics* (New York: Oxford University Press, 1995), looks at forgiveness as a political phenomenon.

On Apology by Aaron Lazare (New York: Oxford University Press, 2004) is an enlightening and readable study of apologies and their potential for healing broken relationships. Jeffrie Murphy's *Getting Even: Forgiveness and Its Limits* (New York: Oxford University Press, 2003) provides an analysis of the topic of forgiveness that is both philosophically profound and highly accessible to the general reader. Linda Radzik, *Making Amends: Atonement in Morality, Law and Politics* (New York: Oxford University Press, 2009) is an excellent philosophical study of the broader subject of the role apology, repentance, reparations, and self-punishment can play in correcting the wrongs we do to one another.

The topic of shame remains an important (and contentious) one in restorative justice. The key text is John Braithwaite's *Crime, Shame and Reintegration* (Cambridge: Cambridge University Press, 1989). Critics of the idea that shaming has a role to play in restorative justice include Gabrielle Maxwell and Allison Morris (see their chapter in Howard Zehr and Barb Toews, eds., *Critical Issues in Restorative Justice* [Monsey, NY: Criminal Justice Press, 2004]). Gilligan, in *Violence: Reflection of a National Epidemic* (New York: Vintage Books, 1997), argues that shame *is* a primary motivator of violence. In "Journey to Belonging" (in *Restorative Justice: Theoretical Foundations*, Elmar G. M. Weitekamp and Hans-Juergen Kerner, ed. [Devon, UK: Willan Publishing, 2002]), Howard Zehr argues that shame operates in the lives of both victims and offenders.

Shame is now the subject of a very large and complex body of literature. For the nonexpert, an excellent way into the subject is *In Defense of Shame: The Faces of an Emotion* by Julien A. Deonna, Raffaelle Rodogno, and Fabrice Teroni (New York: Oxford University Press, 2012). Deonna, et al., provide an accessible account of the nature of shame and an examination of dogmas about it before exploring the subjects of shame, crime, and punishment, in which they include a discussion of restorative justice.

For an invaluable, engaging, and accessible discussion of the meaning of *crime*, Nils Christie, *A Suitable Amount of Crime* (New York: Routledge, 2004) is recommended.

CHAPTERS 5–6: **RETRIBUTIVE JUSTICE; JUSTICE AS PARADIGM**

Law and Crime by Gerry Johnstone and Tony Ward (London: Sage, 2010) includes an account—written with nonspecialist readers in mind—of the historical emergence, fundamental assumptions, and strengths and limitations of the institution of criminal justice critiqued in chapter 5. Declan Roche's essay "Retribution and Restorative Justice" (in Gerry Johnston and Daniel Van Ness, eds., *Handbook of Restorative Justice* [Cullompton: Willan, 2007]) provides an introductory discussion of the complex topic of retributive justice and how it compares with restorative justice. Conrad G. Brunk's chapter "Restorative Justice and the Philosophical Theories of Criminal Punishment" in Michael Hadley, ed., *The Spiritual Roots of Restorative Justice* (Albany, NY: State University of New York Press, 2001), was a key influence upon Howard Zehr's rethinking of the relationship between retribution and restoration. In *Crime, Punishment and Restorative Justice: From the Margins to the Mainstream*, Ross London traces the emergence of restorative justice as a new justice paradigm. A relevant excerpt is reproduced in Gerry Johnstone, ed., *A Restorative Justice Reader*, 2nd ed. (London: Routledge, 2013). In his book, London argues that retributive and restorative justice are compatible rather than conflicting approaches to crime (and hence against the idea of restorative justice as a distinctive paradigm), and he sketches and defends the idea of a comprehensive criminal justice system organized around the idea of restoring trust in the aftermath of crime. For those who wish to go deeper into this topic, an important collection of papers exploring the tensions and overlaps between retributive and restorative justice is Andreas von Hirsch, Julian Roberts, Anthony Bottoms, Ken Roach, and Mara Schiff, eds., *Restorative Justice and Criminal Justice: Competing or Reconcilable Paradigms* (Portland, OR and Oxford: Hart, 2003).

CHAPTER 7: **THE HISTORICAL ALTERNATIVE**

David Cayley's *The Expanding Prison: The Crisis in Crime and Punishment and the Search for Alternatives* (Toronto: House of Anansi Press, 1998) contains a helpful historical discussion. Three books explore in more depth the ways that the development of the Western legal system and of Christian theology mutually influenced each other and, in turn, strengthened the punitive nature of Western culture. Timothy Gorringe, *God's Just Vengeance* (New York: Cambridge University Press, 1996), examines this in the Catholic era of the medieval period and beyond. T. Richard Snyder follows that theme in the Protestant tradition in *The Protestant Ethic and the Spirit of Punishment* (Grand Rapids, MI: Eerdmans, 2001). Gil Bailie, *Violence Unveiled: Humanity at the Crossroads* (New York: Crossroad, 1995), applies Rene Girard's scapegoating framework to this story.

In his fascinating and highly readable book *Returning to the Teachings* (New York: Penguin Books, 1996), Rupert Ross explores the differences between a European and a North American indigenous worldview. His book is part of a growing literature examining indigenous contributions to the restorative field. One piece which gives a good flavor of this literature is Robert Yazzie and James W. Zion's essay "Navajo Restorative Justice: the Law of Equality and Justice." An excerpt from this is available in Gerry Johnstone, ed., *A Restorative Justice Reader*, 2nd ed. (London: Routledge, 2013). In *The Ethic of Traditional Communities and the Spirit of Healing Justice: Studies from Hollow Water, the Iona Community and Plum Village* (London: Jessica Kingsley, 2009), Jarem Sawatsky presents a deeply researched yet very readable exploration of the meaning of healing justice and the conditions which sustain it. Wanda McCaslin, ed., *Justice as Healing: Indigenous Ways* (Saskatoon: Living Justice Press, 2011) is a collection of papers exploring the concept and practice of justice as healing in Aboriginal thought and society.

Chapter 2 of *Law and Crime* by Gerry Johnstone and Tony Ward (London: Sage, 2010) provides an account—written with nonspecialist readers in mind—of ancient traditions of punishment, vengeance, and compensation—emphasizing the community context—and of the formation of modern criminal justice.

CHAPTER 8: **THE BIBLICAL ALTERNATIVE**

Although a variety of articles and chapters examine the biblical roots of restorative justice, two books by Christopher Marshall are essential reading: *Compassionate Justice: An Interdisciplinary Dialogue with Two Gospel Parables on Law, Crime, and Restorative Justice* (Eugene, OR: Cascade Books, 2012) and his earlier *Beyond Retribution: A New Testament Vision for Justice, Crime, and Punishment* (Grand Rapids, MI: Eerdmans, 2001). The focus in *Changing Lenses* is on the Old Testament, whereas Marshall explores restorative themes in the New Testament. A shorter version of his perspective may be found in Christopher Marshall, *The Little Book of Biblical Justice* (Intercourse, PA: Good Books, 2005). John Heagle, *Justice Rising: The Emerging Biblical Vision* (Maryknoll, NY: Orbis Books, 2010) elucidates and asserts the power of a biblical vision of justice and argues in particular for the necessity of embracing it as an alternative to the war on terrorism.

The contributors to Michael Hadley, ed., *The Spiritual Roots of Restorative Justice* (Albany: State University of New York Press, 2001), explore restorative elements in a variety of other faith traditions.

CHAPTER 9: VORP AND BEYOND: EMERGING PRACTICES

No longer called VORP in most communities, victim-offender mediation or conferencing has spread and become more sophisticated. One of the primary researchers following this movement is Mark Umbreit; see, in particular, Mark Umbreit and Marilyn Armour, *Restorative Justice Dialogue: An Essential Guide for Research and Practice* (New York: Springer, 2011). Increasingly it is being applied in cases of severe violence. Mark Umbreit, Betty Vos, Robert B. Coates, and Katherine A. Brown describe and study this phenomenon in *Facing Violence: The Path of Restorative Justice and Dialogue* (Monsey, NY: Criminal Justice Press, 2003). In *After the Crime: the Power of Restorative Justice Dialogues between Victims and Violent Offenders* (New York: New York University Press, 2011), Susan Miller provides a deeply researched account of a scheme which seeks to meet the needs of victims of violent crime by facilitating restorative justice dialogue with offenders. Mark Yantzi, one of the facilitators in the "original" Elmira, Ontario, case, takes on an especially difficult area of application in *Sexual Offending and Restoration* (Scottdale, PA: Herald Press, 1998).

Many other applications of restorative justice have emerged. Paul McCold's paper "The Recent History of Restorative Justice: Mediation, Circles, and Conferencing" (in Dennis Sullivan and Larry Tifft, eds., *Handbook of Restorative Justice: A Global Perspective* [New York: Routledge, 2008]) provides a useful overview. Along with victim-offender mediation, the most developed practices are conferencing and circle processes. Conferencing had its origins in New Zealand's family group conferences, which are explained and discussed in Allan MacRae and Howard Zehr, *The Little Book of Family Group Conferences: New Zealand Style* (Intercourse, PA: Good Books, 2004). The literature explaining, discussing, and evaluating conferencing is now enormous. A useful place to start is the edited collection by Estelle Zinstagg and Inge Vanfraechem, *Conferencing and Restorative Justice: International Practices and Perspectives* (New York: Oxford University Press, 2012). For a shorter introduction, the chapter by Gabrielle Maxwell, Allison Morris, and Hennesey Hayes on "Conferencing and Restorative Justice" (in Dennis Sullivan and Larry Tifft, eds., *Handbook of Restorative Justice: A Global Perspective* [New York: Routledge, 2008]) is useful.

Circle processes are increasingly being used for addressing problems and conflicts, even where there is no justice or disciplinary procedure involved. Kay Pranis, Barry Stuart, and Mark Wedge, in *Peacemaking Circles: From Crime to Community* (St. Paul, MN: Living Justice Press, 2003), describe this in some detail. A short introduction is available in Kay Pranis, *The Little Book of Circle Processes* (Intercourse, PA: Good Books, 2005). *Peacemaking Justice and Urban Youth: Bringing Justice Home* by Carolyn Boyes-Watson (St. Paul, MN: Living Justice Press, 2008) is a fascinating sociological account of the potential and power of peacemaking circles, based on their use in an inner-city project designed to promote positive relationships and bring justice to marginalized youth.

Also worth mentioning here are efforts to apply restorative justice within efforts to build peace and achieve reconciliation and justice in the aftermath of large-scale violent conflict involving gross breaches of human rights. A key work in this area is Pat Howley, *Breaking Spears and Mending Hearts: Peacemakers and Restorative Justice in Bougainville* (Annandale, NSW: Federation Press, 2002). Jennifer Llewellyn and

Daniel Philpott, ed., *Restorative Justice, Reconciliation and Peacebuilding* (New York: Oxford University Press, 2014) is a good overview of the field.

CHAPTER 10: **A RESTORATIVE LENS**

Daniel W. Van Ness and Karen Heetderks Strong, *Restoring Justice*, 5th ed. (Cincinnati: Anderson Publishing Company, 2014), provides an overview of the philosophy and practice of restorative justice. So does Gerry Johnstone, *Restorative Justice: Ideas, Values, Debates*, 2nd ed. (London: Routledge, 2011). But Johnstone also identifies problems and contested issues in the field and suggests ways the field might address them. Johnstone's (ed.) *A Restorative Justice Reader*, 2nd ed. (London: Routledge, 2013) offers in one volume selections of some of the most important sources in the field. Howard Zehr's understanding of the theory and practice of restorative justice is summarized in *The Little Book of Restorative Justice* (Intercourse, PA: Good Books, 2002).

There are now countless books explaining, exploring, and discussing restorative justice. At the risk of leaving out much that is important and interesting, the following are suggested as useful to those beginning to explore the topic: Denis Breton and Stephen Lehman, *The Mystic Heart of Justice: Restoring Wholeness in a Broken World* (West Chester, PA: Chrysalis Books, 2001); Tony Foley, *Developing Restorative Justice Jurisprudence: Rethinking Responses to Criminal Wrongdoing* (Farnham and Burlington, VT: Ashgate, 2014); Carolyn Hoyle and Chris Cunneen, *Debating Restorative Justice* (Oxford: Hart, 2010); Heather Strang and John Braithwaite, eds., *Restorative Justice and Civil Society* (Cambridge: Cambridge University Press, 2001); Dennis Sullivan and Larry Tifft, *Restorative Justice: Healing the Foundations of Our Everyday Lives*, 2nd ed. (Lynne Rienner Publishers, 2005); Margaret Urban Walker, *Moral Repair: Reconstructing Moral Relations after*

Wrongdoing (Cambridge: Cambridge University Press, 2006); Lode Walgrave, *Restorative Justice, Self-Interest and Responsible Citizenship* (Cullompton, UK: Willan, 2008).

CHAPTERS 11–12: IMPLEMENTING A RESTORATIVE SYSTEM; REFLECTIONS TWENTY-FIVE YEARS LATER

The question "Where from here?" is addressed in much of the literature noted in the previous section. In *Critical Issues in Restorative Justice* (Money, NY: Criminal Justice Press, 2004), Howard Zehr and Barb Toews, eds., have invited authors from around the world to look at some of the dangers and problems as restorative justice spreads and becomes more popular. An important book taking stock of restorative justice and charting the way forward is John Braithwaite, *Restorative Justice and Responsive Regulation* (New York: Oxford University Press, 2002).

The question of whether and how restorative justice might be institutionalized, and the issues this raises, are addressed in Ivo Aertsen, Tom Daems, and Luc Robert, eds., *Institutionalizing Restorative Justice* (New York: Routledge, 2012). *Civilizing Criminal Justice: An International Restorative Agenda for Penal Reform*, David Cornwell, John Blad, and Martin Wright, eds. (Hampshire, Waterside Press, 2013), explores and argues for a renewed restorative agenda for penal reform. Joanna Shapland, Gwen Robinson, and Angela Sorsby, *Restorative Justice in Practice: Evaluating What Works for Victims and Offenders* (New York: Routledge, 2011) is an attempt to rigorously evaluate restorative justice initiatives and hence to provide a firm evidence base for future developments. Theo Gavrielides and Vasso Artinopoulou, eds., *Reconstructing Restorative Justice Philosophy* (Burlington, VT: Ashgate, 2013) is a collection of papers, emerging from a distinctive symposium, reexamining the philosophical and social foundations of restorative justice. *In Responsive Regulation: Transcending the Deregulation Debate* (New York: Oxford University Press, 1992), John Braitwaite envisions what a restoratively-oriented system might look like.

As is argued in chapter 11 and in "Safeguarding the Restorative Justice Vision," it is important to think through the implications of restorative justice reforms carefully and to learn lessons from previous efforts to bring about change in the area of law and justice that have gone wrong. In this context, some important critical texts on restorative justice include: Annalise Acorn, *Compulsory Compassion: A Critique of Restorative Justice* (Vancouver, BC: University of British Columbia Press, 2005); George Pavlich, *Governing Paradoxes of Restorative Justice* (London: Glasshouse Press, 2005); Andrew Woolford, *The Politics of Restorative Justice: A Critical Introduction* (Winnipeg, MB: Fernwood Publishing, 2010); and Margarita Zernova, *Restorative Justice: Ideals and Realities* (Burlington, VT: Ashgate, 2010).

Acknowledgments

THIS BOOK EMERGED FROM EXPERIENCE, reading, and discussions over a number of years. As I noted earlier, it is a work of synthesis more than invention. Consequently, it draws on the ideas and experiences of many. I owe appreciation to many more people than I can possibly acknowledge, but at least I want to express my appreciation . . .

To my Canadian colleague Dave Worth, who has encouraged and cajoled me to finish this book and also has provided many ideas and suggestions.

To Martin Wright, Millard Lind, Alan Kreider, and W. H. Allchin, who read the original manuscript, encouraged me to go on, and made many helpful suggestions.

To those whose contributions I have tried to acknowledge in this book. To the many who have made a contribution in ways I am not able to cite specifically. And especially to Nils Christie and Herman Bianchi, whose writings and discussions have helped to point a way.

To the participants in conferences, seminars, and *palavers* in the United States, Canada, and England who have listened to and tested these ideas over the past few years.

To the hundreds of people involved in the restorative justice movement whose determination and examples have given me courage and a grounding in real life.

To Mennonite Central Committee U.S., which gave me encouragement and space to develop my ideas and write them down. H. A. Penner, former director of MCC U.S. program, in particular, encouraged me to carry on.

To John Harding and the Hampshire Probation Service, who invited me to England, made me feel welcome, and gave me a home for working on the original manuscript.

To Doris Rupe, who provided me with a quiet place to write away from my office.

To Judah Oudshoorn and Jennifer Larson Sawin for their helpful suggestions on the Third Edition.

Preparing this twenty-fifth anniversary edition has brought back memories of those early years. I remember a conversation with Dave Worth and Melita Rempel about possible titles; they encouraged me to use the title I eventually chose. Discussions with Dan Van Ness, Wayne Northey . . . so many people and conversations have helped to shape this work. I want to especially acknowledge the contributions of my long-term colleague Lorraine Stutzman Amstutz over many years of working together.

Thanks to Amy Gingerich and Valerie Weaver-Zercher at Herald Press, who persuaded me to do this edition. Emily Hershberger provided invaluable assistance, both with the material itself and by encouraging me along the way. I am grateful to Gerry Johnstone for his willingness to update the bibliography; I know of no better tracker of restorative justice literature than Gerry. And to sujatha baliga, who in the midst of a hectic schedule agreed to provide a contemporary context for this edition—thank you, thank you.

Looking back much further, I want to acknowledge two mentors who impacted the direction of my life. When I first met Dr. Vincent Harding in the early 1960s, he was a colleague of Dr. Martin Luther King Jr. in the civil rights movement. Dr. Harding visited in our home several times during those years. As I look back, I believe it was his patient discussions of justice over the dinner table with this naive white boy that inspired me to seek justice. And my mentor at Morehouse College, history professor Dr. Melvin Kennedy, helped me to make decisions that set the direction of my career. I also want to acknowledge my colleague at Talladega College, Bernard ("Bernie") Bray, who was instrumental in introducing me to the real world of criminal justice while I was teaching there in the 1970s.

Finally, I want to thank my wife, Ruby Friesen Zehr, not only for her support but also for her critical feedback—she helps to keep me grounded and accountable. After nearly half a century of marriage, I am still learning from her.

The Author

HOWARD **ZEHR** is a primary founder of the restorative justice movement and is widely regarded as the "grandfather of restorative justice." A prolific writer and editor, speaker, educator, and photojournalist, Zehr lectures internationally and as director of the first victim-offender reconciliation program in the United States, was an early advocate of making the needs of victims central to the practice of restorative justice. He has helped dozens of communities start restorative justice programs, and he was appointed by the federal court in the Oklahoma City bombing trial of Timothy McVeigh to assist the defense in working with victims.

As codirector of the Zehr Institute for Restorative Justice and distinguished professor at the Center for Justice and Peacebuilding, Eastern Mennonite University, Zehr has led hundreds of events in more than twenty-five countries and thirty-five states. His work on criminal justice matters has had particular influence in the United States, Brazil, Japan, Jamaica, Northern Ireland, Britain, the Ukraine, and New

Zealand, which has restructured its juvenile justice system into a family-focused, restorative approach.

While teaching at Talladega College in Alabama in the 1970s, Zehr's colleague Bernard ("Bernie") Bray helped introduce him to the real world of criminal justice. Together they created the Social Science and the Law project in which they teamed with students to assist defense attorneys in choosing juries in death penalty and other trials.

Zehr and his wife, Ruby Friesen Zehr, live in Harrisonburg, Virginia, and have two adult children and two grandchildren.